CE

The chief aim of this book is the adaptation of some general concepts of the meta-theory of science to normative and more specifically legal discourse. The clarification and definition of a concept of *normative system* and the connected notions of *completeness*, *consistency* and *independence* lead to a new approach to some traditional jurisprudential problems. Most of these problems have a long history in legal philosophy, but very little has been done to apply to them the analytical techniques of modern philosophy of science.

The book contains a critical discussion of the main methodological issues of the science of law and tries to make explicit the ideals of legal dogmatics (especially the ideal of completeness), which are not to be confused with ideological (political) attitudes.

Legal discourse proves also to be an interesting field of application of deontic logic, provided a distinction is made between a prescriptive object-language (in which legal provisions are expressed) and a descriptive meta-language (that of the science of law). This distinction leads to the development of a new branch of normative logic, the logic of normative propositions, which is an extension of the ordinary deontic logic (interpreted as a logic of norms).

Though the main concern of the authors is with legal systems, the definitions of all the crucial notions are given in general terms in order to make them applicable to other kinds of normative (e. g. moral) systems.

Library of Exact Philosophy   5

Carlos E. Alchourrón and
Eugenio Bulygin

Normative Systems

Springer-Verlag New York Wien 1971

mo

Printing type: Sabon Roman
Composed and printed by Herbert Hiessberger, Pottenstein
Binding work: Karl Scheibe, Wien
Design: Hans Joachim Böning, Wien

K
213
. A436
1971

ISBN 0-387-81019-6   Springer-Verlag New York - Wien
ISBN 3-211-81019-6   Springer-Verlag Wien - New York

© 1971 by Springer-Verlag/Wien
Library of Congress Catalog Card Number 75-170895
Printed in Austria

We dedicate
this book to the memory
of Ambrosio L. Gioja

General Preface to the LEP

The aim of the Library of Exact Philosophy is to keep alive the spirit, if not the letter, of the Vienna Circle. It will consequently adopt high standards of rigor: it will demand the clear statement of problems, their careful handling with the relevant logical or mathematical tools, and a critical analysis of the assumptions and results of every piece of philosophical research.

Like the Vienna Circle, the Library of Exact Philosophy sees in mathematics and science the wellsprings of contemporary intellectual culture as well as sources of inspiration for some of the problems and methods of philosophy. The Library of Exact Philosophy will also stress the desirability of regarding philosophical research as a cooperative enterprise carried out with exact tools and with the purpose of extending, deepening, and systematizing our knowledge about human knowledge.

But, unlike the Vienna Circle, the Library of Exact Philosophy will not adopt a school attitude. It will encourage constructive work done across school frontiers and it will attempt to minimize sterile quarrels. And it will not restrict the kinds of philosophical problem: the Library of Exact Philosophy will welcome not only logic, semantics and epistemology, but also metaphysics, value theory and ethics as long as they are conceived in a clear and cogent way, and are in agreement with contemporary science.

Montreal, January 1970

Mario Bunge

Acknowledgements

We shall not attempt to make a complete list of all the sources from which this book has received guidance and influence. But we should like to mention that we have drawn a great deal of inspiration from the writings of GEORG HENRIK VON WRIGHT, RUDOLF CARNAP and ALFRED TARSKI; the footnote references to their works fail to indicate the full extent of our obligations and our gratitude to them. The same is true of the three legal philosophers from whom we have learned most: HANS KELSEN, ALF ROSS and H. L. A. HART.

As for more personal acknowledgements, we owe a lasting gratitude to the late Professor AMBROSIO L. GIOJA who played a unique part in our intellectual development and under whose guidance the Institute of Legal Philosophy of the University of Buenos Aires became an outstanding centre of scientific research, where in many discussions with friends and colleagues we gained stimulation for the development and clarification of our conceptions and their formulation in this book.

Our debt to our friend GENARO R. CARRIÓ is too extensive to permit of detailed acknowledgement. Without his constant assistance, his stimulating criticism and helpful suggestions this book would not have been written. To him we owe our very special thanks for all this and for much besides.

We are most grateful to Professor G. H. VON WRIGHT for his kind encouragement and for many stimulating discussions; to Professor H. L. A. HART, who has taken the trouble to read parts of the manuscript, for a great many useful comments and helpful criticisms, and to the late Professor A. N. PRIOR for his generous friendship, his beneficial advice and many valuable suggestions.

Thanks are also due to MARIA EUGENIA URQUIJO, ISABEL AZARETTO and CARLOS S. NINO who read earlier versions of the manuscript and offered useful comments. The responsibility for any errors in the book rests, of course, entirely with us.

We are also highly indebted to Mrs. J. MACKIE who has revised the English manuscript and we tender her our sincere thanks for her invaluable services. But she should not be made responsible for any linguistic shortcomings. Last, but not least, we should like to thank Professor MARIO BUNGE, editor of the series in which this work appears, not only for having made possible its publication, but also for his lasting contribution to the modernization of philosophical studies in Argentina.

EUGENIO BULYGIN would like to express his gratitude to the British Council whose generous help made it possible for him to spend in 1968/69 an unforgettable year in Oxford, and to the Foundation Alexander von Humboldt and its Secretary General Dr. HEINRICH PFEIFFER for a most rewarding visit to Germany.

Buenos Aires, summer 1971

Carlos E. Alchourrón
Eugenio Bulygin

Contents

Introduction

In consequence of an increased interest in problems relating to human action, normative concepts have been much discussed by philosophers and logicians in the past twenty years. Deontic logic, which deals with the normative use of language and such normative concepts as obligation, prohibition and permission, has become one of the most intensively cultivated areas of formal logic. Important investigations have been carried out which have shed considerable light on various aspects of the normative phenomenon and a great number of different systems of deontic logic have been developed.

This progressive proliferation of deontic logics not only shows the great interest of logicians in normative discourse, but also reflects a basic perplexity: the lack of suitable criteria of adequacy for the interpretation of deontic calculi and hence difficulty in deciding which of the systems provides the best reconstruction of the underlying normative concepts and can therefore be applied with the most fruitful results. This difficulty is so great that some authors have even expressed doubts about the practical usefulness of deontic logic.

One of the sources of this perplexity lies in the absence of a well established pre-analytical basis for formal studies. It is sometimes even uncertain what the intuitive notions are that deontic logicians intend to reconstruct. In talking about obligations, prohibitions and permissions, they usually have in mind moral norms. But the choice of moral norm as an explicandum for the construction of a logic of norms has several disadvantages.

In the first place, there is no well established moral science. Apart from historical or sociological investigations, there is no specific science dealing with the analysis of moral norms and of concrete moral systems. In the second place, it seems to be extremely difficult to identify the content of a moral system. The absence of moral legislator to provide precise formulations of moral norms and record them in an official text makes it almost impossible to identify such norms. It is symptomatic of this fact that moral philosophers usually quote two or three relatively obvious examples of moral norms and that the same examples tend to occur in almost every book on ethics.

From this point of view it would seem that legal norms have considerable advantages over moral norms. They are much more easily identified, since most are created consciously by human beings and recorded in written form, at least so far as positive law is concerned. (The norms of the so called Natural Law are in this respect very much like moral norms.) In addition, there is an old and respectable science that deals specifically with the description and systematization of legal norms. It would certainly be unreasonable to reject without closer inspection the experience accumulated by jurists for hundreds and even thousands of years.

It seems obvious to suggest using legal science as a pre-analytic ground for formal studies (and also as an interesting field for the application of deontic logic). And yet, this suggestion has received scant attention from deontic logicians and the few books that have tried to bring together deontic logic and legal science have had few repercussions on the development of either of these disciplines.

On the other hand, this divorce between deontic logic and legal science has had extremely unfortunate effects for the latter. Jurists have not only paid very little attention to the formal investigation of the normative concepts which they use in their discipline; they have even contrived to remain unaffected by the great revival in foundational studies which in the past hundred years has revolutionized the methodology of both formal and empirical sciences. Methodological studies in the field of law are still at a stage of "underdevelopment" and very little has been done so far to make use of the conceptual tools that have been devised by those who have worked on the foundations of mathematics or physics. It is true that legal science cannot readily be classified as an empirical science; much less readily can it be classified as a formal one. It has its own peculiar features, which would perhaps justify us in speaking of *normative science* as an autonomous category, distinct from both formal and empirical science. But this does not preclude the possibility of transferring to the study of law part of the knowledge gained and some of the methods used in the foundational studies of other, more developed, sciences.

It can thus reasonably be expected that an approach to the traditional problems of legal philosophy in the light of modern logical and methodological investigations would produce interesting results. The notion of normative system seems particularly suitable for such a purpose. On the one hand, although the structure of deductive systems with their formal properties (consistency, completeness and independence) is one of the main topics of modern foundational studies both in their purely formal aspect (uninterpreted, syntactical systems) and their application in the empirical sciences (interpreted systems), specifically normative systems have been studied only by deontic logicians as purely formal (logical) systems. The application of such formal calculi to a concrete subject matter, e. g. to given legal or moral norms, has been explored only to a limited extent probably for the reasons advanced at the beginning of this Introduction.

On the other hand, law has always been conceived of as having some sort of systematic order and the systematization (i. e. ordered arrangement) of legal provisions is traditionally regarded as an important task, assigned both to the legislator (the codification of the law) and to the legal scientist. As a system of norms the law is expected to conform to certain standards of rationality; the self-consistency of legal norms, as well as their collective consistency, is one such requirement. To eliminate the contradictions in legal provisions is, accordingly, a major aim of legal science.

An equally important part in legal theory has been played by the idea of completeness, which has been frequently discussed by jurists and legal philosophers under the heading of "gaps in law". Finally, the independence is also one of the aims pursued by legal scientists.

Thus, the ideas of consistency, completeness and independence, as well as the notion of a legal system in itself, provide suitable intuitive grounds for the analytical treatment (rational reconstruction) of these concepts. This analysis is the main concern of the first part of this book.

Starting with an actual problem in legal theory, we sketch a simplified model of a legal system in order to show how the concept of normative completeness (legal gaps) actually operates in legal science. By generalizing the constitutive elements of the model we are able to give an explicit definition of "gap". This definition shows the relational structure of the concept of normative completeness: it is a relation between a set of norms (a normative system), a set of possible factual circumstances or cases (a Universe of Cases) and a set of possible answers to or solutions of the problem (a Universe of Solutions). This implies that any discussion of the problem of gaps requires, as a preliminary step, the determination of the range of each of the three terms of the relation. It is the omission of this necessary step that has been responsible for the failure of legal philosophers to deal successfully with this problem.

One of the purposes of this book is to give an adequate definition of the concept of a normative system. Two main difficulties had to be avoided. On the one hand, the usual definition of a normative system as a set of norms seems to be too narrow. Legal provisions (statutes, codes, constitutions) contain many sentences that can scarcely be described as norms or, at least, as norms of conduct. Conceptual rules (definitions) play a very important part in legal discourse, a fact that is often overlooked by legal philosophers.

On the other hand, the notion of a legal system or legal order as the set of all the valid provisions whose validity is derived from some common source, such as a sovereign (Austin), a basic norm (Kelsen) or a rule of recognition (Hart) is of relatively little use in legal science. Jurists never discuss problems of completeness (gaps) or consistency in relation to the whole legal order. They often ask whether some particular statute or code or some definite set of norms is complete in relation to some specific problem, but it is only legal philosophers who talk about the completeness of the whole legal order. Thus in order to give an account of the activity of lawyers and jurists a more general concept of normative system is required; the notion of a legal order is merely a special case of this.

In order to meet these difficulties we have elaborated a general concept of normative system which is based on some ideas advanced by Tarski. This involves defining a normative system as a set of sentences that has (some) normative consequences (for some Universe of Cases and some Universe of Solutions). The definition of a normative system in terms of normative consequences allows us to give an account of any non-normative sentences that are included in a system without treating them as incomplete or mutilated norms (KELSEN). At the same time, the stress that we have laid on consequences enables us to dismiss such questions af the number or the origin of the sentences that form the basis of the system. *Any* set of sentences can be used as a basis for a system.

The conception of norms as linguistic entities (sentences that correlate cases with solutions) and normative systems as sets of sentences stands in opposition to a long tradition in legal philosophy. Norms are usually conceived of as ideal entities (meanings, thought-formations). But the treatment of norms at a purely syntactical level has considerable advantages from a methodological point of view and does not necessarily prejudge their ontological status. Logical analysis has proved much more efficacious when applied to linguistic expressions instead of ideal meanings or essences. The whole development of modern logic is an argument in favour of adopting this method, which has also made possible considerable progress in dealing with some traditional philosophical issues, such as the problems of truth (TARSKI) and knowledge (HINTIKKA).

Though the starting point of the discussion is a legal problem, the definitions of all the crucial notions are given in quite general terms, in order to make them applicable to norms of every type.

An application of the conceptual scheme elaborated in Part I to some specific problems of legal science is undertaken in Part II. It is argued that many of the traditional problems of legal theory can be reconstructed as problems concerning the systematization of legal sentences. Empirical questions concerning the identification of those legal sentences which form the basis of a system (the problem of legal validity) must be sharply distinguished from questions concerning the organization of these sentences into a system which is a conceptual (logical) problem. Here the ideas of completeness, consistency and independence play a very important part. A special stress is laid in this book on the concept of normative completeness, as being the most controversial of the three.

The process of the systematization of the law includes several operations whose aim is not only to exhibit the structural properties of the system and its formal defects (inconsistencies and gaps), but also to provide a reformulation of the system that is simpler and more economical. The search for so-called general principles of law and the construction of "general parts" in legal codes — both of which are customarily regarded as a major concern of legal dogmatics — from part of the same demand for a simplification of the law which is tied up with the idea of independence.

It would be a mistake to interpret our characterization of the process of systematization (and our assertion that it is the central activity of legal science) as an attempt to describe what jurists actually do; it is, on the contrary, a reconstruction of some ideals of legal science. These ideals are basic to a scientific and hence rational study of law, and because they are independent of any political ideology they may be characterized as purely rational. Among them, the ideal of completeness plays a very important part in legal thought.

The book contains a discussion of the well known thesis that there can be no normative gaps and that consequently all normative systems are necessarily complete. This thesis is frequently based on the interdefinability of "permitted" and "prohibited". We argue that this thesis derives its plausibility from a systematically ambiguous use of the crucial term "permitted" that results from a failure to draw a clear distinction between norms and normative propositions, i. e. propositions about norms. The so-called postulate of hermetic plenitude (or of necessary completeness) of the law — which is a juristic version of the same thesis — is not justified in its claim that every legal system is complete. It is important to stress the difference between the postulate of completeness, according to which all legal systems are in fact complete, and the requirement that they should be complete. The former is, at best, a mere illusion which nonetheless plays a definite ideological part in legal thought, while the latter is a purely rational ideal independent of any political attitude. The requirement of completeness in normative systems we take to be a special case of a more general principle inherent in all scientific inquiry *qua* rational activity.

It has been a major concern of the authors to avoid as far as possible the use of logical symbolism and other technical devices which would create difficulties of understanding for a general reader without special training in symbolic logic. Thus no previous knowledge of deontic logic or legal philosophy is assumed (though such knowledge would, of course, be helpful for the reader) and on more than one occasion the rigour of the exposition has had to be sacrificed to the demands of simplification. This is the *raison d'être* of the Appendix which contains in the form of definitions and theorems a rigorously formalized presentation of the main lines of thought developed in the book.

Part I

The Logic of Normative Systems

I. A Model for Normative Systems

1. Methodological Considerations

"The essentials of the method of formalization and interpretation are deeply ingrained in the western mind and perhaps constitute the ideal prototype of some aspects of what we call *rational* thought."

R. M. MARTIN
(Truth and Denotation, London 1958)

Our aim is to give an explication of the concept of a normative system in order to examine the formal properties of such systems: completeness, consistency and independence. The explication or rational reconstruction of a concept is the method by which an inexact and vague concept — which may belong to ordinary discourse or to a preliminary stage in the development of a scientific language — is transformed into an exact or, at least, a more exact concept. Or perhaps it might be more accurate to speak of the *substitution* of a more exact concept for a less exact one.

The concept that requires explication is called the *explicandum* and the new concept which is designed to replace it, the *explicatum*.

The process of explication comprises two stages: (1) The clarification of the *explicandum,* and (2) the construction of the *explicatum*. The importance of the first stage is not always sufficiently appreciated; but in order to be able to substitute for one concept another capable of performing with greater efficiency the function of the first, it is necessary to clarify as far as possible the meaning of the *explicandum*. This may be achieved by different methods, such as providing examples and descriptions of the use of the concept in different contexts.

The *explicatum* must fulfil certain requirements: (a) It ought to be an *exact* concept (as exact as possible). This means that the rules for its use must be formulated explicitly (e. g. by means of explicit definitions). (b) It must be a fruitful concept, i. e., it must be useful for the formulation of as many universal statements as possible. (c) The *explicatum* should be *similar* to the *explicandum* in the sense that it should be capable of being used in most cases in which the *explicandum* is used. In other words, the extensions of the *explicatum* and the *explicandum* should be as much alike as possible. This similarity cannot, of course, be so close as to make the two concepts co-extensive and, in general, this requirement is subordinate to the other two. (d) Finally, the requirement of simplicity should be mentioned, though it has less importance than the other three. Other things being equal a simpler concept is preferable to a more complicated one; but a more complicated *explicatum* which is more exact or fruitful is to be preferred to a simpler one.

As has already been pointed out (cf. Introduction), the concepts of normative system, completeness, consistency and independence are frequently used in legal discourse and have been much discussed in legal science. It therefore seems reasonable to take the corresponding legal notions as *explicanda*. We shall pay special attention to the notion of *legal gap* (lacuna) — a much discussed and most controversial topic — in order to elaborate a satisfactory *explicatum* for the concept of normative completeness. The concept of normative gap will prove an extremely useful means of dealing with several methodological problems and will be used, as it were, as a guiding principle throughout the book. But we shall also try to generalize the definitions of all crucial concepts in such a way that our *explicata* can be applied to norms of every type and not to legal norms only.

The starting point for the explication of the concept of a normative system will be the construction of a model which is intended to reproduce — in a slightly simplified and hence more abstract form a "real" problem taken from Civil Law. This model will enable us to give provisional definitions of all the crucial concepts: normative system, completeness, gap, consistency, independence, redundancy, etc. In the next three chapters the generalization of these concepts will be carried out.

Some philosophers seem to believe that the method of rational reconstruction is by its very nature incapable of grasping "the total reality" in all its aspects, because it proceeds by abstraction and leads to an unavoidable impoverishment of our knowledge, as there are necessarily some aspects of things which remain inaccesible to rational explication. Usually some sort of direct intuition is opposed to the method of abstraction. Objections of this kind are based on a misconception of abstraction generally and of the method of rational reconstruction in particular. It may be perfectly true that an *explicatum* does not depict *all* aspects and nuances of the concept it purports to explain. But this does not imply that there is some aspect of the reality (i. e., of the *explicandum*) that is in principle inaccessible to the method of abstraction. No abstract model can depict the total reality, but there is no aspect of the reality that could not be depicted in some model. Thus for every concept we are interested in, an adequate *explicatum* can be constructed. On the other hand, it should be remembered that all scientific knowledge requires some degree of abstraction and, as has been pointed out by R. M. MARTIN, the method of rational reconstruction reflects an essential aspect of all rational thought.

2. A Normative Problem

For the construction of our model we have chosen a typical normative problem, which has been much discussed in legal science (al least in the Argentinian Law). It is the problem of the recovery of real estate from third holders. This problem arises when someone in possession of real estate — which is owned not by him but by someone else transfers it (by way of sale or gift) to a third person. Then comes the question whether (and if so, in what circumstances) the owner of real estate may recover its possession from the third holder. Or to put the question in other terms: in what circumstances has the third holder the obligation to restore it to its owner and in what circumstances (if any) may he keep it, i. e. be allowed to refuse to restore it?

In order to answer this question we must know whether a certain action (restitution of real estate) is obligatory or not. So we are concerned with what we may conveniently call the deontic status of an action. There is a certain set of situations or states of affairs in which this action may take place and this we shall call a *Universe of Discourse* (*UD*).

The states of affairs which belong to a *UD* are the elements of the *UD*. All the elements of *UD* share a certain property which is the defining property of the *UD*. The Universe of Discourse may be described therefore as the set of all elements (states of affairs) identified by a certain property.

In our model the defining property of the *UD* is the property of being the transfer of real estate which belongs to a third person. Therefore, each element of the Universe of Discourse of the model is a state of affairs or situation in which a certain person (the transferor) transfers to another person (the transferee) the possession of real estate which is owned by a third person. The *UD* of the model is the set of all such situations.

A normative problem may be regarded as a question concerning the deontic status of certain actions, i. e. whether these actions are permitted or prohibited or obligatory, etc. Some of these actions are *basic* in the sense that all other actions are truth-functional compounds of them. Any finite set of such basic actions will be called a *Universe of Actions* (*UA*).

In our model there is only one basic action, the action of the third holder that consists in the restitution of the real estate to its owner, which will be called, for short, Restitution (*R*). Thus, the *UA* of the model is a unitary set, because it has only one element (*R*).

The two elements which we have so far distinguished, the *UD* and the *UA*, delimit the scope of a problem. Every variation of any of these two elements would lead to the problem's changing, i. e. becoming a different problem. E. g., if instead of asking in what circumstances the present holder has the obligation to restore the estate, we were interested in knowing whether the holder or the owner has the obligation to pay a certain tax, we should be facing another problem.

If the Universe of Discourse is taken to be constant — as it will be in subsequent discussions — then the identity of the problem will be determined by the Universe of Actions.

3. *The Factual Range of the Problem*

Let us now turn to our primary question: in what circumstances is restitution obligatory and under what conditions is non-restitution permissible? The answer to this question depends on our estimation of the different circumstances that should be taken into account. The selection of the relevant circumstances or properties[1] is there-fore a value problem. If certain properties seem to be quite irrel-evant for our problem (such as, e. g., the colour of the owner or the size of his nose) this is so only because there is a more or less unanimous consensus (in a given social group) concerning certain values. But this is, merely, a contingent fact; there is nothing neces-sary about it. We should certainly consider it very unjust if a law made the obligation to return the estate depend on the colour of its owner, but the possibility that such a law may seem perfectly reasonable to other people (e. g. in South Africa) is not excluded.

We shall regard the following three properties as relevant to our problem: the good faith of the former possessor (the transferor) (*F*), the good faith of the present holder (the transferee) (*G*), and the onerous character of the act of assignment (transfer) (*H*) — that jurists call "consideration".

(In order to simplify the model let us assume that bad faith consists in awareness of the fact that the estate is owned by some-body else and that good faith is simply the absence of bad faith.)

These three circumstances (*F*, *G*, *H*) are properties of the ele-ments of the *UD*. Every property divides the elements of the Uni-verse of Discourse into two classes: the class of those elements of *UD* in which this property is *present* and the class of those elements in which it is *absent*. To say that a property is absent is tantamount to saying that its *complementary* property is present. The com-plementary property is the negation of the property in question,

---

1 The words "circumstance" and "property" are roughly synonymous, but we shall use the latter as a technical term. Cf. J. BENTHAM, Of Laws in General (Hart edition, London, 1970, p. 42—43): "If the import of the word *circumstance* should still be obscure ... it may be made something clearer perhaps by changing it into the word *property* ... Wherever the word *circumstance* is employed with reference to an act, the phrase in which it stands may be changed into another phrase containing the word *property*. ... While logicians and naturalists made use of the word *prop-erty,* people at large made use of the word *circumstance.*"

e. g., $\sim F$ is the complementary property of F, and vice versa. It follows from this that for any property P, every element of UD has either P or its complementary ($\sim P$).

Any set of properties which may be present or absent in the elements of a UD we shall call a *Universe of Properties* (*UP*).

In our model the Universe of Properties includes only three properties: F (good faith of the transferee), G (good faith of the transferor), and H (consideration).

Every property of a UP and every truth-functional compound of such properties (provided that it is not tautological or contradictory) will be said to define a (possible) *case*[2]. Hence the defining property of a case may be either simple or complex.

When the defining property is a conjunction containing every property of a UP or its negation (but not both), the case so defined will be called *elementary*.

Cases which are not elementary are called *complex*.

The set of all elementary cases (corresponding to a UP) will be called a *Universe of Cases* (*UC*). The number of all possible elementary cases may be easily determined. Let n be the number of the properties of the UP; then 2^n is the number of the elementary cases, i. e. of the elements of the corresponding UC. The notion of a UC is, together with the number of the elementary cases, *relative* to a UP.

In our model, such cases as F, $\sim G$, $F \cdot H$, $G \cdot \sim H$[3], etc. are complex. The elementary cases are depicted in Table I-1 (where the sign $+$ symbolizes the presence of the corresponding property and the sign $-$ its absence).

---

2 "The import of this word [i. e. "case"] is nearly allied to that of the word *circumstance*. ... We speak of an act as being attended or accompanied by or with a circumstance: but we cannot speak of it as being attended or accompanied by or with a case. On the other hand we speak of an act as being performed *in* such or such a case: but we cannot speak of it as being performed *in* such or such circumstance. We may speak of it indeed as being performed in such or such circumstances: for an assemblage of circumstances may be considered as constituting a case." (J. BENTHAM, op. cit., p. 44—45; The Limits of Jurisprudence Defined, Everett edition, 1945, p. 130.)

3 We use the usual symbols of truth-functional logic: '.' for conjunction, 'v' for disjunction, '⊃' for (material implication and '$\sim$' for negation. (Sometimes we also use '$\bar{p}$' for the negation of 'p'.)

The table indicates what the possible cases are (in the model) and also makes it clear that these are *all* the possible (elementary) cases. The set of all the possible cases determines what we shall call the factual range of the model.

Table I-1

		UP		
		F	G	H
UC	1.	+	+	+
	2.	—	+	+
	3.	+	—	+
	4.	—	—	+
	5.	+	+	—
	6.	—	+	—
	7.	+	—	—
	8.	—	—	—

In the characterization of the factual range only elementary cases have been taken into account. This is so because these are the strongest properties that can be defined in terms of the corresponding *UP*. Elementary cases are simple in the sense that they cannot be subdivided into other cases, whereas all complex cases may be analyzed in terms of elementary cases. It can easily be shown that every complex case is equivalent to a disjunction of two or more elementary cases. On the other hand, every element of a *UD* must have one and only one such property; in other words, every element of a *UD* belongs to one and only one elementary case. (Cf. *infra*, ch. II, sect. 2.)

4. The Normative Range of the Problem

In the preceding Section we determined the factual range of the problem under consideration. In other words, we identified the possible cases with regard to which it is appropriate to ask whether the restitution of the estate is obligatory.

We must now consider what the possible answers to this question are. As our question is a normative one, i. e. concerns the normative status of certain actions, the range of all possible answers to that question will be called the normative range of the problem.

Every action of a *UA* and every truth-functional compound of actions (provided that it is not tautological or contradictory) will be called a *deontic content*. I will be remembered that the Universe of Actions of our model is a unitary set, whose only element is the action R (restitution of real estate to its owner). Hence there are only two possible deontic contents: R and $\sim R$.

The action R will be said to be obligatory (OR) when it is permitted that R and it is not permitted that $\sim R$ ($PR . \sim P \sim R$). When it is not permitted that R and it is permitted that $\sim R$, the action will be said to be prohibited ($PhR = \sim PR . P \sim R$). When both R and $\sim R$ are permitted, the action will be said to be facultative or optional ($FR = PR . P \sim R$). The expressions P (permitted), O (obligatory), Ph (prohibited) and F (facultative or optional) are the *deontic characters*.

Expressions of the form PR — in which a deontic content is preceded by a deontic character (provided they are not deontically tautological or contradictory) — and the non-tautological and non-contradictory truth-functional compounds of such expressions will be called *solutions*. A deontic content that is preceded by a deontic character will be said to be deontically determined. Hence every solution deontically determines some deontic content.

When the solution is such that it determines *all* the deontic contents which correspond to a UA, we shall call it a *maximal solution*. The set of all maximal solutions (relative to a UA) will be called the *Universe of Maximal Solutions* ($USmax$).

In our model, OR, PhR and FR are the three possible (maximal) solutions and the set of these three maximal solutions is the $USmax$ of the model.

$$USmax = \{OR, PhR, FR\}\,[1]$$

The Universe of Maximal Solutions ($USmax$) is the set of all *complete* answers to our question. A maximal solution is a complete answer in the sense that if it is correlated with a case, then *all* possible actions (contents) are deontically determined in that case. If the solution were not maximal, then the answer would be incomplete, for there would be some action whose deontic status would not be determined. Consider, for instance, the solution PR; from it nothing can be inferred concerning the deontic status of $\sim R$, whereas the maximal solutions determine both R and $\sim R$. Those solutions which are not maximal will be called *partial*. In the construction of the model we shall take into account maximal solutions only. (As may easily be shown, every partial solution is

---

1 The symbol '$\{x, y, z\}$' denotes the class whose elements are x, y and z.

equivalent to a disjunction of two or more maximal solutions, so that every partial solution is definable in terms of maximal solutions.)

The USmax, i. e., the set of all possible maximal solutions determines the *normative range* of the problem.

5. Reconstruction of a Normative System

Sentences (i. e. linguistic expressions) which correlate cases with solutions will be called *norms*. Let us consider the following sentence: "If the present holder (the transferee) is in bad faith, then he has the obligation to restore the estate to its owner." This sentence correlates a certain solution ("OR") with a certain case (the complex case "$\sim F$"); hence it is a norm. This norm may be represented by the expression "$OR/\sim F$", which may be read as "Obligatory R, in case $\sim F$". The case "$\sim F$" is equivalent to a disjunction of 4 elementary cases; thus the norm "$OR/\sim F$" correlates 4 elementary cases with a maximal solution. The following table gives a graphic representation of the norm "$OR/\sim F$":

Table I-2

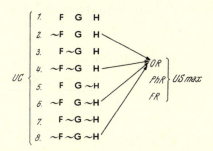

Thus from the norm "$OR/\sim F$" we may infer solutions for cases 2, 4, 6, and 8.

Any set of norms constitutes a *normative system*. (As we shall see later — ch. IV — the converse does not hold; a normative system may contain other types of sentences besides norms.)

Let us consider now a normative system, called S_1. S_1 is the set of the following four norms:

N_1: $OR/\sim F$

N_2: $OR/\sim G$

N_3: $OR/\sim H$ $S_1 = \{N_1, N_2, N_3, N_4\}$

N_4: $FR/F . G . H$

(As a matter of fact, S_1 is a reconstruction of §§ 3877 (2), 3878 (2), 3878 (3) and 3882 (1) of the Civil Code elaborated by the well known Brazilian jurist FREITAS. FREITAS' Code was the inmediate source of the Argentinian Civil Code (1869), especially regarding the problem we are considering. The comparison between the two Codes will prove to be very instructive.)

What are the solutions that can be inferred from the norms $N_1 - N_4$ for the cases of our model? N_1 says that restitution is obligatory when the transferee lacks good faith; hence it correlates the solution OR with all those cases in which $\sim F$ occurs: these are cases 2, 4, 6 and 8. N_2 says that restitution is obligatory when the transferor lacks good faith and consequently correlates cases 3, 4, 7 and 8 with the solution OR. N_3 correlates cases 5, 6, 7 and 8 with the solution OR and N_4 correlates case 1 with the solution FR, because it says that the restitution is neither obligatory nor prohibited (i. e. it is permitted that R and it is permitted that $\sim R$, therefore R is facultative).

The following table (I-3) is a matrix of the system S_1. (Here we use a different mode of representation, which has the advantage of showing the solutions which derive from each norm of the system.)

Table I-3

System S_1

					Norms		
				N_1	N_2	N_3	N_4
				$(OR/\sim F)$	$(OR/\sim G)$	$(OR/\sim H)$	$(FR/F.G.H)$
	1.	F	G	H				FR
	2.	$\sim F$	G	H	OR			
	3.	F	$\sim G$	H		OR		
UC	4.	$\sim F$	$\sim G$	H	OR	OR		
	5.	F	G	$\sim H$			OR	
	6.	$\sim F$	G	$\sim H$	OR		OR	
	7.	F	$\sim G$	$\sim H$		OR	OR	
	8.	$\sim F$	$\sim G$	$\sim H$	OR	OR	OR	

Solutions ($USmax = \{OR, FR, PhR\}$)

The first column (extreme left) is occupied by the eight possible cases. The next four columns correspond to the four norms of S_1. Solutions are placed where the lines corresponding to the cases intersect with the columns corresponding to the norms. Solutions which occur in the same column are those that derive from the same norm. Solutions which are in the same line, are those which can be inferred from the system for the case to which the line corresponds.

The table allows us to give the following definitions:

A case in the line corresponding to which no solution occurs will be called a (normative) *gap*. A normative system is *incomplete* if and only if it has at least one gap. A system that has no gaps will be said to be *complete*.

A system is *inconsistent in a case* C_i if and only if there are two or more different (incompatible) solutions in the line corresponding to C_i. A system is *inconsistent* if and only if there is at least one case in which it is inconsistent. Otherwise it will be called *consistent*.

A system will be called *redundant in a case* C_i if and only if the same solution occurs at least twice in the line corresponding to C_i. The norms of the system will be said to be *independent* if and only if there is no case in which the system is redundant. If there is at least one case in which the system is redundant, the norms of that system will be said to be *redundant*.

6. *Variations of the Model*

As may be easily seen from Table I-3, the system S_1 is complete, consistent and redundant.

S_1 is complete because there are solutions in every line; this means that there is no case which would not be correlated with a solution. Hence S_1 has no gaps.

The system is consistent for no case is correlated with two different solutions (*FR* and *OR* do not occur in the same lines). But the norms N_1, N_2 and N_3 are not independent: N_1 and N_2 are redundant in cases 4 and 8; N_2 and N_3 are redundant in cases 7 and 8; N_1 and N_3 are redundant in cases 6 and 8. Only N_4 is independent of the other three norms.

In spite of the fact that three norms of S_1 are (partially) redundant, none may be removed without giving rise to gaps: the suppression of N_1 would leave case 2 without a solution; without N_2 case 3 would have no solution and the same would happen to case 5 if the norm N_3 were removed. But this does not mean that we must keep all of them if we wish to preserve the completeness of the system.

One way of obtaining a complete, consistent and independent system is to substitute the norms N_5 ($OR/\sim G . H$) and N_6 ($OR/\sim F . G . H$) for the norms N_1 and N_2. The system S_2, constituted by the norms N_3, N_4, N_5 and N_6, is complete and consistent and its norms are independent. Moreover, although the systems S_1 and S_2 are, in a sense, different, as they are constituted by different norms, they nevertheless provide the same solutions for the same cases. We may stress this fact by saying that they have the same normative consequences.

Thus, in an important sense, S_1 and S_2 are (normatively) identical; instead of speaking of two systems, we should say that S_1 and S_2 are two different formulations of the same normative system.

Let us now examine two more systems: S_3 and S_4. S_3 is constituted by the following three norms :

N_2: $OR/\sim G$

N_3: $OR/\sim H$

N_7: $FR/F . G$

The system S_4 is the set of the norms N_6 and N_3.

$$S_4 = \{N_6, N_3\}$$

In Table I-4 we see the matrix of each of the four systems:

Table I-4

Cases	S_1				S_2				S_3			S_4	
	N_1	N_2	N_3	N_4	N_3	N_4	N_5	N_6	N_2	N_3	N_7	N_6	N_3
1. F G H				FR	FR						FR		
2. ~F G H	OR						OR					OR	
3. F ~G H		OR				OR			OR				
4. ~F ~G H	OR	OR				OR			OR				
5. F G ~H			OR		OR					OR	FR	OR	
6. ~F G ~H	OR		OR		OR					OR		OR	
7. F ~G ~H			OR	OR	OR				OR	OR		OR	
8. ~F ~G ~H	OR		OR	OR	OR				OR	OR		OR	

The system S_3 is incomplete (there is a gap in case 2, for no solution occurs in the corresponding line), inconsistent (two different solutions, OR and FR, occur in the line 5) and redundant (in cases 7 and 8).

(We would appear to be stressing the obvious in insisting upon the difference between cases which lack any solution (gap cases) and cases where there are too many solutions (in which the system is inconsistent), were it not that some legal writers regard them as identical[1]. In spite of the fact that in many contexts the practical consequences of the two situations may be similar, it is important to realize that gaps and inconsistencies are two different phenomena, which require different treatment.)

The matrix of S_4 shows that this system is consistent and independent but not complete, for it has three gaps. We are especially interested in S_4 for this system is a reconstruction of two paragraphs of the Argentinian Civil Code. In fact the norm N_6 depicts § 2777 and N_3 § 2778 of the Argentinian Civil Code. These prescribe that the restitution of real estate is obligatory where the transferee is in good faith, the transfer is made with consideration and the transferor is in bad faith (§ 2777), and if the transfer is made without consideration (even if the transferee were in good faith) (§ 2778). This is exactly what our norms N_6 and N_3 say.

A comparison between the systems S_1 (Freitas' system) and S_4 (Civil Code system) reveals considerable impoverishment. FREITAS' four norms have been reduced to two, but the — hardly expected — result is the occurrence of three gaps! (It is interesting to note that FREITAS has been frequently criticized for being too casuistic and among his critics was VELEZ SARSFIELD, the author of the Argentinian Civil Code.)

There is a long-standing controversy among Argentinian jurists about what solution should be assigned to case 1 (in cases 3 and 4 all agree that restitution is obligatory). We are not interested in discussing how gaps should be filled; the important thing for us is to provide an instance of a gap. Of course, to say that the system S_4 which is constituted by §§ 2777 and 2778 is incomplete is not

---

1 Cf. ULRICH KLUG, Rechtslücke und Rechtsgeltung, Festschrift für Hans Carl Nipperdey, München—Berlin, 1965, and Observations sur le problème des lacunes en droit, Logique et Analyse 10, 98—116 (1967), AMEDEO G. CONTE, Décision, Complétude, Clôture. A propos des lacunes en droit, Logique et Analyse 9, 1—18 (1966), and Completezza e Chiusura, Studi in memoria di Widar Cesarini Sforza, Milano, 1968, pp. 141—163; ZYGMUNT ZIEMBINSKI, Les lacunes de la loi dans le système juridique polonais contemporain et les méthodes utilisées pour les combler, Logique et Analyse 9, 38—51 (1966).

equivalent to asserting that the Civil Code is incomplete. It may well be that some other paragraph of the Code provides a solution for those cases to which we can find no solution in §§ 2777 and 2778. But that the system S_4 has gaps is undeniable. This fact has been expressly or tacitly acknowledged by almost all the legal writers who have dealt with this problem. Some explicitly recognize the presence of a gap[2]; but even those who maintain that case 1 has a solution in the Code, solve it not by the application of §§ 2777 and 2778 but by some other norm[3]. This shows, incidentally, the importance of determining what system it is of which we are maintaining that it has gaps.

To ask whether such and such a case has a solution makes no sense unless we first identify the norms of the system that we are speaking about. The same case may have different solutions in different systems. Nor can we ask whether a normative system is complete (or consistent) until we have first determined the range of all possible cases (a UC) and the range of all possible solutions (a US). As has already been pointed out, the idea of completeness requires not only that *all* the cases should have a solution (which means that we must know what the possible cases are), but also that the solutions attached to the cases should be such that *all* possible actions are deontically determined. In other words, the concept of normative completeness has a relational structure and as such can be defined only in terms of the three elements we have distinguished: a Universe of Cases, a Universe of (maximal) Solutions and a normative system.

We are now in a position to give a general definition of the concept of normative completeness and normative gap. To say that a case C_i of a UC is a *gap* in a normative system α in relation to a USmax means that α does not correlate C_i with any solution of the USmax.

A case C_i of a UC will be called a *partial gap* in the system α in relation to a USmax if and only if C_i is a gap in α in USmax,

---

2 Cf. Julio Dassen, La accion reivindicatoria: sus limites, Lecciones y Ensayos 6, 1958: "It is clear that these two paragraphs do not apply where the transferee is in good faith, the transferor in good faith and the transfer is made with consideration."

3 Cf., for instance, Guillermo L. Allende, El acto juridico real, La Ley, vol. 110, 1963, and Alberto D. Molinario, La reivindicacion inmobiliaria y el adquirente de buena fe a titulo oneroso, Santa Fe, 1962.

but α correlates C_i with a disjunction (which is not deontically tautological) of two or more solutions of the USmax.

A normative system α is *complete* in relation to a UC and a USmax, if and only if α has no gaps in the UC, in relation to the USmax. When a system has at least one gap in a UC, in relation to a USmax, it will be said to be *incomplete* (in relation to that UC and that USmax).

These definitions are quite general in the sense that they apply not only to legal norms, but to any set of norms that qualify actions as permitted, obligatory or prohibited.

The relational structure of the concept of completeness has been made explicit in these definitions; the completeness or incompleteness of a normative system is always relative to a Universe of Cases and a Universe of Maximal Solutions. In the chapters that follow we shall discuss these notions in greater detail.

II. The Concept of Case

This chapter and the two that follow constitute a kind of commentary on the definition of the concept of completeness which will be carried out in three stages, corresponding to the three elements of the definition: cases, solutions and normative system.

This first stage will be devoted to the elucidation of the concept of case. We shall first try to formulate explicitly some presuppositions that were implicit in the preliminary characterization given in ch. I.

If what we want is to determine whether a normative system is complete, in the sense that it resolves all *possible* cases, which are those constituting the UC, then it seems to follow that we must so restrict the concept of case that the Universe of Cases contains contingent cases only, eliminating impossible (contradictory) and necessary (tautological) "cases". This, in turn, implies that the properties of the UP, from which the UC originates, will have to obey certain requirements; in particular, they must be logically independent (sect. 1).

It must be pointed out, however, that the UC does not always originate in a finite set of properties (UP), as in the model of ch. I. This makes it necessary for us to revise our definition of the UC, which was relative to a UP. With the help of the concept of division, we shall formulate a more general definition of the Universe of Cases, which will allow the inclusion of Universes with an infinite number of cases (sect. 2).

The term "case" presents some ambiguities. The distinction between generic cases and individual cases allows us to distinguish purely conceptual problems, which arise at the level of general norms and of generic cases, from empirical and semantic problems (application of general norms to individual cases) (sect. 3). The subsumption of individual cases under generic cases gives rise to the so-called problems of penumbra, which should not be confused with the problems of normative completeness. The expressions "gap of knowledge" and "gap of recognition" are introduced in order to distinguish these problems from the problem of normative gaps (sect. 4).

1. The Elements of the Universe of Properties and their Internal Relations

In our account of the Universe of Cases it was tacitly assumed that all cases in the *UC* are possible, in the sense that they are cases which may be exemplified in reality. In fact, cases are circumstances or situations where it is of interest to inquire whether a certain action is permitted, made obligatory or prohibited by a certain normative system. This implies that cases are not logically impossible (contradictory), or necessary (tautological), since circumstances which never occur or always occur are obviously not of interest in this way. Hence our concept of case must exclude those combinations of properties constituting the defining characteristics of cases which are tautological or contradictory.

This implies — if cases are determined by combinations of the properties of the *UP* — that the latter must have certain characteristics ensuring that every combination of the elements of the *UP* is contingent (not necessary, or impossible).

These requirements are:

a) In the first place, the elements of the *UP* must be *logically independent*. Two properties are said to be logically independent when the presence of one in an object is compatible with the presence, and also the absence, of the other in the same object. We shall call the assumption that the properties of a *UP* are logically independent the hypothesis of logical atomism. This hypothesis has great theoretical value if we regard it as a simplified model, without claiming that the reality always corresponds to this model. In fact, it is possible that the properties of a *UP* are not all logically independent; this would mean that some of the combinations of these properties would be impossible, since no object could have the property constituted by a combination of two or more logically incompatible properties. In other words, the presence of properties which are not logically independent would give rise to logically empty cases. To provide for this we should have to introduce meaning postulates[1]. But in order to avoid this complication and not make our exposition excessively long, we shall accept the hypothesis of logical atomism.

The *empirical independence* of the properties of the *UP* gives rise to interesting problems. It may happen that two logically independent properties are empirically not independent. This means that there is a causal relation between them. For example, P_1 may be (in fact) a sufficient condition, a necessary condition, a sufficient and necessary condition or a contributory condition for P_2[2]. In such circumstances, the cases characterized by the property $\sim P_1 . P_2$ (if P_1 is a necessary condition for P_2) or by the property $P_1 . \sim P_2$ (if P_1 is a sufficient condition for P_2) will be empirically empty; they are not exemplified in reality. Such cases are logically possible, but empirically impossible.

A normative system which fails to resolve some empirically impossible cases is logically incomplete, but it is complete in the sense that it resolves all cases which may in fact present themselves. To describe this situation we shall introduce the notion of *empirical completeness,* to distinguish it from that of logical completeness.

Empirical completeness is compatible with logical incompleteness: a system empirically complete may be logically incomplete, but the contrary does not hold: a system which is logically complete is necessarily (for reasons of logic) empirically complete.

Although in practice jurists often content themselves with the empirical completeness of a system, logical completeness is much more important for legal theory.

---

1 On meaning postulates see R. Carnap, Meaning and Necessity, Chicago, 1956, p. 222 ff.

2 On the notion of condition cf. G. H. von Wright, A Treatise on Induction and Probability, London, 1951, p. 66 ff.

It is important to determine whether a system is logically complete because we could know that a logically incomplete system was nevertheless empirically complete only if we had *knowledge* of *all* natural laws. And this knowledge, like all empirical knowledge, is uncertain. It may well happen that a state of affairs which is empirically possible will be considered impossible through error or lack of information. But this problem does not arise with respect to logical completeness, since the latter does not depend on the knowledge of natural facts.

b) We shall also require that the properties of the UP be logically independent of the properties characterizing the actions of the UA. Failure to require this would lead us to identify as possible solutions certain deontic characterizations of certain contents which it would be logically impossible to realize. It is intuitively obvious that we must exclude such deontic characterizations from the list of possible solutions. The above-mentioned requirement is one way though certainly not the only way, of achieving this.

c) Finally, the Universe of Properties and the Universe of Discourse must be two corresponding universes[3], in the sense that each of the elements of the UD can have each of the properties of the UP.

Henceforth, we shall assume that these requirements are met in the UP under discussion[4].

2. The Universe of Cases

The concept of case (in general) may be recursively defined in terms of the properties of the UP:

a) If P_i is a property of the UP, then P_i is (or defines) a case.

b) If P_i is a case, then the negation of P_i ($\sim P_i$) is a case.

---

3 On the notion of correspondence see G. H. von Wright, op. cit. p. 38 and also his On the Idea of Logical Truth, Logical Studies, London, 1957, p. 29.

4 In order to ensure that the cases of the UC are genuinely generic the requirement that the elements of the UP be purely qualitative properties should be added; but we omit this complication here. Cf. C. G. Hempel and P. Oppenheim, The Logic of Explanation, included in H. Feigl and M. Brodbeck (editors), Readings in the Philosophy of Science, New York, 1953, p. 338 ff.

   c) If P_i and P_j are cases, then the conjunction $(P_i \cdot P_j)$ and the disjunction $(P_i \vee P_j)$ are cases, provided that they are not tautological or contradictory.

In ch. I (sect. 3) we have distinguished between elementary cases — that is, those characterized by a conjunction which contains for each property of the UP either the property itself or its negation (but not both) — and complex cases, which are all cases that are not elementary. Then we have gone on to define the Universe of Cases as the set of all elementary cases.

The following table shows how elementary cases arise from a UP:

Table II-1

$$UP = \{P_1, P_2, P_3 \dots P_n\}$$

P_1	P_2	$P_3 \dots P_n$		Elementary cases	Defining Properties
+	+	+	+	C_1	$P_1 . \quad P_2 . \quad P_3 \dots \quad P_n$
—	+	+	+	C_2	$\sim P_1 . \quad P_2 . \quad P_3 \dots \quad P_n$
+	—	+	+	C_3	$P_1 . \sim P_2 . \quad P_3 \dots \quad P_n$
—	—	+	+	C_4	$\sim P_1 . \sim P_2 . \quad P_3 \dots \quad P_n$
+	+	—	+	C_5	$P_1 . \quad P_2 . \sim P_3 \dots \quad P_n$
—	+	—	+	C_6	$\sim P_1 . \quad P_2 . \sim P_3 \dots \quad P_n$
+	—	—	+	C_7	$P_1 . \sim P_2 . \sim P_3 \dots \quad P_n$
—	—	—	+	C_8	$\sim P_1 . \sim P_2 . \sim P_3 \dots \quad P_n$
—	—	—	—	C_{2n}	$\sim P_1 . \sim P_2 . \sim P_3 \dots \sim P_n$

$$UC = \{C_1, C_2, C_3 \dots C_{2n}\}$$

The table has columns for each of the properties of the UP. The different lines show the possible distributions of the two ways in which each property may appear: its presence (symbolized by the sign "+") or its absence (symbolized by the sign "—").

In the last column we find the defining properties of the elementary cases. Each of them is formed by a conjunction in which occurs each property of the UP or its negation.

Accordingly, cases C_1, C_2, etc. are elementary cases and the set of them is the Universe of Cases.

The characterization of the elementary cases in terms of the UP presupposes that the number of the properties of the UP is finite; otherwise it would be impossible to speak about a conjunction of *all* the properties of the UP or their negations. This in turn implies that the number of elements of the *UC* (relative to a *UP*) is also finite (as we have already seen, their number is 2^n, where n is the number of the properties of *UP*).

We shall now attempt to give a more general definition of a *UC* (in order to be able to include Universes of Cases with an infinite number of elements). To do this we shall make use of the notion of division.

A set of properties (or of predicates designating these properties) forms a *division* (or partition)[1] if and only if the following three conditions are fulfilled:

a) The properties are logically disjunct (exhaustive of the *UD*). This means that every element of the *UD* necessarily has some of the properties of the set.

b) Any two distinct properties are logically exclusive. This means that the properties forming a division are mutually exclusive (logically incompatible).

c) None of the properties is logically empty. This means that none of the properties is logically impossible, even though it may happen that in fact it is not exemplified.

We shall now define the *Universe of Cases* as any set of cases which form a division.

This definition has the advantage of making the concept of a *UC* independent of the Universe of Properties and allowing it to be applied to any set of cases forming a division, independently of the genesis of these cases.

It can easily be proved that the set of elementary cases of a *UP* is a Universe of Cases in the sense just defined. In fact, the elementary cases of a *UP* are logically exclusive and exhaustive: the logical independence of the properties of the *UP* (hypothesis of logical atomism) ensures that no elementary case is logically empty. Accordingly, the set of all elementary cases forms a division and is therefore a Universe of Cases.

However, this is only one of the possible kinds of *UC*. Another type of *UC* — also found rather frequently in law, especially in the matter of taxes — is met with when cases are characterized not by a finite set of properties, but by a *numerical value*.

---

1 On the concept of division see R. CARNAP, Logical Foundations of Probability, 2nd edition, Chicago, 1962, § 25, p. 107 ff., and P. SUPPES, Axiomatic Set Theory, Princeton, 1960, p. 83 ff.

Let us suppose that a law establishes a special tax. According to it every citizen with a monthly income below $ 500 has to pay $ 10; those whose income is over $ 500, but below $ 2000 have to pay $ 20 and those who earn over $ 2000 a month must pay $ 30. There are three categories of tax-payers for this law, or, as we might also say, three possible *cases*. These three cases form a division, since they are jointly exhaustive, mutually exclusive and not logically empty. According to our definition of a *UC*, these three cases form a Universe of Cases; nonetheless, this *UC* has not originated from a *UP*.

Examples of Universes of Cases characterized by numerical values are not difficult to find: customs duties, income tax, professional fees, etc. It is interesting that the *UC* that originates in this way usually contains an *infinite* number of cases. The law imposing income tax gives us an example of a *UC* with an infinite number of cases. In order to determine the amount of tax to be paid the income per annum is taken into account. This value can be expressed as a function of a certain quantity of monetary units, for example, dollars.

Any figure expressing the amount of income characterizes a *case*. The number of possible cases is infinite. The possible infinite cases constitute a *UC*, because these cases are logically exhaustive, exclusive and non-empty.

The infinity of the number of possible cases does not imply that it is impossible to resolve all these cases. For, even though it is not possible to point out separately the solution for each of these cases, it is perfectly possible to give a rule that permits the construction of a solution for any case of a *UC* of infinite cases. In our example, the rule would be one giving the percentage of the income per annum that should be paid as income tax. This rule resolves all the cases, since it permits the construction of an infinite number of solutions, in such a way that to each case corresponds a solution.

3. Generic and Individual Cases

The cases we have mentioned up to now have been characterized as *properties* (simple or complex).

Any property may be used to form a *class* of things (individuals) within a given universe of things. This class is constituted by all the things (in the universe) which have the property in question (in which the property is present). The things which lack this property (from which the property is absent) form a complementary class. In this way properties may be used to *classify* the elements of any universe.

The cases may also be used — as may any property — to classify the elements of the Universe of Discourse. We shall call *cases of the UD* the classes of elements of the *UD*, determined by the cases.

The elements of the *UD* are also often called *cases*. For the term "case" is as ambiguous in legal language as it is in ordinary language in general. Thus, for example, we speak about the case of political murder and the case of the murder of Mahatma Gandhi, of the case of divorce and the case of the divorce of Brigitte Bardot and Gunther Sachs. It is obvious that the word "case" has not the same meaning in these phrases. Gandhi's murder is a real event, that happened in a certain place and at a certain moment in time. The expression "case of political murder" does not refer to any concrete event; it is the mere description of certain properties which certain events may have. The property of being a political murder may be instantiated in an unlimited number of concrete occurrences. This ambiguity of the word "case" is the source of numerous misunderstandings in the sience of law, some of which have a direct bearing on the problem of gaps.

In order to remove this ambiguity we shall introduce the expressions "individual case" and "generic case"[1].

We shall call the elements of the Universe of Discourse *individual cases*. These elements are situations or events taking place on a certain occasion (space-time localization) which have the defining property of the *UD*[2]. The Universe of Discourse is the class of all individual cases. The defining property of the *UD* allows us to identify the individual cases belonging to this *UD*. Thus, for example, every situation in which an individual *A* transfers to another individual *B* real estate belonging to a third individual *C*, is an individual case belonging to the *UD* of the model constructed in ch. I.

---

1 For a similar distinction between generic and individual actions see G. H. von WRIGHT, Norm and Action, ch. III, sect. 2.

2 See *supra* ch. I, sect. 2.

Any subclass (subset) of the *UD* defined by a property, and also the defining property of the subclass, will be called a *generic case*. We shall therefore distinguish between generic cases of the *UD* (which are subclasses of the *UD*) and generic cases of the *UC* or simply generic cases (which are properties). (The word "case" has so far been used in the sense of generic case.)

Generic cases may be instantiated in an unlimited number of individual cases: an unlimited number of elements of the *UD* may belong to each generic case of the *UD*.

The classification of individual cases by means of the cases of a *UC* is of special interest. When a Universe of Cases is projected on a Universe of Discourse, the result is a set of generic cases of the *UD* presenting two fundamental characteristics: they are jointly exhaustive of the *UD* and mutually exclusive. Accordingly, any individual case of the *UD* necessarily belongs to one and only one of the generic cases determined by a *UC*.

This implies that *the solution of all the (generic) cases of a UC, also resolves all individual cases of the UD.*

This fact makes legislation possible. To legislate is to issue general norms in order to resolve individual cases. We understand by a general norm one which correlates a generic case with a solution; indirectly, such a norm also resolves all the individual cases belonging to this generic case. It is in this way that the legislator can resolve an infinite number of individual cases by means of a finite number of general norms. He can even resolve *all* individual cases of a *UD*; to succeed in doing so all he need do is to classify the *UD* by means of a *UC* (that is, a set of cases forming a division) and to resolve all the cases of the *UC*. It is only if he does not resolve a generic case that the system will have a normative gap. This shows that the problem of normative completeness arises at the level of generic cases and not at the level of individual cases, as is apparently believed by those writers who maintain that the law always has gaps because the human legislator — since he is a finite being, endowed with a limited capacity of foresight — cannot foresee all the infinite variety of cases that may be found in reality[3]. The fact that reality is infinitely variable is irrelevant to the problem of completeness, since the legislator has no need at all

---

3 "En realité, sans doute, les lois ne peuvent pas embrasser toutes les hypothèses si variées, si nombreuses, que chaque jour la pratique

to foresee all possible individual cases. The legislator does not issue norms for each individual case (this would surely be impossible; moreover, in attempting such a thing he would be ceasing to act as a legislator). His function consists in the creation of general norms, by means of which he resolves generic cases.

We are now in a position to appreciate the part played by the Universe of Cases. To do so, let us recall the main characteristics of the cases of a UC.

In the first place, the cases of a UC are the *minimal* cases: they do not allow a further subdivision and all other cases are equivalent to disjunctions of cases of the UC; accordingly, they can be expressed in terms of the latter. This permits us to assert that all complex cases are reducible to elementary cases, a fact that allows us to ignore the non-elementary cases.

In the second place, the cases of the UC are *mutually exclusive*. This is very important, since it allows to control the consistency of the system. To make sure that the system is consistent all we need is to verify that none of the cases of the UC is correlated with two or more incompatible solutions; if the system is consistent in every one of the cases of the UC, then it is also consistent in respect of all individual cases. This is so because by virtue of the exclusive character of the cases of the UC no individual case may belong to two cases of the UC at the same time, and every non-elementary generic case is equivalent to a disjunction (but never to a conjunction) of elementary cases.

In the third place, the cases of the UC are *jointly exhaustive* of the elements of the UD, that is, of the individual cases. This means that every individual case necessarily belongs to one and only one elementary case. Hence the solution of all elementary cases ensures the completeness of the system in the sense that all possible individual cases (all the elements of the UD) are resolved (even though some of the non-elementary cases do not have a solution).

Thus it may be seen that the exclusiveness of the cases of the UC is related to the idea of consistency and its exhaustiveness to that of completeness.

---

soulève." DEMOLOMBE, Cours de Code Napoleon, Paris, 1880, vol. I, p. 136. Similar opinions may be found in SAVIGNY (Vom Beruf unserer Zeit für Gesetzgebung und Rechtswissenschaft, 1814) and in many other famous jurists.

4. Problems of Application: Gaps of Knowledge and Gaps of Recognition

It is advisable to distinguish problems of a *conceptual* type arising at the level of generic cases and general norms, from *empirical* and *semantic* problems arising from the *application* of general norms to individual cases. The latter is typically the task of the judge, who must resolve individual cases by means of the application of general norms.

In legal theory, the distinction between these two groups of problems is not always as clearly drawn as it should be; they are often dealt with together under the heading of "interpretation". The lack of a clear distinction between generic and individual cases, is one of the sources of this confusion.

One of the main problems that arises in the application of general norms to individual cases is the classification of the individual case as belonging to one of the generic cases. Jurists usually refer to this problem by the name of *subsumption*.

The difficulties of the classification or subsumption of an individual case may arise from either of two sources. The first is *lack of information concerning some relevant fact*. Sometimes we do not know whether or not a concrete fact (individual case) belongs to a class (generic case), because we lack the necessary information; there are some aspects of the fact that we do not know, and this lack of knowledge is the cause of the difficulty in classifying the case. For example, even knowing that every case of transfer is necessarily made with or without consideration, we can very well not know whether the transfer of Ticius' house to Sempronius has been made with or without consideration, simply because we do not know whether Sempronius has paid anything for the house or not.

But the difficulty of knowing whether Ticius transferred his house with or without consideration may arise from yet another source: the *semantic indeterminacy* or *vagueness* of general concepts [1]. Even with full knowledge of the facts of the case, we may not know

---

1 On the concept of vagueness cf. B. Russell, Vagueness, The Australasian Journal of Psychology and Philosophy 1, 84 ff. (1923), F. Waismann, Verifiability, in A. N. G. Flew (editor), Logic and Language (first series), Oxford, 1951, p. 119 ff., G. R. Carrió, Notas sobre Derecho y Lenguaje, Buenos Aires, 1965, pp. 28—35.

whether the transfer was made with or without consideration because we do not know whether the amount of money Sempronius gave Ticius for his house is or is not a price in a technical sense. Let us suppose that the amount of money handed over is markedly less than the economic value of the house. In such circumstances it may be doubted whether it is a sale or a concealed gift.

The first difficulty — lack of empirical knowledge — can to some extent be overcome. Jurists have found an ingenious device for surmounting lack of factual knowledge that is called *legal presumption* and plays a very important part in legal practice generally and in judicial practice in particular. Presumptions allow the judge to forget his ignorance of the facts and act as if he knew all the relevant facts of the case. The central position is occupied by the general principle of the *onus probandi,* according to which all those who assert the existence of a fact must prove it, for if the alleged fact has not been duly proved, it is held to be non-existent. Several other presumptions — good faith, the onerous character of commercial acts, etc. — constitute a set of auxiliary rules for the determination of the legal "existence" of facts (which, as is well known, does not always coincide with their existence in reality).

The second difficulty we have mentioned is much more serious, as it cannot be entirely eliminated, but at most mitigated to a certain extent by means of the introduction of technical terms. This difficulty arises form the vagueness — actual or potential — that legal concepts share with all empirical concepts. Vagueness may be considerably reduced by the use of technical concepts introduced through explicit definitions which expressly stipulate the rules of application of the concepts, but never disappears entirely. It is always possible that an atypical or unusual object may appear which slips through the net of the rules of application of the concept, no matter how numerous and detailed these may be.

The word "gap" is sometimes used to refer to problems of this type[2].

It is obvious that these are questions very different in kind from those that we have analyzed under the same heading, so that to avoid confusion — which is all too frequent among jurists — we shall introduce some distinguishing terms.

---

2 Cf. H. KANTOROWICZ, Der Kampf um die Rechtswissenschaft, Heidelberg, 1906.

To distinguish these problems from normative gaps we shall coin the expressions "gaps of knowledge" and "gaps of recognition"[3].

Where, through ignorance of some of the properties of the fact, we do not know whether a certain individual case belongs to a certain generic case, we shall speak of a *gap of knowledge*.

Where, through semantic indeterminacy of the concepts which characterize a generic case, we do not know whether a certain individual case belongs to it, we shall speak of a *gap of recognition*.

While the problem of normative gaps is of a conceptual (logical) kind, both gaps of knowledge and gaps of recognition appear at the level of the application of general norms to individual cases, and originate in empirical or empirical-semantic problems. The fact that a normative system is (normatively) complete, in the sense that it resolves every possible case, either generic or individual, does not exclude the possibility of gaps of recognition (gaps of knowledge are in fact eliminated from judicial practice thanks to presumptions). There is always the possibility that an individual case whose classification is doubtful may appear. But this does not mean that this case is not resolved by the system; we may know that the case *is* resolved without knowing *how* it is resolved. We may, for example, know that the transfer of Ticius' house must necessarily be made with or without consideration and have a solution for both cases and nevertheless not know which solution to apply, as we do not know whether *this* transfer has been made with or without consideration.

Gaps of recognition arise from what Hart calls problems of penumbra[4]. Following this terminology we may also call them "cases of penumbra". The unavoidable possibility of cases of penumbra is a very important fact — especially for the judicial application of the law — and it is a great merit of legal realism to have called attention to this problem. We have no wish to underrate the importance of problems of penumbra in judicial practice, but feel that a warning should be given against the tendency to

---

3 We have borrowed this last expression from Amedeo G. Conte, Décision, Complétude, Clôture. A propos les lacunes en droit, Logique et Analyse 9, 1—18 (1966), but we use it in an entirely different sense.

4 H. L. A. Hart, Positivism and the Separation of Law and Morals, Harvard Law Review 71, 593—629 (1958).

exaggerate the part played by empirical problems in the application of the law to individual cases, at the expense of logical or conceptual problems arising at the level of generic cases. In particular, many writers dealing with the application of the law to individual cases take the fact that cases of penumbra are always a possibility to mean that the law is essentially incomplete, since it contains gaps[5].

This is, to say the least, a very unfortunate and misleading piece of terminology. To call cases of penumbra mere gaps without introducing a qualifying term to distinguish them from normative gaps may give rise to confusion. Cases of penumbra have nothing to do with the traditional problem of gaps in law, i. e. the problem of normative completeness.

Some writers do in fact speak in this context about the incompleteness of law[6]. This is equally misleading since the term "incompleteness" suggests the absence or lack of something. But cases of penumbra do not arise because the law is lacking in something: if the system is complete in the sense that is solves all the cases in the UC, then it also solves all individual cases, which does not exclude the possibility of the appearance of cases of penumbra. But the latter do not arise from an insufficiency or fault in the normative system; they are due to certain semantic properties of the language in general.

III. The Concept of Solution

This chapter develops the ideas sketched in ch. I, sects. 2 and 4, concerning the notion of solution and its two components, the Universe of Actions (UA) and deontic characters.

In sect. 1 are set down the conditions that the elements of the UA must fulfil. These conditions are analogous to those established for the properties of the UP (ch. II, sect. 1). Expressions describing

---

5 Cf. H. L. A. HART, Positivism and the Separation of Law and Morals, op. cit., The Concept of Law, ch. VII, H. KANTOROWICZ, op. cit., J. DICKINSON, The Problem of the Unprovided Case (Recueil Gény, II, 503), Legal Rules: Their Function in the Process of Decision (79 Pennsylvania Law Review 833).

6 H. L. A. HART, Positivism and the Separation of Law and Morals, op. cit., p. 614: "We can say laws are incurably incomplete and we must decide the penumbra cases rationally by reference to social aims."

the actions of the *UA* and their truth-functional compounds we call
deontic contents and we distinguish between atomic and molecular
contents (sect. 2). A general definition of solution is given in sect. 3.
With the help of the important notion of state-description the concepts of deontic constituent and deontic pair are defined, and these,
in turn, allow us to give account of the concepts of maximal solution and minimal solution and their corresponding universes: *US*max
and *US*min (sects. 3 and 4). In this way an effective method is sup-
plied which makes it possible to identify all maximal and minimal
solutions corresponding to a given *UA* and to establish whether or
not a given solution is maximal in relation to a certain *UA*. In sect. 5
we distinguish between solutions and norms and provide a classification of the latter.

1. Elements of the UA and their Internal Relations

Solutions have been described in ch. I as deontic modalizations of
the elements of the *UA* and their truth-functional compounds. The
elements of the *UA* are *generic* actions. The distinction between
generic and individual actions is analogous to the distinction between generic and individual cases (ch. II, sect. 3)[1]. The solutions
that concern us in this context are therefore generic, not individual
solutions.

As symbols for the elements of the *UA* we shall use the letters
p, q, r, etc. These letters may be interpreted as standing for propositions which describe generic actions, or better: states of affairs
which are the result of an action[2].

It will be assumed that the elements of the *UA* fulfil the following conditions:

a) They are *logically independent*. This implies the acceptance
of the hypothesis of logical atomism (cf. ch. II, sect. 1) regarding
the elements of the *UA*. Were we to abandon the requirement of
logical independence, it would be necessary to introduce meaning
postulates, but by adopting the hypothesis of logical atomism we
avoid this complication.

---

1 Cf. also G. H. von Wright, Norm and Action, p. 35.

2 On this problem see G. H. von Wright, An Essay in Deontic Logic
and the General Theory of Action, Acta Philosophica Fennica 21, 16 and
42 ff. (1968).

b) The elements of the *UA* are logically independent of the properties of the *UP* (cf. ch. II, sect. 1).

To assume a) and b) is equivalent to assuming the logical independence of the set formed by the properties of the *UP* and the elements of the *UA*.

2. Deontic Contents

We have already explained (ch. I, sect. 4) that the term *deontic content* is to be used for any expression describing an element of the *UA* or a truth-functional compound of such elements, provided that the latter is not tautological or contradictory. We shall distinguish between atomic and molecular contents. *Atomic* contents are expressions describing the elements of the *UA*: p, q, r, etc. *Molecular* contents are complex expressions developed from the atomic contents by means of truth-functional connectives: negation ("$\sim$"), conjunction (".") and disjunction ("v").

Starting from a set of atomic contents (a Universe of Actions), we obtain — by means of the successive application of truth-functional operators — a (much more numerous) set of molecular expressions. From this set we exclude all the expressions which are truth-functionally tautological or contradictory. What remains will be the set of all the molecular contents (corresponding to the chosen *UA*).

(Tautological and contradictory molecular expressions are excluded because they do not refer to possible states of affairs, in the sense in which a factual proposition refers to a state of affairs. Strictly speaking, there are no tautological or contradictory states of affairs[1].)

We shall be concerned with a special type of deontic content which, following an established terminology, we shall call *state-description*. A state-description is a conjunction in which occurs each and every one of the atomic contents or its negation, but not both. Thus, for example, if the elements of the *UA* are p, q and r, the following expressions are state-descriptions (for this *UA*): $p \cdot q \cdot r$, $\sim p \cdot q \cdot r$, $\sim p \cdot \sim q \cdot \sim r$, $p \cdot q \cdot \sim r$, etc.

---

1 Cf. L. WITTGENSTEIN, Tractatus logico-philosophicus, 4.461 and 4.463, and F. RAMSEY, The Foundations of Mathematics, London, 1931, p. 10 ff.

The notion of state-description is — as follows from its definition — *relative* to a UA. The set of all state-descriptions of a UA is a finite subset of the set of all the contents (atomic and molecular) corresponding to this UA. This subset occupies a special position, since any content (atomic or molecular) may be expressed in terms of state-descriptions. In fact, it can be proved (though we do not intend to prove it here) that any deontic content is truth-functionally equivalent to a state-description or a disjunction of state-descriptions[2].

The number of possible state-descriptions for a UA can be easily calculated by means of the formula 2^n, where n is the number of the elements of the UA.

3. Deontic Sentences and Solutions

Any expression formed by a deontic operator (character) followed by a deontic content and also any truth-functional compound of such expressions will be called a *deontic sentence*.

Deontic characters or modalities have been subjected to intensive scrutiny by logicians in the past twenty years. Different systems of deontic logic have been developed since 1951, when von Wright's classic essay "Deontic Logic" was published.

Among the various possible deontic characters[1], those that are most frequently used and are hence most frequently analyzed are P (permitted), O (obligatory), Ph (prohibited or forbidden) and F (facultative or optional)[2]. Deontic logicians desagree on the question whether each and every deontic operator can be defined in terms of any other. The definition of prohibition in terms of obligation (and negation) seems to be entirely uncontroversial, but the definition of permission in terms of obligation (and negation) is more problematic. (This problem will be discussed later — ch. VII, sect. 2).

We shall adopt P (permitted) as the primitive operator and assume that all the other can be defined in terms of P. (This has

---

2 On the notion of state-description see R. Carnap, Logical Foundations of Probability, Chicago, 1962, p. 70 ff.

1 Cf. A. G. Conte, Saggio sulla completezza degli ordinamenti giuridici, Torino, 1962.

2 The term "facultative" used here corresponds to von Wright's "indifferent". Cf. Deontic Logic, op. cit., Logical Studies, London, 1957, p. 61.

already been tacitly assumed in ch. I, sect. 4.) The following for-
mulae show the relations between P and the rest of the operators
and allow us to translate any expression in which one of the other
operators appears into an expression where only P occurs (preceded
sometimes, of course, by the negation sign "$\sim$").

$$Ph\,p \equiv \sim Pp \tag{D-1}$$

$$Fp \equiv Pp \,.\, P \sim p \tag{D-2}$$

$$Op \equiv \sim P \sim p \tag{D-3}$$

If from the set of all the deontic sentences (corresponding to a UA)
we exclude those which are deontically tautological or contradictory,
we obtain a set of sentences which we have called *solutions*. This
is the set of all possible solutions (for this UA). A solution is, accordingly, any deontic sentence that is neither deontically tautological
nor contradictory. (The meaning of the expressions "deontic tautology" and "deontic contradiction" depends, of course, on the
deontic logic that we choose to adopt, since they may be defined
in different ways in the different systems of deontic logic. Here we
shall use — mainly for the sake of illustration — the deontic logic
of von Wright, with slight modifications[3]. But what we say about
solutions and norms can also be adapted to other systems of deontic
logic, in which the terms "deontic tautology", "deontic contradiction", "deontic equivalence", etc. may have different meanings.)

Within the set of solutions special attention will be paid to
a subset of deontic sentences which we shall call *deontic constituents*. A deontic constituent is any expression formed by a state-
description preceded by the operator P or $\sim P$. As the expression
"$\sim P$" may be read as "prohibited" — by virtue of D-2 — we
can say that any permission or prohibition of a state-description
is a deontic constituent. Thus, for example, for $UA = \{p, q, r\}$,
the following expressions are deontic constituents: $P\,(p\,.\,q\,.\,r)$,
$P\,(\sim p\,.\,q\,.\,\sim r)$, $\sim P\,(p\,.\,q\,.\,\sim r)$, etc.

---

3 The deontic logic adopted throughout the book is Hanson's
system D (cf. W. H. Hanson, Semantics for Deontic Logic, Logique et
Analyse 8, 177—190 [1965], which differs from von Wright's first deontic calculus (that of Deontic Logic) only in abandoning the Principle of
Deontic Contingency for the axiom Ot.

It can be proved (though we do not intend to prove it here) that any deontic sentence can be transformed into (i. e. is deontically equivalent to) a truth-function of the deontic constituents. Thus, for example, the expression "Op" is deontically equivalent (for a $UA = \{p \cdot q\}$) to "$\sim P(\sim p \cdot q) \cdot \sim P(\sim p \cdot \sim q)$".

For any state-description (e. g. "$p \cdot q$") we can construct two deontic constituents: the permission and the prohibition of this state-description ["$P(p \cdot q)$" and "$\sim P(p \cdot q)$"]. For these two deontic constituents that correspond to the same state-description we shall use the term *Deontic Pair*.

4. Maximal and Minimal Solutions

By means of the notion of deontic constituent we shall define two special types of solutions: maximal solutions and minimal solutions.

What we shall call a *maximal solution* is any conjunction of deontic constituents formed by taking one constituent from every Deontic Pair, provided that this conjunction is not deontically contradictory. (For the deontic logic we are using, this restriction means the elimination of the conjunction in which all the constituents are prohibitions of state-descriptions, since in von Wright's logic the prohibition of all possible states is deontically contradictory.)

The maximal solution is a function of the Universe of Actions; the number of possible maximal solutions may be easily calculated by means of the formula $2^{2^n} - 1$, where n is the number of the elements of the UA. The following diagram illustrates the relation between the UA, state-descriptions, deontic constituents and maximal solutions:

Table III-1

UA	State-descriptions	Deontic Pairs	Deontic constituents	Maximal solutions
n	2^n	2^n	$2^n \cdot 2$	$2^{2^n} - 1$
1	2	2	4	3
2	4	4	8	15
3	8	8	16	63
4	16	16	32	255
.	.	.	.	.
.	.	.	.	.
.	.	.	.	.

An example:

p	p	$\{Pp, \sim Pp\}$	Pp	$Pp \cdot P \sim p \quad (\equiv Fp\ )$
	$\sim p$	$\{P \sim p, \sim P \sim p\}$	$\sim Pp$	$Pp \cdot \sim P \sim p (\equiv Op\ )$
			$P \sim p$	$\sim Pp \cdot P \sim p (\equiv Php)$
			$\sim P \sim p$	

As can be seen from this table, the number of maximal solutions increases considerably when the number of elements of the *UA* increases.

The set of the maximal solutions of a *UA* will be called the *Universe of Maximal Solutions* (USmax).

We define a *minimal solution* as any disjunction of deontic constituents formed by taking one constituent from every Deontic Pair, provided that the disjunction is not deontically tautological. (As in VON WRIGHT's logic the expression "$Pp \vee P \sim p$" is a deontic tautology, this restriction eliminates the case in which all the disjuncts are permissive constituents, i. e., permissions of state-descriptions. This disjunction of permissions of all possible states is a deontic tautology.)

The number of possible minimal solutions is a function of the elements of the *UA* and is obtained by means of the formula $2^{2n} - 1$, which means that the number of minimal solutions is the same as the number of maximal solutions. For a *UA* composed of only one element ($UA = \{p\}$), we obtain the three possible minimal solutions as follows:

$$Pp \vee \sim P \sim p \ (\equiv Pp) \tag{1}$$

$$\sim Pp \vee P \sim p \ (\equiv P \sim p) \tag{2}$$

$$\sim Pp \vee \sim P \sim p \ (\equiv \sim Fp) \tag{3}$$

(The fourth case: $Pp \vee P \sim p$ is eliminated on the ground that it is deontically tautological.)

This table shows that the characters O, Ph and F give rise to maximal solutions (when the *UA* contains only one element, as was the case in the model in ch. I), while P, $P \sim$ (which may be read as permitted not to do) and $\sim F$ (nonfacultative, that is, obligatory or prohibited) provide minimal solutions.

The set of all the minimal solutions of a *UA* will be called the *Universe of Minimal Solutions* (*US*min).

These two concepts, *US*max and *US*min, are equally important. In contexts where the aim is to establish the completeness of a system, it is necessary to have recourse to the Universe of Maximal Solutions, since it is only the elements of the *US*max which determine (when they are correlated with each one of the cases of the corresponding *UC*) that the system is complete. On the other hand, the concept of the Universe of Minimal Solutions is required in contexts where the aim is to determine whether a certain set of sentences (e. g. a statute) establishes any correlations between a given *UC* and the *US*min, i. e., whether it has any normative consequences for certain cases. Here it does not matter that the solutions are not maximal (and that therefore there may be partial gaps), since the aim is to determine whether there is any solution at all.

In the first chapter, when we dealt with the problem of completeness, we used the concept of *US*max only. In ch. IV we shall make use of the concept of *US*min to define the concept of normative system.

5. Solutions and Norms

It can be proved that any solution is deontically equivalent to a maximal solution or to a disjunction of maximal solutions. But any solution is also deontically equivalent to a minimal solution or to a conjunction of minimal solutions. In short, any solution, that is, any deontic sentence which is not deontically contradictory or deontically tautological is deontically equivalent to a disjunction (of one or more terms) of maximal solutions and is also equivalent to a conjunction (of one or more terms) of minimal solutions. This means that any solution can be expressed in terms of maximal or minimal solutions indifferently.

From this it follows that maximal solutions are equivalent to conjunctions of minimal solutions and, viceversa, minimal solutions are equivalent to disjunctions of maximal solutions.

We shall now give some examples of these equivalences:

$$UA = \{p\}$$

Maximal solutions		Expressed in terms of deontic constituents		Expressed in terms of minimal solutions
Fp	$\equiv$	$Pp \cdot P\sim p$	$\equiv$	$(Pp \vee \sim P\sim p) \cdot (\sim Pp \vee P\sim p)$
Op	$\equiv$	$Pp \cdot \sim P\sim p$	$\equiv$	$(Pp \vee \sim P\sim p) \cdot (\sim Pp \vee \sim P\sim p)$
$Ph\,p$	$\equiv$	$\sim Pp \cdot P\sim p$	$\equiv$	$(\sim Pp \vee P\sim p) \cdot (\sim Pp \vee \sim P\sim p)$

Minimal solutions		Expressed in terms of deontic constituents		Expressed in terms of maximal solutions
Pp	$\equiv$	$Pp \vee \sim P\sim p$	$\equiv$	$(Pp \cdot P\sim p) \vee (Pp \cdot \sim P\sim p)$
$P\sim p$	$\equiv$	$\sim Pp \vee P\sim p$	$\equiv$	$(Pp \cdot P\sim p) \vee (\sim Pp \cdot P\sim p)$
$\sim Fp$	$\equiv$	$\sim Pp \vee \sim P\sim p$	$\equiv$	$(\sim Pp \cdot P\sim p) \vee (Pp \cdot \sim P\sim p)$

Maximal solution and minimal solution are not contradictory concepts, since there are solutions which are neither maximal nor minimal (even though they can be expressed in terms of both maximal or minimal solutions). The solutions which are not maximal will be called *partial*. The concepts of maximal solution and partial solution are contradictory; minimal solutions are a subclass of partial solutions.

At this point we must make some comments on terminology. It is usual for authors dealing with deontic logic to use the term "norm" in a wide sense, embracing all the expressions in which a deontic operator occurs. Among norms, two subclasses are distinguished: categorical norms and hypothetical or conditional norms (cf. G. H. von Wright, Norm and Action, chs. VIII and IX). We have preferred to use the term "norm" in a more restricted sense (which is more in accordance with legal terminology), confining it to expressions correlating cases with solutions. Therefore it is only von Wright's hypothetical norms that are norms according to our terminology; von Wright's categorical norms correspond to what we call solutions.

The distinction between elementary and complex cases and the correlative distinction between maximal and partial solutions suggest the following classification of norms. (This classification is, of course, relative to a UP and a UA.)

When a norm establishes a correlation between an elementary case and a solution (of any kind) it will be called *simple*. When a norm correlates a complex case with a solution, it will be said to be *complex*.

Norms are *complete* when they correlate cases (of any kind) with a maximal solution; when the solution is partial, the norms will be called *incomplete*.

Norms will be called *elementary* when they correlate an elementary case with a maximal solution. Elementary norms are simple and complete. Non-elementary norms may be of three types: complex and complete, simple and incomplete and complex and incomplete.

IV. The Concept of Normative System

Having analyzed the concepts of case and solution, we shall now examine the third element, in relation to which the concept of normative completeness was defined: the normative system. But before giving a definition of the concept of a normative system, we must clarify the notion of a deductive system in general, as this concept plays a very important part in scientific methodology and is intimately linked with the very notion of science.

The conception of science, and together with it the conception of system, have undergone an important change in the past hundred years. This change has in turn been conditioned by the abandonment of the Aristotelian ideal of science, an ideal which had from ancient times been extremely influential. For this reason we shall begin this chapter with a historical digression; after characterizing the Aristotelian ideal of science and briefly describing its influence on scientific and philosophical thought (sect. 1), we shall contrast with it the modern theory of science and the new conception of system. To characterize the latter we shall adopt A. TARSKI's definitions of deductive system and axiom system which show the shift of emphasis, in the modern conception, from principles (axioms or postulates) to the concept of deductive consequence (sect. 2).

In sect. 3 we shall discuss the influence of ARISTOTLE's ideal of science and his conception of system on the legal science of the past four centuries. Our main thesis is that some errors of legal dogmatists are related to the classical conception of system; this same conception is shared by the so-called realists who, however, deny that legal science can satisfy this ideal. They attack not only the errors of the dogmatists but the ideal of systematization itself; that is, they cure the illness by killing the patient.

One of the major theses of this book is that the modern conception of system allows us to reconstruct a large part of jurist's work without falling into the errors which can be attributed to classical dogmatics.

In order to do this it is necessary to define the concept of normative system, after clearing up any ambiguities to which the different conceptions may give rise. We shall define normative system on the basis of TARSKI's conception in terms of normative consequence, which is in turn defined by means of the notions of deductive correlation and normative correlation. We shall distinguish six related concepts of normative system and point out their uses (sect. 4).

Sect. 5 will be devoted to commenting on the definition. We shall try to show its advantages, which consist primarily in its neutrality with regard to questions about the logical status of the sentences of the system or the origin and number of its basic sentences. It will be argued that not all the sentences belonging to a normative system (or to its basis) are norms, though they are frequently called by this name. Some non-normative sentences which typically occur in legal systems well be examined in sect. 5.

Finally, we shall give exact definitions of such formal properties of normative systems as completeness, normative gap, independence and consistency (sect. 6).

1. Aristotle's Theory of Science and its Influence

As is pointed out by E. W. BETH[1] — whose ideas are followed in this section — the modern conception of scientific methodology cannot be fully understood unless it is contrasted with the conception of ARISTOTLE, whose theory of science has exercised a strong influence on scientific and philosophic thought from ancient times to the present day. The modern conception of science and scientific method owes its origin in great measure to the incompatibility of the main theses of the Aristotelian theory with certain developments in modern science. Among these the non-Euclidean geometries, symbolic logic, the theory of relativity and quantum mechanics should be mentioned. This incompatibility led to a crisis in the Aristotelian conception and brought about the emergence of a new theory of science, which we shall call the "modern conception".

ARISTOTLE takes as a general ideal of science the kind of deductive or apodeictic science which is exemplified by EUCLID's geometry.

---

1 E. W. BETH, The Foundations of Mathematics, Amsterdam, 1959, p. 31 ff. Cf. also H. SCHOLZ, Die Axiomatik der Alten, Mathesis Universalis, Darmstadt, 1961, p. 27 ff.

That is, the deductive structure of geometry is taken to be the ideal of science as such. According to this ideal every science must have: (i) a set of self-evident principles, (ii) a deductive structure, and (iii) a real content. This means that every science must fulfil the following conditions, which BETH lays down in the form of four postulates[2]:

I. *Postulate of Reality:* Any sentence belonging to a science must refer to a specific domain of real entities.

II. *Truth Postulate:* Any sentence belonging to a science must be true.

III. *Deductivity Postulate:* If certain sentences belong to a science, any logical consequence of these sentences must belong to it.

IV. *Postulate of Evidence:* In any science there must be a finite number of sentences, called principles, such that (a) the truth of these sentences is so obvious as to require no further proof; (b) the truth of any other sentence belonging to the science may be established by logical inference starting from these sentences[3].

According to BETH, ARISTOTLE's theory of science demands a metaphysics as a science of the principles (philosophia prima). The role of metaphysics is that of analyzing the principles on which the special sciences are based and which they admit without definition or proof. This conception of metaphysics has persisted until very recently, as titles such as "Metaphysics of Morals" (KANT) or "Metaphysics of Mathematics" (GAUSS) reveal, though the rôle played by the science of principles has been transferred in modern times to the theory of knowledge. Indeed, if all scientific knowledge is acquired by means of logical deduction from some principles which must be admitted to be self-evident, the problem inevitably arises of accounting for our knowledge of these principles and justifying our use of them. In this sense, DESCARTES' innate ideas, LEIBNIZ' *primae veritates* and KANT's synthetic judgements a priori are epistemological versions of ARISTOTLE's metaphysical principles.

---

2 Cf. BETH, op. cit., p. 32.

3 An analogous postulate might be formulated (and is in fact formulated by BETH) for the terms which occur in a science: There is a finite number of terms, such that (a) their meaning is so obvious that it does not require any explanation, and (b) all other terms may be defined by means of these terms. But as we are concerned only with sentences and not with terms, we have omitted this version of the Postulate of Evidence.

The first crisis of ARISTOTLE's scientific ideal arose round about 1600, when scientific practice made it clear that it was impossible to satisfy all four postulates at the same time. This crisis resulted in a splitting of the Aristotelian ideal and hence a division of the sciences into two radically different types: rational sciences and empirical sciences. In philosophy also two main branches have emerged: *rationalism* (which shows a clear preference for rational science) and *empiricism,* inspired by empirical science.

Rational science, whose paradigm is still mathematics, conforms to the Aristotelian postulates of evidence and deductivity though not necessarily to the postulate of reality. This science starts from principles accepted as self-evident and proceeds by logical deduction.

Empirical science, on the other hand, represented principally by the new physics of GALILEO and NEWTON, starts from experimental data and proceeds by analysis, thus conforming to the postulates of reality and truth, but not necessarily to the postulates of deductivity and evidence.

KANT's attempt to reconcile rational science with empirical science and thereby restore ARISTOTLE's unitarian ideal was not succesful, so that the clear-cut division between rational and empirical sciences persisted until the end of the nineteenth century.

2. Modern Conception of Science and the Notion of System

The latest developments in the methodology of science are characterized by a new conception of deductive system which makes a decisive break with the Aristotelian tradition by abandoning the Postulate of Evidence and by the attenuation of the traditional dichotomy between rational and empirical science.

In the rational — or, as it is now costumary to call them, the *formal* sciences — the Postulate of Evidence has been completely abandoned, and with the emergence of symbolic logic a much more rigorous conception of deduction has been developed. In the empirical sciences the Postulate of Reality has been weakened in order to permit the construction of deductive systems. In both, the formal and the empirical sciences, the same concept of deductive system operates, and the point of disagreement between the two kinds of science has now shifted to the problem of selection or the establishing of the primitive sentences of the system. In the empirical sciences these sentences are established on the basis of experience and even though it is not required that they should be self-evident, they must be true sentences about reality. In the formal sciences the primitive sentences are no more regarded as self-evident truths; neither do they have an empirical content. The criteria for the selection of axioms are their formal properties: consistency, completeness, independence, etc. This means that there are two types of problems: empirical problems concerning the selection of the basis of an empirical science (the primitive sentences or axioms of the system) and rational or logical problems concerning the deduction of the consequences that follow from the basic sentences. The latter are problems of *systematization*, which are fundamentally of the same kind in the formal and the empirical sciences.

A comparison between EUCLID and HILBERT shows clearly the great gulf that separates the classical and modern conceptions of geometry. EUCLID's geometrical system, which was for centuries the paradigm of the scientific ideal and of logical rigour, was shown to have serious deficiencies, and modern axiomatics springs in large measure from the attempt made to remedy these deficiencies[1].

In the first place, the modern conception of deductive system rejects the view that the principles (EUCLID's postulates and axioms) are self-evident truths about the real space and in so doing abandons the Postulates of Evidence and Reality. The difference between postulates and axioms also disappears, since the modern conception distinguishes only between primitive sentences or axioms (which take the place of Aristotelian principles but are devoid of the attributes of truth and self-evidence) and the derived sentences or theorems.

In the second place, the extraordinary refinement of the logical apparatus produced by the development of symbolic logic has made possible the detection of serious errors in the deduction of the theorems of classical geometry. Many of EUCLID's proofs are based not on logical inference, but on intuition[2]. This is why HILBERT, in his axiomatization of geometry[3], has taken special care to make explicit the rules of inference admitted in the system. These rules

---

1 R. BLANCHÉ, L'Axiomatique, Paris, 1955; English translation by G. B. KEENE, Axiomatics, London, 1962.

2 Cf. BLANCHÉ, op. cit.

3 D. HILBERT, Grundlagen der Geometrie, 1899; English translation by E. J. TOWNSEND, Foundations of Geometry, Chicago, 1902.

determine with precision and rigour the notion of *deductive consequence* which forms the core of modern axiomatics [4].

An axiom system may be defined, generally, as the totality of consequences derivable from a finite set of sentences, called the *axiomatic basis* or simply the basis of the system. Any set of sentences may be used as the basis of an axiom system. The only requirement is that this set should be finite, but it may have any number of sentences. It is not required that the sentences of the basis should be true, independent or even consistent. The consistency of the sentences of the basis has a bearing on the consistency of the system, but not on its existence. (An inconsistent system is still a system, just as incomplete and redundant systems also are systems.)

In this way the concept of system is based on that of deductive consequence. The notion of consequence depends on the rules of inference that are admitted, as it is these rules which determine what sentences follow from a given sentence or a set of sentences. (By "sentence" we understand here a certain type of linguistic sign or expression, since we are operating on a purely syntactical level. The criterion of a well formed sentence (which in semantic terms would be called a meaningful sentence) in any given language depends on particular formation rules of the language in question. It should also be remembered that we are dealing here with systems of sentences and not with systems of concepts.)

The specification of the rules of inference corresponds to the elucidation of each particular system, but we can indicate here the minimum conditions that any notion of consequence must satisfy in order to correspond to our intuitive notion. According to TARSKI [5], every definition of deductive consequence must satisfy the following requirements:

(1) The set of the consequences of a set of sentences consists solely of sentences. This means that it is only sentences which will be regarded as consequences.

---

4 See for the following discussion A. TARSKI, Logic, Semantics, Metamathematics, Oxford, 1956, especially the following chapters: III. On some fundamental concepts of metamathematics, p. 30 ff., IV. Investigations into the sentential calculus, p. 38 ff., V. Fundamental concepts of the methodology of the deductive sciences, p. 60 ff., XI. On the foundation of Boolean algebra, p. 320 ff., and XII. Foundations of the calculus of systems, p. 342 ff.

5 A. TARSKI, op. cit., ch. V, and XII.

(2) Every sentence belonging to a given set is to be regarded as a consequence of this set. Hence it follows that every sentence is a consequence of itself and that axioms are also theorems. (This is why the axiom system has been defined as the totality of the consequences of a basis and not as the basis plus its consequences.)

(3) The consequences of the consequences are, in turn, consequences. That is, if p is a consequence of q and q is a consequence of r, then p is a consequence of r.)

(4) If a sentence of a conditional form $(y \supset z)$ is a consequence of the set of sentences X, then z (the consequent of the conditional) is a consequence of the set of sentences resulting from adding to X the sentence y (the antecedent of the conditional). And also conversely, if z is a consequence of the set formed by X and y, then $y \supset z$ is a consequence of X[6].

As we shall see later, this last requirement, known as the Deduction Theorem, is particularly important. To illustrate its operation let us consider a set (which we shall call A) composed of the following two sentences:

(i) Those who are 21 years old are of age.

(ii) Those who are of age may administer their property.

According to the Deduction Theorem the conditional sentence "If x is 21, then he may administer his property" is a consequence of the set A if and only if the sentence "x may administer his property" (i. e. the consequent of the conditional) is a consequence of the set composed of A [i. e. the sentences (i) and (ii)] and the sentence "x is 21" (i. e. the antecedent of the conditional).

The definition of an axiom system as the set of all the consequences of a finite set of sentences, which emphazises the concept of consequence, makes possible a generalized concept of system. In fact, TARSKI distinguishes between deductive and axiom system. He defines a deductive system as any set of sentences which contains all its consequences[7]. From this definition it follows that a set of sentences A is a deductive system if and only if all the consequences of A belong to A, that is, if there is no consequence of A which is not included in the set A.

---

6 Here only the main requirements are mentioned. For a more complete exposition see TARSKI, op. cit., ch. XII, p. 346.

7 Cf. TARSKI, op. cit., ch. V, p. 69—70.

Deductive systems can sometimes, but not always, be axiomatized; this process consists in finding a finite subset of sentences such that all the other sentences of the system can be derived as consequences from this subset, which constitutes the basis of the new presentation of the system (as an axiom system)[8]. When a deductive system possesses at least one axiomatic basis, it is said to be axiomatizable. It must be stressed that not all deductive systems can be axiomatized; it is precisely the existence of sets which cannot be axiomatized that makes it necessary to distinguish between the generic concept of deductive system and the specific concept of an axiom system.

It is perfectly possible for a deductive system to be axiomatized in different ways, that is with different bases. But each of these bases will necessarily have the same consequences, since they are axiomatizations of the same deductive system. We shall say that these axiomatic bases are *equivalent*. We can generalize the notion of equivalence by saying that two sets of sentences are equivalent if and only if their consequences are the same. This definition may be applied both to systems and to axiomatic bases, since both systems and bases are sets of sentences. Hence it follows that two equivalent systems are *identical* and that two or more equivalent bases determine the same system (since they have the same consequences).

The *construction* of an axiom system may be performed in two ways[9]:

(1) When the starting point is a deductive system, the problem is to find an axiomatic basis, that is, a finite set of sentences, from which all other sentences of the original system may be inferred as consequences.

(2) When the starting point is a finite set of sentences, the problem is to infer all the consequences of the original set.

It is the latter method which is more frequently used, especially in legal science.

3. The Concept of System in Legal Science

The evolution of the scientific ideal outlined in the two first sections of this chapter could not fail to have an influence on legal

---

8 For TARSKI a basis must be independent (op. cit., p. 88), but we drop this requirement for practical reasons.
9 TARSKI, op. cit., ch. IV, p. 40.

science. Even though it never fully attained the Aristotelian ideal, attempts were made, nevertheless, to give legal science a deductive structure after the fashion of geometry. Perhaps the most outstanding results of this tendency have been the great rationalist systems of the seventeenth and eighteenth centuries. After the division of the sciences into rational and empirical, legal science was placed by the majority of jurists and legal philosophers in the sphere of rational science. The conception of legal science which we find in the rationalistic systems of Natural Law, from GROTIUS and PUFENDORF to KANT and FICHTE, answers fully to the ideal of rational science.

All these systems have in common certain very typical features. In the first place, they start from self-evident principles, the norms of Natural Law. In the second place, these systems are deductive developments (or at least claim to be such) of the principles of Natural Law. Every legal proposition is inferred logically and derives its truth from this, so that legal science satisfies the Postulates of Evidence and Deductivity. The weakening of the Postulate of Reality, which is typical of the rational science of that period, is reflected in the *ideal* character of legal science, which claims to describe not the rules that are actually in force in a given society, but ideal rules which, in accordance with the principles of Natural Law, ought to be in force. Thus the concept of system which is used at the time in the science of law is — in general terms — the same that operates in the classical conception of EUCLID's geometry.

A major change in the conception of legal system occurred in the nineteenth century. This change was the product of several factors, both legal and philosophical, the most important of which were the codification of law in France (which soon spread to the rest of Europe), SAVIGNY's historical school in Germany and utilitarianism (BENTHAM and AUSTIN) in England.

The characteristic feature of this change is the abandonment of the doctrine of Natural Law and a new conception of legal system which resulted in the so-called *legal dogmatics*. The dogmatic legal science preserves the deductive structure, but resolutely abandons the Postulate of Evidence, rejecting the principles of Natural Law and replacing them by the norms given by the legislator (positive law). The positivism of the new science of law consists in the "dogmatic" acceptance of the norms issued by the positive legislator; the axioms of a legal system are no longer self-evident, immutable principles of Natural Law, but contingent norms issued by human beings [1].

The task of the dogmatic jurist is twofold: it consists, on the one hand, in discovering the general principles underlying the positive norms, which is performed by means of an operation called "legal induction" (cf. infra, ch. V, sect. 5) and, on the other hand, in deducing consequences from these general principles and from positive norms so as to solve all the cases (including individual cases) which may occur.

In spite of the abandonment of the Postulate of Evidence, legal dogmatics is still a rational and not an empirical science. Experience as a source of verification for scientific propositions has no place in dogmatic science; the jurist's preoccupation is with deducing the consequences of his "dogmas" and he does not worry very much about the "real content" of his sentences. The important thing is not what men (including judges) really do, but what they ought to do in accordance with legal norms. It is therefore not surprising that the system's formal properties such as consistency, completeness and independence absorb a large part of the dogmatic jurist's interest.

In the first half of the twentieth century an important attempt was made to found a legal science on an empirical basis. The school of *libre recherche scientifique* (GENY), the jurisprudence of interests *(Interessenjurisprudenz)* and the *Freirechtsschule* (KANTOROWICZ), different sociological schools (DUGUIT in France, ROSCOE POUND in the United States), American Realism (HOLMES, CARDOZO, GRAY, LLEWELLYN, FRANK) and Scandinavian Realism (HÄGERSTRÖM, LUNDSTEDT, OLIVECRONA, ALF ROSS), all tried to perform this task in different ways, some of these programmes being more far-reaching than others.

Legal empiricism or realism constitutes a reaction against the attempt of legal dogmatics to construct a legal science as a deductive system. Hence its violent attacks on all systematization, its rejec-

---

1 In spite of their confessed positivism, many dogmatic jurists still ascribe to positive legal norms certain characteristics that were traditionally ascribed to Natural Law. Thus, for example, the reverence shown by some authors of the French exegetic school for the Code Napoleon is well known. Even today it is not unusual to find among the jurists the belief that certain absolute and immutable principles are embodied in positive law.

tion of the very idea of system and its attempt to base the truth of the sentences of legal science on the observation of empirical facts, as in any other empirical science.

Realist movements have generally formed a salutary corrective to the formalist excesses of legal dogmatics. But from the point of view of modern scientific methodology, this attitude is much less revolutionary than may appear at first sight. Far from superseding the old ideal of science, realism seeks to remove legal science from the class of rational sciences and place it in that of empirical sciences, both understood in the traditional way. Furthermore, the realist's rejection of the very idea of systematization (that is, of the deductive structure of legal science) reveals that his conception of system is the same as that of the legal dogmatist (i.e. the "classical" conception of system). In effect, the old idea of rational science is bound up with the Aristotelian concept of system, but instead of introducing a new concept of system (which would make it possible to avoid the errors of legal dogmatics), the realist uses the same notion of system. Consequently his rejection of the rational character of legal science leads him to reject the whole idea of systematization as such. But as we have already pointed out, a science's being empirical in character is in no way incompatible with its having deductive structure. The systematization of its sentences is one of the basic requirements of any science, either formal or empirical. The difference between the two types of science consists, above all, in the criteria used for the selection of their primitive sentences, not in the deduction of the derived sentences.

But to recognize this is to abandon the classical conception and adopt the new ideal of system. This precisely what we aim at to do in this work: to apply to legal science the methodological tools developed in other fields of knowledge (above all in the methodology of mathematics and physics) in order to show (1) that there is a concept of system which so far has not been used in the domain of legal science; (2) that systematization is one of the legal scientist's fundamental tasks; and (3) that, in legal science, there are empirical as well as logical — that is, purely rational — problems. To characterize it as a purely formal science is as misleading as to think of it as being a purely empirical one. And this is so because the classification itself is already obsolete: even though there are purely formal sciences, there are no purely empirical sciences.

4. Definition of Normative System

As a starting point for the definition of normative system we shall take TARSKI's definitions of deductive and axiomatic systems, which have been outlined in sect. 2. According to TARSKI a deductive system is a set of sentences which contains all its consequences. An axiom system is the set of all the consequences of a finite set of sentences.

As we have seen in ch. I, the function of a normative system is to establish correlations between cases and solutions. On the basis of this we can outline the following *adequacy criterion* for the definition of a normative system; for this purpose we shall make use of the concept of *normative set*.

A normative set is a set of sentences such that among its consequences there are some sentences which correlate cases with solutions. Every normative set which contains all its consequences will accordingly be called a *normative system*.

When among the consequences of a set of sentences there is some sentence such that it correlates a case with a solution, we shall say that this set has *normative consequences*. A normative set may be characterized now as a set of sentences which has some normative consequences, and a normative system as a system which has some normative consequences.

This is not a definition of normative system, but only a criterion that states certain conditions which must be satisfied by any definition of the concept of normative system. In order to give a satisfactory definition we must first clarify the notion of normative consequence. For this task we shall introduce a new concept, that of a deductive correlation.

A *deductive correlation* of a set of sentences α is an ordered pair of sentences such that the second is a *deductive consequence* of the first in conjunction with the set α[1].

By virtue of the Deduction Theorem (cf. sect. 2), if a sentence y is a consequence of α in conjunction with the sentence x, then the conditional $x \supset y$ is a consequence of α. It follows that the sentences x and y are deductively correlated by the set of sentences α if and only if the conditional $x \supset y$ is a consequence of α.

---

1 It would perhaps be more accurate to say: " ... is a deductive consequence of the set of sentences resulting from adding the set α to the first sentence of the ordered pair."

When a deductive correlation is such that the first sentence of the ordered pair is a *case* and the second a *solution,* it will be called *normative.* If among the deductive correlations of the set α there is at least one normative correlation, we shall say that the set α has *normative consequences.* A system of sentences which has some normative consequences will be called a *normative system.*

Therefore, to say that a normative system correlates cases with solutions is to say that at least one solution is a consequence of the set which results from adding to the system a sentence which describes a case.

With the aid of these elements we can define several concepts of *normative set* and, consequently, of normative system.

(1) A set of sentences α is normative in relation to a Universe of Cases UC_i and a Universe of Minimal Solutions $USmin_j$ if and only if α deductively correlates some element of UC_i with some element of $USmin_j$.

This concept of normative set is relative to a certain UC and a certain $USmin$. For the definition of completeness it was necessary to use the concept of maximal solution; but here we are concerned with the question whether a system is normative and for this it is enough that there should be *some* solution (not necessarily a maximal one) for some case. And as every solution (of any kind) entails at least one minimal solution, the definition of normative system is made in terms of minimal solutions only. It is easy to see that if a case has no minimal solution, then it has no solution at all.

(2) A set of sentences α is normative in relation to a UC_i if and only if α deductively correlates some element of UC_i with some element of some Universe of Minimal Solutions.

(3) A set of sentences α is normative in relation to a $USmin_j$ if and only if α deductively correlates some case of some UC with an element of $USmin_j$.

These three concepts of normative set are relative concepts: the first is relative to a UC and a $USmin$, the second is relative to a UC and the third to a $USmin$. The next one is not relative to any UC nor to any US; it is therefore an absolute concept.

(4) A set of sentences α is normative if and only if α deductively correlates some element of some UC with some element of some $USmin$.

When a normative set of sentences (in any of the four senses that we have so far distinguished) is a system, i. e. when it contains all its consequences, then it is a normative system. It is easy to see that a normative system may be relative (to a *UC* and a *US*min, to a *UC* or to a *US*min) or absolute.

All these four concepts of normative system are widely used in legal science. The choice of one rather than another at any time is a matter of convenience. Sometimes jurists are interested in determining whether a certain set of sentences (e. g. a statute) has some normative consequences for a given *UC* and/or a given *US*min. Sometimes they want to know whether it has some normative consequence, not for a definite *UC*, but for any *UC*.

These concepts of normative system are related in such a way that the first implies the other three; the second implies the fourth, and the third implies the fourth. This needs no proof: if α has normative consequences for a certain *UC*, then clearly there is at least one *UC* such that α has normative consequences for it, etc. The following diagram shows — by means of arrows — in which directions the relations of implication hold.

Diagram IV/1

In all four senses, a normative system correlates some case with some (minimal) solution. But there is a particular situation which deserves special consideration. Suppose that a certain normative set is such that it correlates a certain solution (belonging to a *US*min) with all the cases of a certain *UC*, so that every case of the *UC* is correlated by that system with the same solution. It may easily be shown that in such a situation, the solution in question is also correlated with all the possible cases of all the possible *UCs*. This is so because the disjunction of all the cases of a *UC* is a tautology. (We need hardly remind the reader that a *UC* is a division and hence its cases are logically disjunctive.)

To illustrate this point let us consider the following: suppose we have a UC_i with only two cases q and $\sim q$. Suppose further that α correlates both q and $\sim q$ with the solution Pp, i. e. the sentences

"Pp/q" and "$Pp/\sim q$" are consequences of α. Then it follows that Pp holds in every case of UC_i and the sentence "$Pp/q \vee \sim q$" is a consequence of α. Let us consider now another UC_j which has four elementary cases: $r . s$, $\sim r . s$, $r . \sim s$ and $\sim r . \sim s$. The disjunction of these four cases is a tautology, just as "$q \vee \sim q$". From "$Pp/q \vee \sim q$" it follows that "$Pp/r . s \vee \sim r . s \vee r . \sim s \vee \sim r . \sim s$" is also a consequence of α. We may generalize this result by saying that Pp/t, where 't' stands for any tautology.

To sum up: if a solution is correlated by α with all the cases of a UC_i, then this solution is correlated by α with all the cases of every UC.

These considerations enable us to define the concept of a *categorical normative system:*

(5) A normative system α is categorical in relation to a $USmin_j$ if and only if every solution of $USmin_j$ which α correlates with some case of some UC, is also correlated by α with every case of this UC.

From this definition it follows that when a normative system α is categorical for a $USmin$, then any solution which is correlated by α with some case, is a direct consequence of α.

The notion of a categorical normative system has little bearing on legal theory and we shall make use of it only in connection with the problem of closure (ch. VII, sect. 6).

Finally we shall introduce the notion of a *purely normative system.*

(6) A system α is purely normative if and only if it is normative (i. e. it has some normative consequences) but has no factual consequences, that is, no factual (descriptive) sentence is a consequence of α.

It follows that no sentence descriptive of a case is a consequence of a purely normative system.

It seems reasonable to believe that all legal or moral systems should be purely normative in the above sense, since their function is to regulate human actions, not to describe them. A statute containing factual statements would certainly be regarded defective. But a requirement (an ideal rule in VON WRIGHT's sense[2]), however reasonable, should not be confused with a fact. Even if it is widely accepted that legal systems should be purely normative, some of

---

2 Cf. G. H. VON WRIGHT, Norm and Action, ch. I, sect. 9, p. 13—15.

them may not be pure; there are well known examples of declarative sentences in some constitutions.

We shall come back to purely normative systems when dealing with the problem of consistency (sect. 6).

5. *Comments on the Definition of Normative System*

The definition of normative system based on the notion of consequence offers considerable advantages from the methodological point of view.

a) In the first place, the definition is neutral with regard to the sentences composing the system. The one thing that is required to make a set of sentences normative (in one of the several senses of the expression that we have distinguished) is that it should have normative consequences, but we are not passing judgement on the logical structure of the other sentences of the system.

To see clearly that this is a very important advantage, it is convenient to consider the — very common — definition of normative system as a *set of norms*[1]. To speak of a normative system (or order) as a set of norms seems to imply that all the sentences composing this system are normative sentences (norms). However, it is very common to find in a normative system sentences which can hardly be called norms. This is especially true of legal systems. Even a superficial examination of a legal text (a code, a constitution, a statute) reveals the existence of sentences which do not establish obligations, prohibitions or permissions, but serve very different ends: e. g. definitions ("By the term 'goods' all kinds of things which may be sold are meant", § 77 of the Argentine Penal Code), political declarations, expressions of purposes, conceptual rules, etc.[2]. It would certainly not be advisable to call all these sentences norms, since this would mean widening the extension of the term "norm" to such an extent that its meaning became indeterminate.

A way of surmounting this difficulty consists in saying that such sentences are not norms but fragments of norms, which must be

---

1 Cf. Kelsen, General Theory of Law and State, Cambridge, Mass., 1945, p. 110 ff., Reine Rechtslehre, 2nd ed., Wien, 1960, p. 196 ff.

2 Cf. G. H. von Wright, On the logic and ontology of norms, in J. W. Davis et al. (ed.), Philosophical Logic, 1969.

integrated with other sentences in order to form complete norms. But then, when speaking about a set of norms we are not speaking about a set of normative sentences; norms are for this doctrine entities of a different kind, which may be expressed by means of several sentences.

This solution, which might be called "the theory of the incomplete norm" has been adopted by KELSEN, among others. The chief disadvantage of such a theory — which comes out particularly clear in KELSEN's doctrine — lies in the difficulty of specifying the conditions of idendity of a norm. KELSEN gives no criterion to decide whether a sentence (or a set of sentences) expresses a complete norm or not. What are e. g. the sentences which must be added to art. 79 of the Argentine Penal Code ("He who kills somebody will be imprisoned for a period from eight to twenty five years . . .") in order to make it a complete norm? Will it be enough to add to it the majority of the articles of the General Part of the Code or is it also necessary to integrate it with the relevant dispositions (and which are they?) of the Code of Procedures, of Administrative Law (e. g. regarding the appointment of the judge, etc.), and of the Constitution? It is significant that KELSEN himself never gives an example of a complete legal norm[3].

In view of all these difficulties, there are obvious advantages in defining a normative system in terms of consequences, which leaves open the question of a further analysis of the different types of sentences that occur in legal systems or in other kinds of normative system.

b) In the second place, it is necessary to emphasize that our definition of normative system does not say anything about the sentences constituting the basis of the system. These sentences may have different origins, may be of different types and of any number. Questions about the choice of the basis and the criteria governing this choice have no bearing on the notion of system. Thus, in the case of a legal system the basis may be composed by sentences contained in a Code or in a statute, or extracted from judicial decisions or from Natural Law. Nor does the number of the sentences of the basis matter: it is possible to construct a system starting

---

3 Cf. HART's criticism in The Concept of Law, p. 35 ff. and p. 239. There is an interesting discussion of KELSEN's theory of legal system in J. RAZ, The Concept of a Legal System, Oxford, 1970.

from all the articles of a Code or from some of them only; provisions belonging to different legal texts may be adopted as a basis of a system; they may also be mixed with customary norms or precedents. In each case the result will be a different system; the choice of one basis rather than another depends entirely on the interest of the person who is constructing the system. The construction of omnicomprehensive systems trying to embrace very extensive matters, such as all the laws of a country or the whole civil law, are no more than programmatic postulations of legal philosophers; in scientific practice jurists seem to be much more interested in the systematization of small areas of law (such as the law of torts, of extracontractual responsibility, of customs procedure, etc.). They choose a certain number of sentences (taken from statutes, from judicial decisions or from customary rules) and try to determine their consequences and, in particular, their normative consequences for a certain area of problems.

c) Our definition of normative system does not pass judgement on the ontological status of the norms. The treatment of norms as sentences (i. e. linguistic entities) is not incompatible with the view that they have extra-linguistic (ideal) existence. The only thing presupposed in the definition is that norms can be expressed in a language, that is, by means of sentences. This seems incontrovertible.

d) We shall not discuss in this work the logical structure of the sentences that usually occur in normative systems, especially in legal systems. We shall be content to make a few informal remarks about two types of sentences which are extremely common in law and which are often called "norms", even though they do not always fit into our definition of "norm". These are sentences correlating cases with cases and sentences correlating solutions with solutions.

As an example of the first type we may mention art. 126 of the Argentine Civil Code: "Persons who are not 21 years old are under age." This article defines the concept of being under age in terms of the property of being less than 21. In other words, the article correlates the *case* characterized by the property of being "less than 21 years old" with the *case* characterized by the property of being "under age". According to our definition of "norm" this article is not a norm, since it does not establish any obligation, or prohibition, or permission, that is, it does not correlate a case with a solution (and, therefore, has no normative consequences). Nevertheless, it is quite usual to call this a "legal norm". There are at least two reasons why this is so; in the first place, it is usual to call the articles of any code or statute legal norms. In the second place, even though this article is a definition, and as such a conceptual rule and not a norm of conduct, it is a definition that is closely related to other sentences correlating the case of being under age with a solution (e. g. arts. 134 and 135 which establish a series of prohibitions and rights for those who are under age)[4]. But it is convenient to bear in mind that a sentence correlating a case with a case is not a norm, in the sense that it does not establish any obligation or permission; it is a definition of a concept (e. g. the concept of being under age), that is, a meaning postulate.

As for sentences correlating solutions with solutions, two possibilities must be distinguished. Sometimes, such sentences can be interpreted as meaning postulates, especially when they define the extent of a right. For instance, arts. 2862—2909 of the Argentine Civil Code establishing the rights and obligations of the usufructuary determine the extent of the real right of usufruct, i. e. define the concept of usufruct.

But, a sentence correlating a solution with another solution can also be a genuine norm. For instance, a law imposing the obligation of paying a special tax on the owners of real estate. This obligation is not contained in the concept of property; it is a new obligation imposed on those who have the right of property. The fact of being owner of real estate functions here like a case, but it is a case characterized by deontic properties and not by natural ones.

6. Formal Properties of Normative Systems

We are now in a position to give general definitions of such structural properties of normative systems as completeness, independence and consistency.

a) *Completeness:* In ch. I (sect. 7) completeness has been defined in terms of gaps: a normative system α is said to be complete in

---

4 Cf. G. H. VON WRIGHT, On the logic and ontology of norms, op. cit., pp. 99—100.

relation to a UC_i and a $USmax_j$ if and only if α has no gaps in UC_i in relation to $USmax_j$.

This definition can be reformulated in terms of relational logic. As we have already seen, a normative system establishes a deductive correlation between the elements of a UC and the elements of a $USmax$. Let us define $R\,(\alpha, UC, USmax)$ as the deductive correlation that the system α establishes between the elements of a given Universe of Cases and a given Universe of Maximal Solutions. $R\,(\alpha, UC, USmax)$ is a binary relation; any binary relation has two members: the first and the second member. Let us use the term '*domain* of R' for the class of all first members of R and the term '*counterdomain* of R' for the class of all second members of R. If a relation is a *many-one relation* it is called a *function*.

With these elements we can now define the concept of completeness as follows:

A normative set α will be called *complete* in relation to UC_i and $USmax_j$ if and only if the domain of $R\,(\alpha, UC_i, USmax_j)$ is identical with UC_i.

The concept of a normative gap may be defined as follows: x is a normative gap of α in relation to UC_i and $USmax_j$ if and only if x is an element of UC_i and x does not belong to the domain of $R\,(\alpha, UC_i, USmax_j)$.

b) *Independence:* Two norms will be said to be *redundant in a case* C_i of a UC_j in relation to a $USmin_k$ if and only if each norm correlates C_i with the same element of $USmin_k$. If two norms are not redundant in a case, they are *independent in this case*.

A normative set α is *redundant* in relation to UC_i and $USmin_j$ if and only if α contains at least two norms which are redundant in some case of UC_i in relation to $USmin_j$. A normative set which is not redundant in relation to UC_i and $USmin_j$ is *independent*.

We can generalize this definition of independence by stating that a normative set α is *independent* in relation to UC_i and $USmin_j$ if and only if it has no proper subset β such that the relation $R\,(\beta, UC_i, USmin_j)$ is equivalent to the relation $R\,(\alpha, UC_i, USmin_j)$.

It should be observed that for the definition of independence the concept of $USmin$ (instead of $USmax$) has been used.

c) *Consistency:* Generally speaking, a normative system α is *inconsistent* in a case C_i of a UC_j if α correlates C_i with two or more solutions in such a way that the conjunction of these solutions is a deontic contradiction. The notion of deontic contradiction is, of course, relative to the system of deontic logic that is used. But it is easy to make this definition independent of any particular concept of deontic contradiction. In fact, it is a general law of logic that from a contradiction any sentence may be inferred; so that if a case is correlated with two or more deontically contradictory solutions, then it is correlated with any solution whatsoever. This observation makes the following definition possible:

A normative set α is *consistent* in relation to a UC_i if and only if no element of UC_i is correlated by α with all solutions.

The concept of consistency is thus not relative to a particular US (maximal or minimal), but only to a UC.

From this definition it follows that a normative set α is consistent in relation to a UC_i and a $USmax_j$ if and only if the relation $R(\alpha, UC_i, USmax_j)$ is a function, because to say that $R(\alpha, UC_i, USmax_j)$ is a function means that no case of UC_i is correlated by α with more than one solution of $USmax_j$; so α is consistent.

A normative set α is complete and consistent (in relation to UC_i and $USmax_j$) if and only if $R(\alpha, UC_i, USmax_j)$ is a function whose domain is UC_i.

Some writers seem to regard consistency as a necessary property of a system. On this view, an inconsistent set of norms would not be a system[1].

Such a restriction of the meaning of "system" would hardly be advisable. Inconsistent normative sets are extremely common as every jurist knows by experience. Of course, an inconsistent normative system may justly be called "irrational"; in this sense, consistency is a rational ideal. (As we shall argue later — ch. IX — completeness is a rational ideal too.) But there seems to be no reason for confining the term "system" to consistent sets, unless by "normative system" we understand a purely normative system, i. e. a system which has no factual consequences. Consistency certainly is a necessary property of purely normative systems, since from an inconsistent system factual consequences may be easily

---

1 KELSEN is very emphatic that only consistent sets of norms can be regarded as systems; cf. Reine Rechtslehre, 2nd ed., Wien, 1960, pp. 209 ff., 280, and 329.

G. H. VON WRIGHT seems to share this conception; see Norm and Action, p. 206.

derived. (In fact: if "$\sim t/q$" is a consequence of α, then "$\sim q$", i. e. the negation of the sentence q which is descriptive [factual] is a consequence of α; where "$\sim t$" stands for any contradiction.) Hence the fact that a system has no factual consequences (that is, is a purely normative system) implies that the system is consistent, though the converse does not hold. A system may have factual consequences and still be consistent.

Part II

Some Problems of Legal Theory

V. Problems of Systematization in Legal Science

1. *Introduction*

The aim of this chapter is to emphasize the importance of the concept of normative system, which we discussed in the previous chapter, as a methodological tool by showing that systematization occupies a central place among the problems of legal science.

Legal science deals with legal systems; the latter are normative systems whose sentences present certain specific characteristics that permit us to label them *legal sentences*[1]. What these characteristics are depends on the *definition* of law; this is a problem that lies outside the scope of this book.

It is particularly important to draw a sharp distinction between *logical problems*, which arise in the course of the activity of jurists that we call the *systematization* of legal sentences and *empirical*

---

1 We use deliberately the neutral expression "legal sentences" instead of the more usual "legal norms" or "legal rules", because — as we have already pointed out — not all sentences occurring in legal discourse (e. g. in a statute) are normative. Furthermore, legal norms or rules are not identical, for the majority of legal philosophers, with sentences; they are abstract entities (meanings). Our discussion, on the contrary, is conducted at a purely syntactical level and this enables us to avoid the difficult problem of the identification of such norms. On this problem see J. RAZ, The Concept of a Legal System, Oxford, 1970. We thank Dr. RAZ for his kindness in making the manuscript of his work available to us before it has been published.

problems which arise in the course of the prior activity of identifying these sentences. (This division does not claim to exhaust the whole set of problems of the science of law.)

Different problems demand different methods and confusing them may result in serious methodological difficulties. In fact, in legal theory we find two tendencies which are diametrically opposed to each other in character, but equally distorting in their effects. The first called *rationalism* or *formalism* consists in ignoring or minimizing the importance of empirical problems and claiming to solve all the problems confronting the science of law by purely rational (deductive) methods. The opposite trend — *empiricism* or *realism* — places too much emphasis on empirical problems and even denies any importance whatsoever to systematization.

However, it would be a mistake to accept without question the account given by jurists of their own scientific procedures. It is a well known fact that distinguished scientists frequently show far less competence when they attempt to expound the foundations of their own sciences. In legal science — where the study of methodology has been sorely neglected — the danger that the facts may inadvertently be distorted as a result of false theoretical conceptions is all the greater.

For this reason, the jurists' own theories about the character of the problems and the methods of their science have comparatively little value. It is not the programmatic declarations of different schools that are of interest, but their scientific activity. Thus it is much more important to observe what jurists do when they are concerned with the law, than to take note of what they say when they are engaged in controversy about theoretical conceptions.

On the other hand, we must remember that methodology is not a description of the psychological processes of the scientist but a rational reconstruction of the logical procedures by which he justifies his assertions[2].

In sect. 2 we shall sketch the different stages of the process of systematization of the law and at the same time indicate the elements that constitute the material from which a system is constructed. But the logical manipulation of a given material is one

---

2 Cf. K. POPPER, The Logic of Scientific Discovery, New York, 1959, pp. 31—32; R. CARNAP, Logical Foundations of Probability, 2nd ed., Chicago, 1962, pp. 37—51.

thing; another (and a very different) thing is the prior identification of this material. It is to the elucidation of this last problem that sect. 3 is devoted, being specifically concerned with the identification and selection of legal sentences which are to constitute the basis of the system.

In sect. 4 we examine the second stage of systematization which is usually undertaken for purely practical reasons and consists in reformulating the system in order to provide a basis that is more general and hence more economical. The discovery of the general principles "implicit in law" raises the question of the logical character of this operation (sect. 5). Contrary to the opinion of many legal theorists, we maintain that this operation is deductive and draw attention to the danger of characterizing logical deduction as a purely mechanical activity, when in fact the use of deductive methods is perfectly compatible with the creative character of a science (sect. 6). Finally, in sects. 7 and 8 some questions related to changes in legal systems and the part played by the so-called "interpretation of law" in such changes are discussed. These considerations bring out the importance of the rules of inference for the identification of a system.

2. Legal Science and the Systematization of the Law

Legal philosophers seem to agree that *the* task or, at least, the most important task of legal science consists in describing the law and presenting it in a "systematic" way, thus making possible the knowledge of the law and facilitating its application by individuals subject to the legal order, especially those who must deal with it for professional reasons (lawyers, judges, officials, etc.).

Nevertheless, this basic agreement is only apparent; such terms as "description" and "systematization" often conceal very real divergences of opinion. It is therefore important to determine by detailed discussion exactly what is involved in these typical activities of the jurist, which the philosophers of law call "description" and "systematization".

To begin with, it seems clear that the description of the law is not a mere transcription of statutes and other legal norms, but that it also involves the operation which jurists refer to under the vague term "interpretation" and which fundamentally consists in the determination of the consequences that can be derived from such norms. Jurists are particularly interested in discovering the solutions that the law provides for certain cases. (The cases dealt with by legal science are normally generic cases.) Thus a great part of what jurists call "interpretation" in this context may be reformulated as a determination of the normative consequences of a set of legal sentences for a certain problem or topic. And this, in our terminology, means the construction of an axiomatic system, adopting these sentences as axioms. (This is what we did on a small scale in ch. I; when determining the consequences of the corresponding paragraphs of FREITAS' Code or the Argentinian Civil Code we adopted a specific interpretation of those norms.)

The identification of the system by means of the derivation of its consequences in general, and its normative consequences for a certain topic in particular, does not exhaust the process of systematization. Jurists, moreover, frequently try to find a new axiomatic basis: one that has fewer components and is hence easier to apply. This is what is usually meant when jurists speak about the systematic presentation of legal material. (In sects. 4 and 5 we shall examine this operation in more detail.)

Thus, the first stage of the systematization of a set of sentences consists in the determination of the normative consequences for a given topic. This presupposes the existence of certain elements which are the starting point for the systematization. These elements are: (1) a problem or a group of problems (a topic), whose regulation by the law is of interest to the jurist; (2) a set of legal sentences, relevant to the topic in question; (3) a set of rules of inference used by the jurist in the derivation of the consequences. Let us examine these elements briefly.

(1) The Topic:

Jurists are usually concerned with determining the normative status conferred by law on certain actions (UA) in certain circumstances (Universe of Discourse). The Universe of Actions and the Universe of Discourse determine the extension of the problem or topic. The scope of the problem depends, of course, on the scientist's interest, and is therefore in a certain sense arbitrary. A jurist may want to deal with the recovery of real estate, with extracontractual responsibility, with the law of torts or with legislative procedure. But it must be emphasized that the jurist is always concerned with a limited field of problems and although every legal problem is studied by some jurist, no jurist can take an interest in all the problems at the same time[1].

(2) *Legal Sentences:*

The second element is a set of legal sentences that constitute the axiomatic basis of the system. Jurists call *valid* sentences (or valid norms) those sentences which are considered admissible as part of the basis of a legal system (and also the consequences of such sentences). To identify valid sentences certain criteria are used, which we shall call the *criteria of identification*. The problems involved in the identification of the sentences of the basis will be discussed briefly in the following section, but it is important to bear in mind that, no matter what procedure is used to identify the sentences of the basis, we cannot speak about a system or systematization unless a set of legal sentences has been delimited and identified. In positive law this set will always be finite, but its extension is subject to considerable variation. In fact, this set will usually contain not all the legal sentences identified as valid by a certain criterion, but only a sub-set of such sentences, because jurists use to take into account only those sentences that have consequences for the problem that has been selected.

(3) *Rules of Inference:*

The fact that jurists consider as valid law not only sentences identified as valid according to certain criteria of identification, but also the sentences which are *consequences* of those sentences is of the utmost importance. So to give an example which is somewhat trivial but is nevertheless a good illustration of what we want to say, it seems indubitable that if a law contains the sentence "All

---

1 To simplify matters we shall confine ourselves to normative consequences, that is to say, sentences correlating cases with solutions. Accordingly, our characterization of the notion of a topic is somewhat narrow. The conceptual scheme outlined in this book can be directly applied only to normative problems (cf. ch. I, sect. 2). But normative systems may also contain other types of sentences, e. g. sentences correlating cases with cases or solutions with solutions (cf. ch. IV, sect. 5). Nevertheless, taking into account the fact that all these sentences are correlations between certain elements belonging to two different Universes, it is easy to extend the scheme of the model to such situations.

citizens over the age of 22 have the right to vote" and this is accepted as valid, then the sentence "All 30-years-old citizens have the right to vote", which is a consequence of the first sentence, will also be considered a valid legal sentence, even if it has not been expressly formulated by the legislator. (This fact justifies our characterization of legal system as a deductive system.)

In order to determine the consequences of a set of sentences it is necessary to use some rules of inference. The rules of inference define the notion of consequence. It is quite obvious that the consequences of the same set of sentences will be different if different rules of inference are used. A sentence which is a consequence of a basis with certain rules of inference may cease to be a consequence if some of the rules are suppressed and, vice versa, a sentence that is not a consequence may become a consequence if a new rule of inference is introduced.

The content of an axiomatic system (whether normative or not) is, in other words, determined not only by the sentences of the basis, but also by the rules of inference.

The rules of inference have rarely, if ever, been discussed by legal writers, who often are not aware of their existence. The traditional philosophy of law has never dealt with this question and it is only very recently that legal philosophers have shown any interest in it, usually dealing with it under the heading of "juristic logic"[2]. This is hardly surprising since the logic of normative discourse has only recently emerged as a subject of study.

The three elements (topic, legal sentences and rules of inference) determine the content of a normative system and the task of jurists consists in formulating it explicitly and, eventually, in reorganizing it. (This reflects the idea that science does not "create", but only describes the law.)

The systematization of the law consists, accordingly, in the following procedures:

(a) *Determination of a UC and a US:*

To identify the normative consequences, that is, the correlations between cases and solutions, we must know what the possible cases

---

2 Cf. U. Klug, Juristische Logik, 3rd ed., Berlin, 1967; R. Schreiber, Logik des Rechts, Berlin, 1962; J. Kalinowski, Introduction a la logique juridique, Paris, 1965, and I. Tammelo, Outlines of modern legal logic, Wiesbaden, 1969.

and the possible solutions are, i. e. we must identify the Universe of Cases and the Universe of Solutions.

The determination of the *US* does not present major problems, since the *US* is a function of the *UA*. The *UC*, on the other hand, is not determined by the *UD*, since the *UC* is the result of a classification of the elements of the *UD* by means of certain properties (the *UP*). Accordingly, in order to determine the *UC* it is necessary to identify the relevant properties. Jurists usually take these properties from the legal sentences of the basis, but this is not necessary, since the choice of the *UP* may also be made on the basis of other criteria. This question gives rise to important logical and axiological problems discussed in ch. VI.

(b) *Derivation of the consequences of the basis:*

Once the *UC* and the *US* have been determined, the next step is to derive, using the rules of inference, the normative consequences of the basis for the given *UC* and the *US*, in order to identify the solutions that the system provides for the different cases of the *UC*.

The explicit formulation of the consequences of the basis exhibits the formal properties of the system (consistency and completeness) and that of the basis (independence).

(c) *Reformulation of the system:* consisting in the substitution for the original basis of another one. This usually occurs when the number of sentences in the basis is very large. The replacement of a very extensive basis by another that is more restricted but deontically equivalent is considered by jurists to be an advantage, since applying the system thereby becomes simpler. On the other hand, this operation does not modify the system itself but only its presentation. Frequently when jurists speak about the systematization of the law, they mean precisely what we call reformulation of the basis[3].

As the first stage of systematization (i. e. formulation of the system) has been already analyzed, we shall be concerned in this chapter mainly with the second stage (reformulation). But first, we shall discuss briefly the empirical problem of the identification of the sentences of the basis.

---

3 The criticism of legal systems that takes the form of pointing out defects and putting forward suggestions for its improvement is sometimes considered to be a part of the task of legal science. But it is an activity that goes beyond mere systematization.

3. Indentification of the Basis
and the Problem of Legal Validity

Before proceeding with systematization the jurist must determine the material he is to systematize, that is, he must identify the sentences that he will use as the axiomatic basis of his system. Following traditional terminology, we shall use the term *"valid"* for those legal sentences which jurists accept as admissible as components (of the basis) of a legal system. For the identification of the sentences of the basis certain criteria are used. These *criteria of identification* establish what requirements legal sentences must satisfy in order to be valid. The notion of legal validity is therefore *relative* to a criterion or a set of criteria of identification.

Criteria of identification consist of two types of rules: (a) *rules of admission,* stipulating the conditions under which a sentence becomes valid; and (b) *rules of rejection,* establishing when a legal sentence, valid according to the rules of admission, is no longer so.

The rules of admission indicate the various *sources* of law: legislation, precedent, custom, etc. The rules of rejection indicate the ways in which a valid legal sentence may lose its validity (derogation rules, desuetude, etc.).

A significant proportion of the controversy between different legal schools is concerned not with logical problems (systematization), but with the choice of criteria of identification and therefore with sources of law. Part of the disagreement between supporters of the Natural Law doctrine and legal positivists is a disagreement about admissible sources of law. Positivists admit as valid only those sentences issued by an empirical (human) authority, while the supporters of the doctrine of Natural Law admit other sources as well. There are also important differences among positivists. For some of them (the exegetic school in France) legislation is the only source of law; others admit, together with legislation, several other sources, such as custom or precedent. The attack of GENY on the exegetic school or that of HECK and his supporters (jurisprudence of interest — *Interessenjurisprudenz*) on the school called the jurisprudence of concepts *(Begriffsjurisprudenz)* had, among others, the object of enlarging the set of criteria of identification, advocating as they did the admission of new sources of law.

The rules of admission, together with the rules of rejection, *define* the notion of a valid legal sentence[1]. They are, therefore, *conceptual rules* (definitions). The definition of legal validity usually takes the form of a recursive definition: through the application of these rules in succession it is possible, in a finite number of steps, to establish whether a given sentence is valid or not (according to the criterion in question).

Conceptual rules (definitions) must not be confused with rules of action; the latter establish that an action is obligatory, forbidden or permitted. Conceptual rules, on the contrary, merely regulate the use of a concept (or a term) and do not forbid or permit anything. It is important to stress this difference because in the philosophy of law there is a certain tendency to identify criteria of validity with norms of competence[2].

Norms of competence are (a special class of) permissive norms; they are norms of action permitting the creation of new norms[3]. Criteria of identification often make reference to norms of competence, but this gives us no ground for confusing them. An example will probably make this distinction clearer.

A rule of admission which institutes legislation (in a wide sense) as a source of valid legal sentences may have (and as a matter of fact frequently has) the following form:

(a) All sentences belonging to the set C (e. g. a Constitution) are valid.

(b) If there is a valid sentence permitting a normative authority x to issue the sentence p, and x has issued p, then p is valid.

---

1 In this context we are interested only in the descriptive meaning of the term "valid"; the possible prescriptive or evaluative connotations of this term are therefore not taken into account.

2 So, for instance, the basic norm *(Grundnorm)* in KELSEN not only provides the ultimate criterion of the validity of the whole legal order, but also confers law-creating power (competence) on the first legislator. But it is clear that a definition cannot confer competence to create legal norms. Similarly, HART fails to discriminate between the logical status of the *rule of recognition* (which corresponds to our criterion of identification and hence must be a conceptual rule) and that of the *rules of change* which seem to be norms of competence (i. e. norms of conduct). The very use of the same expression "secondary rule" to refer to both is open to criticism, since it tends to conceal the distinction.

3 Cf. G. H. VON WRIGHT, Norm and Action, p. 192 ff.

(c) All sentences which are the consequence of (are inferred from) valid sentences are valid.

(a), (b) and (c) together constitute a recursive definition of "valid sentence". This means that by applying these rules in succession we can establish whether or not a given sentence is valid. (In fact, rules of admission are usually complemented by rejection rules, but this is a complication which we can disregard for the sake of simplicity.)

As may easily be seen, rule (b) refers explicitly to norms of competence (i. e. norms permitting the issuing of sentences); thus in order to be able to establish the validity of a sentence it may be necessary to know the content of certain norms of competence. But rules (a), (b) and (c) themselves are not norms of conduct, but mere definitions.

It is the concern of the philosophy of law (or general jurisprudence) to elucidate the criteria of identification which legal scientists in fact use to identify valid sentences of law, i. e. criteria which are actually in force in a given society[4]. This problem is usually dealt with under three different headings: (1) definition of the concept of law, (2) sources of law, and (3) unity of the legal order[5].

The set of *all* legal sentences which are valid according to a certain criterion of identification we shall call a *legal order*. The unity of an order is ensured by the criterion of identification of valid sentences.

The concept of an order is a special case — in a certain sense a limiting case — of the more general concept of *legal system*. In fact, it is the system formed by all valid sentences. (Let us recall that the consequences of valid sentences are also valid.)

When legal philosophers speak about "legal systems", they nearly always use this expression in the sense of "legal order", that is, to refer to the totality of norms which are valid according to

---

4 Cf. H. L. A. HART, The Concept of Law, p. 98: "For the most part the rule of recognition is not stated, but its existence is *shown* in the way in which particular rules are identified, either by courts or other officials or private persons or their advisers."

5 The most important contributions to the analysis of this last topic are found in BENTHAM and AUSTIN, and more recently, in H. KELSEN, ALF ROSS, and H. L. A. HART. Cf. J. RAZ, The Concept of a Legal System, Oxford, 1970.

a criterion of identification[6]. It is notable that they have shown virtually no interest in the more general concept of system which we have tried to outline in this book (*any* set of legal sentences containing all their consequences). But it is the latter concept — the generalized concept of legal system — which is nearly always used in legal science, or perhaps it would be better to say that this is the one that makes possible the rational reconstruction of the scientific practice of jurists. Indeed, jurists always construct their systems by initially taking some subset of a legal order, made up entirely of those valid sentences which are relevant to the problem that concerns them. Nobody has ever suggested identifying *all* the valid sentences of an order and such a Cyclopean task would have little value precisely because the properties of normative systems such as consistency, completeness and independence, as well as the very notion of normative system, are relational concepts. What the jurist is interested in is determining of the normative consequences for a certain topic (i. e. a given *UC* and a given *UA*) and this involves adopting a selective criterion which limits the extension of the basis to a considerable degree, for those sentences which obviously have no consequences for the problem in question are discarded at the very beginning[7]. Hence identifying the valid sentences is only the first step towards determining the basis. For this initial stage, all that the jurist needs is a criterion which will enable him to decide whether a given sentence is valid or not, but he is not interested in determining what *all* the valid sentences are. The second step consists in selecting — form the class of valid sentences — those that have consequences (and, above all, normative consequences) for the given problem.

Even though the choice of the problem is arbitrary in the sense that it depends entirely on the interest of the jurist, the selection of the sentences which are to integrate the basis of the system is

---

6 See, for example, H. KELSEN, Reine Rechtslehre, 2nd ed., Wien, 1960, ALF ROSS, On Law and Justice, 1958, H. L. A. HART, The Concept of Law, 1961, and J. RAZ, The Concept of a Legal System, 1970.

7 As we have pointed out, legal philosophers habitually consider problems of completeness (gaps) and consistency in relation to the whole order, and this is precisely what renders their analyses sterile. It is one of the topics in which the divorce between science and the philosophy of law is most clearly exhibited.

not, since it is determined by two factors: (1) the sentences of the basis must be valid sentences of law, and (2) the basis must contain all the sentences which have normative consequences for the given problem[8].

The difficulty of the problem of selecting all the sentences that are relevant to the problem in question varies according to the different sources of law. When the source is legislation, the problem has usually been solved in advance (at least in part) by the legislator himself who normally orders the statutes and their contents according to some criterion. This means that he also is engaged in the activity of systematization. This tendency to legislate in a systematic way has increased remarkably since the enactment of the Code Napoleon (the trend towards codification of the law). The characteristic feature of this procedure is that the statutes or the paragraphs of a code are grouped according to different topics. (The presence of the so-called "general parts" in modern codes corresponds to the second stage of systematization that will be discussed in the next section.) It should be noted that so far as theory is concerned, the legislator who draws up a statute is engaged in exactly the same activity as the dogmatic jurist: both are constructing a normative system, although the former is not bound by pre-existing (valid) sentences, but chooses them more or less freely. (These sentences become valid only when the legislator sanctions the project and transforms it into law.)

When the valid sentences are taken from judicial decisions (precedents) — as occurs in case law — the selection of the sentences of the basis presents considerable difficulty. In the first place, judicial decisions are not systematized as codes are. This fact compels the jurist to review a great number of decisions in order to be

---

8 In fact, since law is formulated in ordinary language, the inferences of jurists are seldom rigorously formal, and the question whether or not a certain sentence is a consequence of a given set cannot always be solved by purely rational methods. In these situations all that the jurist can do, as a scientist, is to point out the possible alternatives and their consequences, leaving the choice between them to the decision of the competent authority. On this subject see H. FIEDLER, Juristische Logik in mathematischer Sicht, Archiv für Rechts- und Sozialphilosophie 52, 93—116 (1966), and H. FIEDLER, Derecho, Logica, Matematica, Buenos Aires, 1968.

reasonably sure that he has not overlooked any legal sentence that is relevant for his problem. A further complication is the need to extract the *ratio decidendi* from each decision he is considering, since a precedent is not the whole decision (i. e. not all the sentences issued by the judge for the solution of an individual case), but only the *general* sentences which are used to justify the decision. (We have already pointed out that legal science is concerned with the solution of generic cases, so that the basis must be made up of general sentences and, in particular, of general norms[9].)

Now, the *ratio decidendi* of a decision is not always clearly formulated by the judge. Though the judge is obliged to justify his decision in explicit terms, the justification very often contains too many or too few things. Sometimes, the judge does not state all that is necessary in order to justify his decision (for example, because he considers it obvious); at other times he adduces arguments that are superfluous to the justification of his decision. Extracting the *ratio decidendi,* that is, the general rule of which the decision is application, is one of the most important tasks of the jurist concerned with case law[10].

The integration of the basis of a system is conditioned not only by criteria of identification used by the jurist and the problem or topic chosen by him, but also by a *temporal factor:* the particular time with respect to which the identification of valid sentences is made. The different sources of law are constantly producing new sentences that have acquired validity, while other sentences lose their validity by derogation or desuetude. This is why the application of the same criteria of identification at different times brings about different results. The identification of the sentences of the basis is an empirical problem precisely because the criteria of identification and of selection are applied to a material acquired through experience; the content of experience varies at different times. In this sense, legal systems are relative to a particular time: they are *momentary* systems[11].

---

9 Cf. E. BULYGIN, Sentenza giudiziaria e creazione di diritto, Rivista Internazionale di Filosofia del Diritto 44, 164—180 (1967).

10 Cf. G. R. CARRIÓ, Recurso de Amparo y Técnica Judicial, Buenos Aires, 1959, where there is an excellent illustration of the difficulties which the determination of the general norm applied by a court may present.

11 We shall return to this problem at a later stage; cf. *infra,* sect. 7.

4. Reformulation of the System and the Genesis of General Principles of Law

The importance of the task we have described as the first stage of systematization (derivation of consequences) lies in the fact that it makes explicit the content of the system and hence exhibits any defects such as gaps, inconsistencies and redundancies. The surest way of avoiding these defects would be to solve each case, step by step, by means of elementary norms. (By "elementary norm" we understand a norm correlating an elementary case with a maximal solution; cf. ch. 3, sect. 5.) This fact has led to a tendency in legislative technique which is habitually called "casuistry".

As a legislative technique, casuistry offers certain advantages, the most important of which is that it facilitates the construction of complete and consistent systems, but it also has great disadvantages. Its main fault consists in the proliferation of norms that it entails; if a norm is required for every case, it is clear that the number of norms of the basis will be extremely large if the system is to be complete in relation to a relatively complex problem.

On the other hand, the absence of gaps, contradictions and redundancies is not the only criterion used by jurists in evaluating systems. There is another which we shall call, following JHERING, the *principle of economy*[1], according to which the basis of a legal system should be as small as possible, i. e. should contain the smallest possible number of sentences. This implies that the sentences of the basis, and in particular, its norms, must be as *general* as possible. A norm is general — in the relevant sense of the term — when it solves a plurality of cases. This concept of generality is a comparative one: one norm is more general than another when it solves a greater number of (elementary) cases. General norms in this sense are those which we have called *complex* norms (ch. III, sect. 5): they provide a solution for a complex case and so resolve all elementary cases included in that complex case. This concept of generality must be distinguished from another which is also widely used in legal theory and which is not a comparative but an absolute concept. In this other sense, a norm is general when it provides a generic solution for generic cases in contradistinction to individual norms, which solve individual cases. Elementary norms

---

1 R. JHERING, Geist des römischen Rechts (Spanish translation: El Espiritu del Derecho Romano, Madrid, 1891, vol. III, pp. 25 ff.).

are general in the latter but not in the former sense. Since the term "general" is widely used in both senses, we thought it inadvisable to propose a change in terminology and trust that the context will make clear which concept of generality is meant in each situation.

The advantages of a system with a small but general basis are manifest: the relatively small number of sentences makes it easier to grasp the structure as a whole and to apply it in practice. But there are corresponding dangers: it is difficult to foresee all the consequences of very general norms and consequently the system may be incomplete or inconsistent.

Legislation through general (complex) norms seems to be the dominant technique among jurists, except perhaps in the Anglo-Saxon world, where the tendency towards casuistry has traditionally been very strong. The reduction in the number of the paragraphs of a code is usually regarded as a progressive measure. One of the most frequent criticisms of FREITAS has been that his code is too casuistic and, accordingly, excessively ample (there are 4908 paragraphs in FREITAS' code, though he left it unfinished). VÉLEZ SARS-FIELD, the author of the Argentinian Civil Code, managed to reduce the number of paragraphs to 4051 and the German Civil Code (BGB), which is considered to be one of the most perfect from a technical point of view, has only 2385 paragraphs. (The comparison of VÉLEZ SARSFIELD's code with that of FREITAS illustrates, by the way, the dangers of hasty generalizations. In ch. I we saw that VÉLEZ SARSFIELD reduced to two the four norms of FREITAS regarding the problem of recovery of real estate, with the result that three gaps appeared in his system!)

Generally speaking, the reformulation of a system consists in the replacement of the basis by a new one, that is less extensive, more general and normatively equivalent.

One purpose of the reformulation is to remove certain defects from the system. The possible defects in a system have varying degrees of importance. Incompleteness and inconsistency affect the system itself, in the sense that to eliminate them one must modify the system. In other words: if a system presents normative gaps or inconsistencies, the only way of removing them is the construction of a new and different system. If we believe (as most dogmatic jurists do) that a scientist must not modify a system imposed by a legislator, we must hold that he cannot eliminate gaps or inconsistencies. All that he may do is advocate their elimination. He can, however, eliminate redundancies and casuistry — simply by reformulating the basis of the system, because they do not affect the system as such, but only its presentation or formulation. And it is possible to modify the basis of a system without modifying the system itself, provided that the new basis is normatively equivalent to the original one.

The requirement of *normative equivalence* is most important: only if the new basis has the same normative consequences as the original can we regard the result as the same system reformulated. If the new basis lacks some of the normative consequences of the original, or has new consequences, we are confronted not by the same system, but by a different one. The modification of the law, however, is outside the province of legal theorists, since it is properly the concern of legislators. For this reason there is some justification in the attacks made on the jurisprudence of concepts, which purports to find new norms (new normative consequences) by means of the method of legal construction, although this should go no farther than the definition and analysis of legal concepts. This claim for the jurisprudence of concepts is either vacuous, if all that it provides is an explicit formulation of norms which are already implicit in the system, or an admission that it transgresses the limits of the purely cognitive function of science by creating new norms — which is a political function proper to the legislator.

When the sentences of the basis are taken from the body of enacted law (statutes), the reformulation becomes a complementary task, provided that the legislator has already proceeded systematically when creating the law. But the importance of the reformulation becomes evident when this prior systematization is lacking; for instance, when the sentences of the basis come from judicial decisions. To reduce the multiplicity of sentences taken from judicial decisions to a few general sentences from which all others can be deduced is one of the aims of legal science. This involves the substituting for the basis of the system — formed by all the general sentences used by judges to justify their decisions — a new basis consisting only of a few sentences, which have, nevertheless, the same normative consequences.

The reformulation of the basis of a legal system has been traditionally regarded as one of the most important tasks of legal dogmatics, since such reformulation is closely linked to the elaboration of the so-called "general parts" and of the general principles of law[2]. These activities seem substantially the same, consisting as they do in the formulation of more general norms. Between the norms that jurists call "general principles" and the norms integrating the "general parts" of a code, there is a difference only in degree, in the sense that the former are more general than the latter. It is very difficult, if not completely impossible, to draw a sharp distinction between norms and principles[3]. One of possible criteria seems to be that the principles are so general that they may be applied to different topics, while "general parts" refer to a more limited subject matter. But the procedure used for the elaboration of the general part of a code and the formulation of a general principle seems to be exactly the same.

5. "Juristic Induction"

What is the logical nature of the operation by means of which the jurist transforms a multiplicity of norms into a more general norm, normatively equivalent to the original norms? The analysis of this question may shed some light on the methods and character of legal science.

A distinguished dogmatic jurist, SEBASTIAN SOLER, after pointing out that the main part in the technical reconstruction of legal system is not purely deductive, maintains that a generalization that consists in deriving general rules and principles from isolated, concrete precepts of positive law is an *inductive* operation[1]. But SOLER contrasts this "juristic induction", where the conclusion is fully warranted by the premises, with the "induction by enumeration" that is used in factual sciences and provides conclusions that are merely probable. At the same time, SOLER stresses, in his controversy with KANTOROWICZ, the fact that juristic induction is not syllogistic and that the syllogism "is not the only possible way of arriving at logically valid conclusions[2].

---

2 R. JHERING, op. cit., vol. III, pp. 49 ff.; S. SOLER, Interpretación de la ley, Barcelona, 1962, pp. 171—181.

3 This is, of course, only *one* of the meanings that the term "general principles" has in juristic parlance. We shall not examine here all the possible meanings of this extremely ambiguous expression. Cf. C. R. CARRIÓ, Principios jurídicos y positivismo jurídico, Buenos Aires, 1970.

1 S. SOLER, Interpretación de la ley, Barcelona, 1962, p. 176.

2 SOLER, op. cit. p. 178.

That the syllogism is not the only logically valid form of reasoning is an established fact. Nevertheless, SOLER's observation is not without importance, for quite a number of jurists — even among those who write about logic — are curiously ignorant of many advances in the theory of logic. There is, however, a more interesting question, the question whether the operation that jurists call "juristic induction" is, in fact, induction or deduction.

ARISTOTLE[3] defines induction as "a passage from individuals to universals". Following this definition, Aristotelian tradition characterizes the difference between deductive and inductive reasoning in the following terms: deductive reasoning is a conclusion from the universal to the particular, inductive reasoning is a conclusion from the particular to the universal[4]. This characterization is obviously unsatisfactory; there is no reason why the conclusion drawn by deductive reasoning should be particular, nor is it necessary that its premisses should be universal. For this reason modern logicians introduce another criterion of differentiation: a deductive inference is logically valid, i. e. the conclusion is logically implied by the premisses, so that if the premisses are true, the conclusion cannot be false. In an inductive reasoning, on the other hand, there is no such relation of logical implication; the premisses do not guarantee the truth of the conclusion, but merely indicate its degree of probability or confirmation[5].

By this criterion it is clear that the operation called "juristic induction" is deductive inference, if it really leads, as SOLER asserts, to logically valid conclusions and the premisses fully guarantee the truth of the conclusion[6]. Nevertheless, it is interesting to observe that this piece of legal terminology — even if it does not agree with the terminology used in modern logic — has very illustrious antecedents. ARISTOTLE was the first to discuss this form of inference, which consists in a generalization starting from all the cases of a genus, and it was he who called it *induction*[7]. ARISTOTLE points out that in some respects this induction — which is clearly different

3 Topica, I, 12 (105ª 10—16).

4 ÜBERWEG, System der Logik und Geschichte der logischen Lehren, 1857.

5 R. CARNAP, Logical Foundations of Probability, op. cit., p. 43 ff.

6 SOLER, op. cit. p. 176 ff.

7 Analythica Priora, II, 23 (68ᵇ 15—29).

from the induction he characterizes in Topics[8] — can be contrasted with syllogism, even though it might also be regarded as a special case of it, and he insists that "induction proceeds through an enumeration of all the cases"[9]. The example mentioned by ARISTOTLE is, as PRIOR points out[10], not a happy one, since it is drawn from natural history, where it is impossible to examine all instances of a generalization, though PRIOR also remarks that the Aristotelian "induction" has many uses in the more abstract sciences, such as logic and mathematics. He also discusses the attempts of ARISTOTLE and DE MORGAN to reduce this type of inference to one of the figures of syllogism. We need not enter into these technicalities; it is sufficient for our purposes to state that the Aristotelian "induction" is a form of logically valid inference and hence deductive. This type of inference is widely employed in mathematics[11] and, apparently, also in legal science.

In order to decide whether juristic induction is really a logically valid inference of the same type as the Aristotelian induction and inductive reasoning in mathematics, we must examine its presuppositions. We have already seen that the validity of Aristotelian induction depends essentially on the possibility of surveying *all* the cases of a genus. The difference between this kind of inference and an ordinary syllogism may be expressed — as pointed out by PRIOR — by saying that instead of proving the result in the case by the rule, we prove the rule by observing the result in all the cases[12].

One condition that must be satisfied if observation of all the cases is to be a possibility is the existence of a finite number of cases. Jurists maintain that juristic induction is a logically valid inference because the law satisfies this condition: the material handled by the jurist is limited, since the number of rules from which he takes the general principles is finite[13]. This thesis seems to rest on the assumption that the set of originally valid sentences is necessarily finite.

---

8 Topica, I, 12 (105^a 10—16).

9 Analythica Priora, II, 23 (68^b 28—29).

10 A. N. PRIOR, Formal Logic, Oxford, 1955, pp. 141—145.

11 Cf. J. BARKLEY ROSSER, Logic for Mathematicians, New York, 1953, pp. 34—35.

12 A. N. PRIOR, Formal Logic, op. cit., p. 144.

13 S. SOLER, op. cit., p. 178: "Juristic induction is legitimate only in the measure that the general principle is taken out of the totality of the

This is certainly true for positive law, for since positive law is the law created by human beings, the set of sentences in the basis cannot be infinite, since they must have been formulated in a finite number of steps. Therefore, if we accept the positivist contention that all law is positive law, the finitist thesis is valid without qualification. But this does not necessarily follow for a natural law position. The basis of a system of natural law may (though it need not) be formed by an infinite number of sentences, created, for example, by God (who, as an infinite being, may well create an infinite number of sentences). In this case, the task of systematization (or axiomatization) would be to find a finite basis equivalent to the system of natural law. But it is also possible that it cannot be axiomatized.

From a practical point of view, there is no doubt that legal scientists have operated exclusively with positive law, for the past 150 years. Sentences that do not belong to positive law are hardly, if ever, admitted to the basis. This is true even of those dogmatic jurists who declare themselves supporters of the doctrine of natural law on an ethical or philosophical level. Accordingly, the condition of finitude which is necessary for the logical validity of reasoning by cases, is met — at least where positive law is concerned — in legal science. Juristic induction is therefore a deductive (logically valid) inference of the same type as that used in the formal sciences.

6. Creative Function of Legal Science

The fact that the relation between the sentences of the original basis and "general principles", i. e. the sentences of the new basis, is one of logical implication and that, consequently, the inference of the latter from the former is deductive, does not mean that systematizing in legal science is a purely mechanical activity. Yet there is a deeply rooted prejudice — not only among jurists — which consists in regarding all operations in the field of deductive logic as mechanical, and it is perhaps for this reason that dogmatic jurists insist that their methods are not purely deductive[1].

However, the conception of logical deduction as a mere mechanical activity is not only a mistake in itself but also one that is

provisions, and the operation is possible because the series of legal provisions is always finite."

1 S. SOLER, Interpretación de la ley, p. 176.

responsible for a good deal of confusion in legal theory. A theoretical activity can be described as mechanical only if there are effective procedures for solving the problems in question. By an effective procedure we understand the existence of a set of rules determining univocally each one of the steps in the procedure, which leads, in every case where it is applied, to the desired solution in a finite number of steps. A decision procedure which is effective for a class of sentences is, in logical syntax, a procedure which enables us to determine in a finite number of steps whether or not a given sentence of this class is a theorem, and in semantics, whether it is true or false[2].

It is therefore desirable to separate very carefully questions for which there are effective procedures from those which lack — sometimes necessarily, i. e. for logical reasons — such procedures. CARNAP, whom we are following on this point, distinguishes three types of problem[3].

I. First Problem: To Find a Conclusion

Given a set of sentences as premisses, a conclusion (logically implied by the premisses) suitable for a certain purpose is wanted. There is no effective procedure for the solution of problems of this kind. Unlike mere computation (for which there is an effective procedure), problems of the kind just mentioned cannot be solved by mechanical activity. But, as CARNAP points out, the work of a logician or a mathematician consists to a great extent in attempts to solve problems for whose solution there are no fixed rules. It is an activity in which rational und intuitive factors are combined; it requires talent, creative imagination and sometimes luck[4].

II. Second Problem: To Examine a Result

Given two sentences, the problem is to find out whether one logically implies the other or, in other words, whether the second is deducible from the first. Here, again, we have a kind of problem

---

2 Cf. R. CARNAP, Logical Foundations of Probability, op. cit., § 43, p. 193; The Logical Syntax of Language, London, 1937, § 15; Formalization of Logic, Cambridge, Mass., 1961, § 29.

3 R. CARNAP, Logical Foundations or Probability, § 43, pp. 192—199.

4 Cf. K. POPPER, The Logic of Scientific Discovery, New York, 1959, pp. 31 and 55.

which plays an important part in logic and mathematics and for which there is, in general, no effective procedure of decision. Not only finding an interesting new theorem, but also constructing a proof is an operation which is not subject to rational control. For although there are logical rules regulating the deduction of a theorem, these merely indicate which steps are permitted and which are not; but they do not say which steps (among those permitted) must actually be chosen for the construction of the desired proof. Only in the most elementary part of deductive logic are there effective procedures of decision (as, for example, the method of truth-tables in propositional logic).

III. Third Problem: To Examine a Given Proof

Given two sentences and an alleged proof that the first logically implies the second, the problem is to discover whether the alleged proof is actually a proof, i. e. whether it is in accordance with the rules of logic. For the solution of this third problem there is, in general, an effective procedure of decision. It may be verified whether each of the steps of the alleged proof conforms to the rules of inference. This task may be described as purely "mechanical".

The two first problems, finding a conclusion and constructing a proof, belong to what REICHENBACH[5] calls the "context of discovery", for which there are no logical rules which could replace man's creative powers. The third problem, the examination of a given proof, belongs instead to the *context of justification:* it is justification of a given proof by means of the rules of logic. This is the proper field of formal logic.

Bearing in mind the essentially limited character of mechanical procedures in the light of this distinction, we can now examine the allegation that systematization as performed by dogmatic jurists is a mere mechanical activity. It should be clear that although the reasoning of the jurist, deriving as he does general principles (complex norms) from given legal sentences, is deductive in character, and although the relation between the premises and the conclusion (i. e. the new basis) is one of logical implication, the activity of reconstructing the system (or rather, of reformulating its basis) is nevertheless very far from being a mere mechanical operation, since,

---

5 H. REICHENBACH, The Rise of Scientific Philosophy, Berkeley, Calif., 1951, ch. XIV.

among other things, it involves discovering the general principles that are implicit in the basis. This task requires a considerable degree of creative ability and a special kind of intuition that Germans call "Einfühlung". It is this activity that shows up the difference between genius and sheer industry, and demands the presence of the former for success. But it is not only the finding of general principles that qualifies as a creative activity; so also does the construction of the proof that they are really deducible from sentences of the original basis.

This creative side of legal science does not, of course, consist in the creation of new norms; in other words, it should not be confused with the activity of the legislator. Yet many jurists have in fact failed to draw this distinction and to recognise that the two tasks are creative in different senses of that word[6]. In reaction to such confusions, many modern theorists draw a sharp line between the function of the legislator which is regarded as creative (since he introduces new norms), and the function of the scientist which is regarded as purely cognitive and is, furthermore, characterized as being merely descriptive[7]. The distinction itself is quite justified, but the characterization of scientific activity as mere description is not very happy, since it withholds recognition from the creative element in scientific investigation.

Consequently, there is no justification for the fears of those jurists who — mistakenly equating logical deduction with mechanical activity — issue warnings against an excessive "mathematization" of law and look with deep mistrust, if not with open hostility on attempts to apply symbolic logic to legal science[8]. Such fears arise from ignorance of the nature of logic and mathematics, and of the important and, indeed, indispensable part that creative imagination plays in these sciences[9]. The progressive rationalization of a field of knowledge that is achieved as a result of the explicit for-

---

6 See, as an example of such confusion, W. JELLINEK, Schöpferische Rechtswissenschaft, 1928.

7 E. g. H. KELSEN, Reine Rechtslehre, Wien, 1960, and ALF ROSS, On Law and Justice, London, 1958.

8 Typical for this position is L. RECASENS SICHES, Nueva Filosofia de la Interpretación del Derecho, Mexico, 1956.

9 Cf. H. FIEDLER, Mathematik und moderne Logik, Archiv für Rechts- und Sozialphilosophie 47, 4 (1961), and Derecho, Lógica, Matematica, Buenos Aires, 1968.

mulation of the conceptual apparatus and logical rules (which have been refined to a high degree of precision) leads inevitably to the elimination of irrational fears, emotive factors, mythical superstitions, pseudo-arguments and pseudo-problems, but creative genius cannot thereby be rendered superfluos or superseded by robots and computers.

7. Changes in a System

We have characterized a legal system as a normative system whose basis is composed of legal sentences. The fact that jurists reformulate the basis of a system, substituting some sentences for others, does not affect the identity of the system, provided that the new basis is normatively equivalent to the original. There is no change in that system, in the sense that its normative consequences remain the same.

However, jurists often speak of changes in a system — a mode of speech which is highly misleading and a source of confusion. When a jurist says that a system has changed — because some of its normative consequences have been modified — what he intends to assert or at least what he is entitled to assert is that it is no longer the same system, that it has become another system different from the former. This is a direct consequence of our definition of system: the criterion of identity is provided by its consequences. Therefore, expressions like "change in a system" or "change of a system" must be taken to mean not a modification of the same system (which would retain its identity despite the change), but the substitution of a new and different system for the original one. This is a perfectly natural meaning of the term "change".

What holds true for normative systems in general also holds true for *legal orders,* which are a species of the genus normative system. (Let us recall that an order is a system which contains all sentences which are valid according to a criterion of identification.) A legal order cannot change without losing its identity. A so-called change in a legal order is in fact the substitution of a different order for the original.

These reflections show that our concept of legal order does not reflect the meaning that expressions such as "Austrian law" or "French legal order" have in ordinary language. There is no doubt that French law changes in the course of time without losing its identity, that is, without ceasing to be the same French law. In other words, French law is not a momentary order, i. e. one that belongs to a given temporal moment, in contradistinction to our concept of legal order which is momentary in the sense that it is a legal system containing all legal sentences that are valid at a certain moment.

However, the expression "French law" can be translated into our language, in the sense that its meaning can be rendered in terms of "momentary order". Indeed, in our terminology, French law is not *one* legal order, but a temporary and discrete succession of (momentary) legal orders. It is certainly not easy to determine a criterion of unity for these orders and what seems most likely is that there are several criteria in ordinary language (which are rather vague and not always consistent). One of these seems to be the territory in which these orders are efficacious (in force). According to this criterion, French law would be the sequence of all momentary legal orders that have been in force in France[1].

---

1 It is not easy to determine the exact meaning of such expressions as "legal order" or "legal system" in the writings of legal philosophers. KELSEN, for example, defines "Rechtsordnung" as the set of norms which derive their validity from the *Grundnorm* (basic norm). Cf. Reine Rechtslehre, 1960, p. 32 and pp. 196 ff. But it is not clear whether his concept of legal order is a momentary one and therefore comprehends only those norms that are valid at a particular time, or whether it comprehends all norms that are valid at any time. The second interpretation is supported by the fact that KELSEN speaks of a change of a legal order only if there is a change of the basic norm, e. g. as a consequence of a revolution. (Cf. Reine Rechtslehre, 1960, pp. 213—214, and General Theory of Law and State, Cambridge, Mass., 1945, p. 118). In such a case, the criterion of identity of a legal order would be given by the identity of the criterion of validity (basic norm), and the system would still be the same throughout time, until the basic norm changed. On the other hand, this interpretation is difficult to reconcile with KELSEN's assertion that the unity of a legal order is ensured by the absence of contradiction between its norms (Reine Rechtslehre, 1960, p. 209). For if the validity of the norms is not referred to a particular time and the order contains all norms that are valid at any time whatever, then norms that have been derogated (i. e. norms that were once valid but have ceased, meanwhile, to be so) also belong to the legal order. It would therefore be virtually impossible that no contradictory norms should be present, since a norm that is

Bearing in mind these considerations about the meaning of the term "change", let us now examine the different ways in which a change, that is, the substitution of one system for another, may be produced.

I. Change of the Basis

It is obvious that any modification of the basis which alters the normative consequences of a system produces a change of the latter. But the modification of the normative content of the basis may arise from either of two different causes.

(a) Change in the criterion of identification: Any modification of the criteria of identification may produce a change in the basis. The fact that the adoption of different starting points leads to different results is hardly surprising.

(b) Application of the same criteria at different times: This is the usual, we might perhaps say "normal" case of a change of a system. The enactment of a new statute, the appearance of a new custom, the abrogation of a norm, all normally give rise to a modification of the corresponding system. What changes here is not the criterion of identification, but the sentences identified as valid according to this criterion. (Naturally, there may be some laws which do not modify the normative content of a system and which, accordingly, produce no change.)

---

derogated is usually replaced by a new norm which is incompatible with the previous norm. For this reason we are inclined to believe that KEL- SEN's legal order *(Rechtsordnung)* is, after all, a momentary order. But even if his order were not momentary, it still would not coincide with what is understood by a legal order in ordinary language. French law does not lose its identity because of a revolution; it remains the same legal order. Changes in the criteria of identification do not affect its continuity.

A good deal of what has been said about KELSEN may be applied, *mutatis mutandi,* to HART's concept of legal system. Even though HART does not give an explicit definition of "legal system" and does not expressly indicate what his criteria of identity are, his legal system does not appear to be a momentary one, since its identity is determined, mainly, by the identity of the rule of recognition. (Cf. The Concept of Law, pp. 114 ff.). See also J. RAZ, The Concept of a Legal System, Oxford, 1970.

II. Change of the Rules of Inference

As the content of a system is determined not only by the sentences of the basis but also by the rules of inference used to infer consequences from these sentences, a change of system may arise not only from a modification of the basis but also from a modification of the rules of inference. In a sense, changing the latter is an easier matter, for these rules are very seldom, if ever, explicitly stated. But since a change in rules of inference involves a change in the criteria of identification, this case may be regarded as analogous to I a.

8. Changes in Interpretation

Sometimes it is not easy to determine what it is that has changed in a system: its basis or its rules of inference. In this context, the phenomenon that jurists call a "change in interpretation" creates very interesting problems. It seems clear that a change in the interpretation of a legal text (e. g. of a paragraph of a code or a statute) made by judges is likely to produce a modification of its normative consequences. But any modification of the consequences means that the system is no longer the same. How then are such changes in interpretation to be "interpreted"? Of the two elements that determine a system, the sentences of the basis and the rules of inference, which is affected by the change in interpretation?

This is not an easy question to answer. We shall begin by considering an example. The Argentinian Civil Code provides, in § 450 (18): "A guardian is absolutely forbidden, even if a judge illegally allows it ... to lend money belonging to his ward, no matter how advantageous the conditions are." The absolute prohibition against lending money belonging to wards was, for a long time, applied to loans of every kind, including mortgages, since the Code makes no exceptions, until in 1951 the courts decided to authorize a guardian to lend his ward's money for a mortgage[1].

We shall not discuss the details of the case which resulted in this decision, or the arguments advanced by the court to justify it. What we are concerned to do is to analyze the effects of this decision. Now it is clear that the decision caused a change in the consequences of § 450. Before this decision guardians could not invest

---

1 We have taken this example from C. Cossio, Teoría de la Verdad Jurídica, Buenos Aires, 1954, pp. 194—195.

the money of their wards in mortgages; after it, this action ceased to be regarded as forbidden and became perfectly lawful. There are two possible ways of explaining this phenomenon. One, which we shall call *version A*, consists in saying that the decision has changed § 450 by substituting for it another norm. The alternative explanation of the same fact, which we call *version B*, consists in maintaining that § 450 has not been modified, and that the change in the consequences arises from a change in the rules of inference.

Both versions present considerable difficulties. Jurists are reluctant to admit that a change in interpretation implies a modification of the legal sentences themselves, especially where enacted law is concerned. The idea that a judge changes the statute itself by interpreting it in a different way seems to be repugnant to deeply rooted habits of thought and, implying as it does that judges create law, suggests that the judicial function in fact exceeds the bounds assigned to it in theory. It is therefore likely that most jurists would reject this account of the phenomenon, even though it is not very clear whether they would be prepared to accept version B.

This also presents great difficulties, since it implies an excessive enlargement of the rules of inference, for by this account any change in interpretation would mean the introduction of new rules of inference. But if, apart from the logical rules of inference, the introduction of *ad hoc* rules for each term is allowed, then the notion of consequence which defines the system, becomes too vague. The rules of inference are then no longer *a priori* (necessary), but merely contingent. Now, there are good reasons for giving the status of necessary *(a priori)* laws to the laws governing the notion of consequence as this notion lies at the core of the whole conceptual scheme of science[2]. And this involves excluding any rules of inference other than logical ones.

Before deciding between one of the two versions we must emphasize two points:

(i) These two versions constitute a dilemma from which there is no escape. If we admit that the consequences have changed, we are bound to admit that either the sentences of the basis or the rules of inference have been modified. There is no other possibility.

---

2 Cf. WILLARD VAN ORMAN QUINE, Methods of Logic, 2nd ed. 1962, Introduction, and also QUINE's Two Dogmas of Empiricism, From a Logical Point of View, Cambridge, Mass., 1953, pp. 20—46.

This may require some amplification. Many jurists would be prepared to say that what a change of interpretation modifies is the *meaning* of a term, and that judges, when interpreting, define or rather redefine the terms occurring in a legal text. This is perfectly true. But there is no doubt that changing the meaning of a term implies modifying the consequences of the sentences in which this term occurs, and modifying the consequences means either changing the sentences or changing the rules of inference.

(ii) The two versions (A and B) are descriptively equivalent, that is to say, their empirical content is exactly the same, since they describe the same facts, even though in different languages. Their difference, therefore, lies not in their content, but in the form given to the expression of this content. This means that, in principle, either of the two versions may be adopted, which in turn means that there is no one description of a system that is uniquely true; instead there are several (that is, a whole class of) true descriptions[3]. Nevertheless, among these equivalent descriptions there is one and only one in which the rules of inference are *logical rules,* and this we shall call a *normal system,* defining it as a system where no rules of inference other than logical ones are admitted (though there is no commitment to any particular system of logic).

In a normal system, any change in the consequences — for example, one that comes about through a change in interpretation — will mean that the sentences of the basis have been modified.

We shall adopt a usage by which the expressions "system", "normative system" or "legal system" mean a normal system, that is, we shall choose a description of system which leads to a normal system, except when indicated otherwise. By adopting this convention we are accepting version A, since any change in the system will be described as a change in the sentences of the basis and not as a change in the rules of inference.

We are now in a position to put forward a possible interpretation of one of the arguments advanced by Cossio against the existence of gaps in law[4]. Cossio's thesis that "There are no legal gaps because there are judges" and "There are no gaps because

---

3 This problem is similar to that of congruence discussed by H. REICHENBACH in his The Rise of Scientific Philosophy, Berkeley, Calif., 1951, ch. VIII.

4 For the discussion of other arguments put forward by Cossio see below ch. VII, sect. 5, and ch. VIII, sect. 5.

there is interpretation"[5] may be understood as follows: There are no legal gaps because any set of legal norms (taken as a basis) is able to supply solutions for all possible cases, provided that the criterion used for the admission of the rules of inference is sufficiently elastic. When a case is not explicitly solved by the norms of the basis, an appropriate rule of inference is introduced by the judge, which enables him to infer a solution for this case. The task of interpretation would thereby amount to deriving solutions for cases for which there is no explicit solution by introducing *ad hoc* rules of inference. This means — if our interpretation of Cossio's theory is correct — that Cossio adopts version B. However, although it is legitimate to describe a change in interpretation as a change in the rules of inference, we cannot infer from this that there are no gaps in the law. The adoption of version B entitles us to say only that an incomplete system (a system with gaps) can be transformed through interpretation, that is, by the introduction of new rules of inference, into a complete system (a system without gaps). But since it is clear that what we have here are two different systems, the argument we are discussing does not entitle Cossio to maintain that gaps do not exist. Indeed, far from supporting his thesis, his own arguments — provided that our interpretation is correct — presuppose the existence of normative gaps.

VI. The Problem of Relevance and Axiological Gaps

In this chapter we shall discuss some logical and axiological issues related to the problem of determining the Universe of Cases and provide definitions of some important concepts commonly used in legal and other forms of normative discourse.

Determining the Universe of Cases belongs — as has been shown in the preceding chapter — to the procedure that we called systematization. The jurist, after delimiting his problem and identifying the corresponding legal sentences (which form the basis of his system), must determine the possible cases in order to see how these cases are solved, if at all, by the system.

The Universe of Cases is generated from the Universe of Properties. We shall speak of Universes of Cases of different levels,

---

5 C. Cossio, La Plenitud del Ordenamiento Jurídico, 2nd ed., Buenos Aires, 1947, pp. 58 ff.

basing our distinction on the varying number of properties of *UP*, i. e. properties that are selected to characterize the cases. Some interesting relations hold between the *UCs* belonging to different levels, one of which (the relation of being finer) is especially important for us (sect. 1).

In sect. 2 we analyze the ways in which one and the same normative system resolves cases which belong to different *UCs*.

What emerges is that if a system is complete in relation to a *UC*, then it is also complete in relation to all *UCs* which are finer than the *UC* in question, but if we choose a less fine *UC*, then the occurrence of normative gaps is possible. However, even if a system which is complete in relation to a certain *UC*, is also (necessarily) complete in relation to all *UCs* which are finer, in all these finer *UCs* there are some properties which are *irrelevant* for the solutions of the system, in the sense that the solution is the same, whether the property is present or absent.

The definition of the concept of relevance is elaborated in three stages in sect. 3 and is most important for the discussion that follows. We can show that for every normative system there is one and only one Universe of Properties that contains all the properties which are relevant and none beside, a fact which enables us to give a criterion of adequacy for the selection of the Universe of Cases. This criterion we call the *thesis of relevance* and according to it, the Universe of Cases should be constructed out of the Universe of Relevant Properties (*UPR*).

On the other hand, to ask which properties ought to be relevant, i. e., should be taken into account for the solutions, is to raise a question of valuation.

The proposition which identifies those properties that ought to be relevant according to some axiological criterion we call *the hypothesis of relevance*. This is a criterion of the axiological adequacy of normative systems in the sense that a coincidence between the hypothesis of relevance and the thesis of relevance of the system is a necessary though not sufficient condition for the axiological adequacy of the system (sects. 3 and 4).

The situation in which there is a property such that it ought to be relevant (according to some hypothesis of relevance), but is, in fact, not relevant for the system, deserves special attention. Such cases are in legal parlance sometimes called "axiological gaps". An explicit definition of this concept is worked out in sect. 5.

In sect. 6 we try to show, by means of concrete examples, that the frequent confusion between axiological and normative gaps in legal theory arises from an imperfect understanding of the nature of both these concepts, so that more exact definitions of these concepts are badly needed. The same sort of confusion underlies the well known distinction between primary and secondary gaps, the so called primary gaps being what we call normative gaps, whereas the secondary gaps are, in most cases, axiological gaps or gaps of recognition.

1. Universes of Cases of Different Level

In the following discussion we shall consider only those UCs which are generated from a set of properties (Universe of Properties). As we have already pointed out, this is not the only way in which a UC may come into existence, but for the sake of simplicity we shall take into account only Universes of Cases of the first type, which are, certainly the most common ones. On the other hand, most of what we shall say in this section is also applicable — *mutatis mutandis* — to the other type of UC.

According to the generalized definition of UC (ch. II, sect. 2) every set of cases that forms a division is a UC. We shall now examine the relations between different UCs.

Given a set of properties, different UPs and, accordingly, different UCs may be constructed out of the properties included in this set (because any given number of logically independent properties and their negations form a division). We shall call the *width* of the UP the finite number n of the properties contained in this UP.

(Clearly, the number n cannot be infinite, because we are concerned only with properties which can be expressed in a language and even if the properties of a thing or a state of affairs were infinite, the number of primitive predicates available in any language would still be finite. This is not to say that there are inexpressible properties, i. e. properties which cannot be expressed in any language. Any property can be expressed in some language, but there is no single language that provides names for all possible properties).

Every Universe of Cases is a function of a UP of a finite number n of properties. This number n will be said to measure not only the width of the UP, but also the *level* of the corresponding UC.

Different *UPs* of the same width *n*, will give rise to different *UCs* belonging to the same level *n*. Of special interest is the situation in which the *UCs* are characterized by sets of properties (*UPs*) which are included in (are subsets of) a given set of properties, as illustrated in the following diagram. (The expression "*UC (p q r)*" is to be read: the Universe of Cases characterized by the properties *p*, *q* and *r*.)

Diagram VI-1

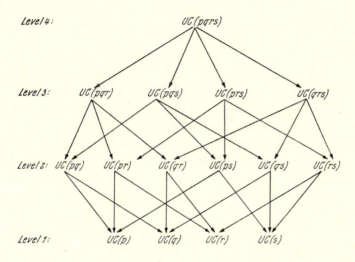

Diagram VI-1 shows that for a set of properties α of width 4, 4 different *UCs* of level 1, 6 *UCs* of level 2, 4 *UCs* of level 3, and 1 *UC* of level 4 may be formed out of *UPs* which are subsets of α. The number of cases of each *UC* may easily be obtained by means of the formula 2^n (where *n* is the level of the *UC*). According to it, each *UC* of level 1 has 2 cases; each *UC* of level 2, 4 cases; each *UC* of level 3, 8 cases, and each *UC* of level 4 has 16 cases.

Between Universes of Cases which belong to different levels and also between the cases of these Universes certain relations hold that are worth mentioning.

The arrows in the Diagram VI-1 indicate the relation of fineness.

A division D_1 is said to be finer than another division D_2 if and only if every element of D_1 logically implies some element of D_2 and at least one element of D_1 is not implied by any element of D_2.

The relation of fineness holds between Universes of Cases, because they are divisions (ch. II, sect. 2). If we take the Diagram VI-1, we see that $UC(pqrs)$ is finer than $UC(pqr)$; this last is finer than $UC(pq)$ and so on. The relation holds in the direction of the arrow. It is transitive, asymmetrical and irreflexive.

Those UCs which are not (directly or indirectly) connected by means of an arrow are not comparable so far as fineness is concerned. It can be seen that the UCs which belong to the same level are not comparable with one another regarding fineness. But there are some UCs of different levels which are also not comparable. E. g., between $UC(pqr)$ and $UC(rs)$ the relation of being finer does not hold, so these two UCs are not comparable.

Our definition of the relation of fineness entails that if UC_i is finer than UC_j, then every case of UC_i logically implies some case of UC_j but not viceversa. (The relation of logical implication holds between the cases of two UCs which are comparable regarding fineness, but it holds in one direction only.)

Diagram VI-2 shows the relations of logical implication between the cases of two UCs of different levels; these relations are indicated by arrows.

Diagram VI-2

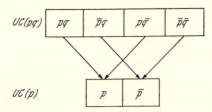

2. Completeness of a System and the Problem of Relevance

The completeness of a normative system has been defined (ch. I, sect. 6, and ch. IV, sect. 6) as a relation between a normative system and (among other things) a UC. It follows from this that a system which is complete in relation to a certain UC may be incomplete regarding another UC even in relation to the same UA. Let us now see how a system which is complete in relation to a certain UC stands in relation to other UCs which belong to different levels.

We shall first consider two Universes of Cases related in such a way that the first is finer than the second. Let the first be $UC(pq)$

and the second $UC(p)$. Suppose that a certain normative system α is complete in relation to $UC(p)$, i. e. the UC which is less fine. This means that cases p and $\bar{p}$ are solved by α, and this implies that among the consequences of α there are two sentences which correlate case p and case $\bar{p}$ with two (not necessarily different) maximal solutions. Suppose that these solutions are S_1 for p and S_2 for $\bar{p}$. We may also say that the sentences "if p then S_1" and "if $\bar{p}$ then S_2" are consequences of α.

The question is: how does α solve the cases of $UC(pq)$, which is finer than $UC(p)$? The arrows in Diagram VI-2 show that the case pq logically implies the case p and given that case p is correlated with the solution S_1, it follows that case pq is also correlated with S_1. Hence the system solves the case pq, as it correlates this case indirectly with the solution S_1. Similarly, it may be shown that all other cases of $UC(pq)$ are correlated by α with one of the two solutions S_1 or S_2, viz., the cases pq and $p\bar{q}$ are correlated with S_1 and the cases $\bar{p}q$ and $\bar{p}\bar{q}$, with the solution S_2. We may conclude that the solution of all cases of $UC(p)$ holds also for all cases of $UC(pq)$. This conclusion may easily be generalized in the following way:

(T_1) If a normative system α is complete in relation to a UC_i then it is also complete in relation to all UCs which are finer than UC_i.

Suppose now that the system α is complete in relation to $UC(pq)$ and we want to know what happens in relation to a UC which is less fine, say $UC(p)$. Suppose that the case pq is correlated with S_1 and the case $p\bar{q}$ with S_2. Which solution is correlated by the system with the case p?

It is clear that from the sentences "If pq then S_1" and "pq implies p" we cannot determine which solution applies to the case p. But as p is equivalent to the disjunction "$pq \vee p\bar{q}$" the sentences "If p then S_1 or S_2" may, in fact be derived from the given sentences. This means that p is correlated with the disjunction of two solutions (S_1 and S_2) and is therefore a (partial) gap (provided the system is consistent). (Cf. ch. I, sect. 6). We do not know which solution applies to the case p, for to know this we should first need to know whether or not the property q is present. The solution of the cases of a UC which is finer than UC_i, does not imply that all the cases of UC_i are solved. Only if all cases of $UC(pq)$ that imply the same case of $UC(p)$ were correlated with the same solution

7*

(say S_1) would the cases of $UC(p)$ be solved as well. But this is a very special instance; from the mere fact that all the cases of a finer UC have solutions it does not follow that all the cases of a less fine UC are solved as well. So we may state:

(T_2) The fact that a normative system is complete in relation to a UC_i does not imply its completeness in relation to any UC less fine than UC_i.

Let us now turn to our first example (Diagram VI-2). The solution of the cases of a less fine UC — $UC(p)$ — holds also for all cases of a finer division — $UC(pq)$. In our example, S_1 was the solution for the cases pq and $p\bar{q}$ and S_2 for the cases $\bar{p}q$ and $\bar{p}\bar{q}$. It follows that those cases in which the property p is present are correlated with the solution S_1 whether the property q is present or absent. The same happens with the two other cases: here the solution is also independent of the presence or absence of the property q. This shows that the property q is quite irrelevant as its presence or absence does not affect the solutions of the cases of $UC(pq)$. We may generalize this observation, saying:

(T_3) If a normative system is complete in relation to a UC_i, then it also solves all the cases of any UC_j finer than UC_i, but those properties which characterize UC_j but do not characterize UC_i are irrelevant for the solutions of the system (provided the system is consistent in UC_j).

This last restriction is necessary, for if the system is not consistent in UC_j, then the properties of UC_j that do not characterize the UC_i may, nevertheless, be relevant for the solutions of the cases of UC_j. Consider, e. g., a normative system β containing the norms "S_1/p", "$S_2/\bar{p}$" and "S_2/q". This system is complete (and consistent) in relation to $UC(p)$; but in relation to $UC(pq)$ — which is finer than $UC(p)$ — β is no longer consistent, because case pq is correlated by β with two different solutions (S_1 and S_2 are supposed to be maximal and so incompatible solutions). Nevertheless the property q is not irrelevant in $UC(pq)$: its presence (case pq) gives rise to an inconsistency, whereas its absence (case $p\bar{q}$) does not.

This example suggests that the consistency and completeness of a normative system are differently related to more and less detailed UCs. Completeness holds in one direction: from a less fine UC to finer UCs, but not vice versa. Consistency holds in the opposite direction: from a finer UC to less fine UCs, but not vice versa. We have just considered a normative system β which was consistent in relation to $UC(p)$ and inconsistent in relation to $UC(pq)$.

These observations regarding consistency may be generalized as follows:

(T_4)   If a normative system is consistent in a UC_i, then it is also consistent in any UC_j *less fine* than UC_i.

(T_5)   If a normative system is inconsistent in a UC_i, then it is also inconsistent in any UC_j *finer* than UC_i (though it may be consistent in relation to a UC_k less fine than UC_i)[1].

3. *Relevant and Irrelevant Properties*

Our next task will be to give a definition of relevance, a concept which made its appearance at the end of the preceding section and will be referred to frequently in the sections that follow.

First we shall introduce the following terminological convention: two cases will be said to be *complementary regarding a property p* if and only if p is present in one case and absent in the other, and all the other defining properties remain constant. (This is an extension of the notion of complementary property — ch. I, sect. 3 — to cases.) Hence the cases characterized by the properties $pqrs\ldots n$ and $\bar{p}qrs\ldots n$ are complementary in relation to p.

From this definition it follows that a case C_i has one and only one complementary case in relation to each defining property of C_i *in a certain Universe of Cases*. For instance, in the $UC(pqr)$, the case pqr is complementary to $\bar{p}qr$ in relation to p, is complementary to $p\bar{q}r$ in relation to q and is complementary to $pq\bar{r}$ in relation to r.

By means of the notion of complementary case we shall define three concepts of relevance, because a property may be relevant in relation to a case, in relation to a Universe of Cases and in relation to a Universe of Actions. The three concepts of relevance — and its negation (irrelevance) — are, moreover, relative to a normative system and to a Universe of Minimal Solutions.

(D_1)   The property p is *relevant in the case C_i* of a UC_j in relation to a normative system α and a $UA_k = $ Df. the case C_i and its complementary case relative to p have a different normative

---

1 Regarding the relation of fineness between the Universes of Solutions see Appendix (T 42 and T 43).

status in relation to α and the USmin which corresponds to UA_k. To say that two cases have a different normative status in relation to a normative system α and a UA means that there is an element (solution) of USmin such that it is correlated by α with one of the cases but not with the other.

(D_1') The property p is *irrelevant in the case* C_i of a UC_j in relation to a normative system α and a $UA_k = $ Df. p is not relevant in C_i, i. e. case C_i and its complementary case relative to p in UC_j have the same normative status in relation to α and USmin (corresponding to UA_k).

To say that two cases have the same normative status means either that both cases are correlated with the same solution or that neither is correlated with any solution.

(D_2) The property p is *relevant in a Universe of Cases* UC_i in rela-tion to a normative system α and a $UA_k = $ Df. there is at least one case of UC_i in which p is relevant in relation to α and the USmin (corresponding to UA_k).

(D_2') The property p is *irrelevant in* UC_i in relation to a normative system α and a $UA_k = $ Df. p is not relevant in UC_i, i. e. p is irrelevant in all possible cases of UC_i (in relation to α and the USmin of UA_k).

(D_3) The property p is *relevant in a Universe of Actions* UA_i in relation to a normative system $\alpha = $ Df. there is at least one UC_j such that p is relevant in UC_j in relation to α and UA_i.

(D_3') The property p is *irrelevant in a Universe of Actions* (UA_i) in relation to a normative system $\alpha = $ Df. p is not relevant in UA_i, i. e., there is no UC_j such that p is relevant in UC_j in relation to α and UA_i.

The three concepts of relevance and the three corresponding concepts of irrelevance are logically related in the following way:

If a property is relevant in a case it implies that it is also rele-vant in the UC to which this case belongs and in the correspond-ing UA.

But, from relevance in a UA nothing can be inferred regarding relevance in a UC, nor in the cases of this UC, and from relevance in a UC nothing can be inferred regarding relevance in a certain case of this UC.

4. *The Thesis and the Hypothesis of Relevance*

The term "relevant", as it is used in expressions like "the relevant property" or "the irrelevant property" is ambigous. The definitions we have given in the preceding section do not pretend to reflect all the meanings these terms may have in different contexts, but only to reconstruct *one* typical meaning which we shall call the *descriptive meaning* of "relevant".

To say that a property is relevant in its descriptive meaning (in a case and in relation to a normative system and a UA) is to say that a certain state of affairs exists; this state of affairs is the fact that the case in question and its complementary case *have* different normative status in this system.

But the expression "relevant" is also frequently used in another sense, which may be called its *prescriptive* meaning. To say that a property is relevant in the prescriptive meaning is to say that a certain state of affairs ought to be or should be the case, i. e. that a case and its complementary ought to have different normative status. E. g. in the sentence "The property p is relevant, though the legislator did not consider it when he solved the case C (i. e., did not take it into account for the solution of the case C)" the term "relevant" is clearly used in its prescriptive meaning (if it were used in its descriptive meaning the sentence would be self-contradictory).

This ambiguity has given rise to confusions in legal discourse, and to avoid these difficulties we shall adopt a terminology that distinguishes between the two meanings, using the term "relevant" exclusively in its descriptive sense (as we already have done in the preceding section) and the expression "ought to be relevant" to refer to the prescriptive meaning.

We are now in a position to distinguish between two notions which are very frequently confused in legal theory. We shall give special names to these two notions.

The proposition that identifies the set of all properties which are relevant in relation to a normative system α and a UA_i, will be called *thesis of relevance* of α for UA_i.

The proposition that identifies the set of all properties which ought to be relevant for a UA_i, will be called the *hypothesis of relevance* for UA_i.

When a Universe of Properties contains all and only relevant properties (in relation to α and UA_i), we shall say that this UP satisfies the thesis of relevance of the system α for UA_i and accordingly it will be called *Universe* of *Relevant Properties* (*UPR*), in relation to α and UA_i. It should be observed that this notion is *relative* to a normative system and a Universe of Actions.

The concept of relevance may be extended to the Universes of Cases. The division formed by the properties of *UPR* will accordingly be called the *Universe of Relevant Cases* (*UCR*) in relation to a normative system and a *UA*.

It may easily be proved that for every normative system and for every *UA* there is at most one *UP* such that it satisfies the thesis of relevance, i. e. at most one *UPR*. Hence there is at most one *UCR*. (The qualification "at most" is necessary in order to allow for the situation in which a system has no normative consequences for a certain *UA*, because in such a situation there are no relevant properties for this system and this *UA*; hence there is no *UPR*. But if the system has normative consequences for *UA*, then there is one and only one *UP* such that it satisfies the thesis of relevance and there is one and only one *UCR*.)

The *UCR* occupies a special position among all possible *UC*s. This is so because — as we already know by virtue of T_3 (section 2) — every *UC* which is finer than *UCR* necessarily has some irrelevant properties (i. e. some superfluous distinctions which do not affect the solutions of the system). On the other hand, in every *UC* which is less fine than the *UCR* there are gaps (provided the system is consistent). This last assertion may be proved by means of the following *reductio ad absurdum*. Suppose that a UC_i, which is less fine than the consistent *UCR*, has no gaps: this means that the system is complete in relation to UC_i. But then, by virtue of T_3, every *UC* which is finer than UC_i must have some irrelevant properties and as the *UCR* is, by hypothesis, finer than UC_i it follows that *UCR* has irrelevant properties which contradicts the definition of *UCR*.

Hence we may conclude: (i) that a system which is consistent and complete in relation to *UCR* is incomplete in relation to every *UC* less fine than *UCR*; (ii) if a system has gaps in *UCR*, then it has more gaps in every *UC* less fine than *UCR*; and (iii) if a system is complete in relation to *UCR*, it is also complete in relation to every *UC* finer than *UCR* and all the additional properties which characterize the *UC* finer than *UCR* are irrelevant.

It follows that in order to establish whether a normative system is complete in relation to a *UA* we must select the *UCR* of this *UA* (in relation to the system), and this requires that the thesis of relevance of the system (for this *UA*) should first be identified.

For instance, in the model of ch. I, the *UP* which contains the properties "good faith of the transferee", "good faith of the transferor" and "consideration" satisfies the thesis of relevance of the systems S_1 to S_4, because all these properties are relevant and these are all the relevant properties (for the *UA* of the model and the systems $S1—S4$). Therefore, the Universe of Cases constructed out of these properties is the *UCR*.

The foregoing considerations show the importance of the thesis of relevance. But equally important is the hypothesis of relevance.

This identifies the set of properties which ought to be relevant for a *UA*. The question whether a given property ought or ought not to be relevant for a certain *UA* is a question of value. Therefore, the hypothesis of relevance presupposes a value judgement, or as we shall call it, an axiological criterion: a property which ought to be relevant according to an axiological criterion may not be relevant (in its prescriptive meaning) according to another criterion. This does not imply that the axiological criterion (value judgement) that underlies a hypothesis of relevance is necessarily subjective (in the sense that it is relative to a person or group of persons). All we are saying is that every hypothesis of relevance presupposes the existence of a certain axiological criterion, and this, although it *may* be subjective, e. g. when it expresses the personal preferences of an individual (who may be a judge, a jurist or a mere mortal), *need* not be so; it may well be objective; its objectivity may be relative to some value or set of values or it may even be absolute (e.g. if the axiological criterion is based on Natural Law). We need not discuss here such debatable questions as the possibility of absolute value-judgements or the existence of Natural Law. Such problems lie outside the scope of this book. All that need concern us in this context is that the hypothesis of relevance always presupposes some axiological criterion, whatever its ultimate nature may be.

It should be noted that the hypothesis of relevance is relative only to a Universe of Actions. In this it differs from the thesis of relevance which is relative both to a *UA* and to a normative system. This difference might be expressed by saying that the thesis of relevance is a criterion for selecting the *UP* and, consequently, for selecting the *UC* in order to determine the formal properties (consistency and completeness) of a given system, whereas the hypothesis of relevance is a criterion of axiological adequacy for normative systems.

Accordingly we shall say that a normative system satisfies the criterion of axiological adequacy given by a hypothesis of relevance (in relation to a *UA*) if and only if its thesis of relevance is coextensive with the hypothesis of relevance in question.

Generally speaking: a normative system is axiologically inadequate (unjust, bad) for a *UA*, if its solutions are inadequate (unjust, bad). If the solutions that can be derived from the system are adequate (just, good), the system is axiologically adequate.

But the satisfaction of the hypothesis of relevance is only a necessary and not a sufficient condition for the axiological adequacy of a system (for a *UA*). In other words, a system which does not satisfy the hypothesis of relevance is, *eo ipso*, axiologically inadequate, but a system which satisfies it may nevertheless be inadequate for other reasons. This is so because a system in which all properties which ought to be relevant are relevant (i. e., a system which takes into account all the circumstances which ought to be taken into account) may correlate some case with a solution with which it ought not to be correlated. In this sense a system may still give inadequate (bad or unjust) solutions in spite of the fact that it satisfies the hypothesis of relevance.

We may generalize these observations saying: a normative system may be regarded as axiologically inadequate (bad or unjust) for a *UA* for two different reasons: (1) because it does not satisfy the hypothesis of relevance (what is wrong then is the selection of the cases); (2) because it fails to correlate the cases with the right solutions (what is wrong then is the solution given to the cases which have been selected correctly). As is obvious, these two defects are not incompatible: a system may solve wrongly cases wrongly selected.

5. Axiological Gaps

The expression "gap in law" is often used in legal language (and especially in judicial parlance) to refer to situations in which there is a solution (so that these situations are not normative gaps in our sense), but one that is axiologically inadequate. However, not every

bad or unjust solution is regarded as a gap; jurists speak of gaps —
in this new sense which we are trying to characterize — when the
solution is inadequate *because* the legislator did not take into
account some distinction which he should have taken into account.
This type of gap presupposes the existence of some relevant property (relevant in the prescriptive sense of the term), which is, nevertheless, irrelevant (in the descriptive sense) for the system in question. In other words: a property which ought to be relevant is
irrelevant for the system.

The use of the term "gap" is not entirely arbitrary here; the idea
is that the legislator did not take into account the property in question because *he did not consider it* and if he had considered it, he
would have given a different solution; instead of solving the case as
he did, he would have given it a specific solution. (This, of course,
may be true in many cases.)

This type of gap will be called *axiological gap,* in order to
distinguish it from normative gap. The concept of axiological gap
plays an important part in legal theory and practice and for this
reason an exact definition of this concept is badly needed, as the
indiscriminate use of the term "gap" conceals important conceptual
differences and consequently leads to confusion. But this is not an
easy task; in a sense, the first four sections of this chapter may be
regarded as prolegomena to the definition of axiological gap.

We shall propose the following definition:

A case C_i of a Universe of Cases UC_j is an *axiological gap* of the
normative system α in relation to a $UA_k = $ Df. the case C_i is correlated by α with a maximal solution of the USmax (corresponding
to UA_k) and there is a property p such that p *ought* to be relevant for
C_i (according to a certain hypothesis of relevance) and p *is* irrelevant
for α in relation to UA_k.

This definition, which is in fact not as complicated as it looks,
requires some explanatory comments.

a) An axiological gap is a property of a case. It is moreover
a concept which is *relative* to a normative system, to a UA and to
a hypothesis of relevance. This last point is very important.

b) There can be no axiological gap if the case has no solution:
the existence of a solution is a necessary condition for the existence
of axiological gaps. This means that the concepts of normative gap
and axiological gap are mutually exclusive (logically incompatible).

c) The definition requires the existence of a property such that it ought to be relevant according to some axiological criterion (hypothesis of relevance). In the case of an axiological gap the existing solution is regarded as axiologically inadequate *because* a property which ought to be relevant has not been taken into account; in other words, the system fails to make a distinction which should be made. Moreover, this property must be prescriptively relevant *in the case in question.*

d) The property which is valued as relevant must be *irrelevant for the UA* and not only for the case in question. In other words, it must be a property which does not satisfy the thesis of relevance of the system. This is so, because if the property were irrelevant only for the case in question, and relevant for some other case, then — in spite of the fact that the solution would be axiologically inadequate — it would no longer be true or even plausible that the legislator did not foresee or consider this property. Our definition rules out this case, though the linguistic usage of jurists is probably not very precise on this point.

The definition we consider clarifies a very common use of the term "gap" and enables us to draw important conceptual distinctions which often remain obscure from lack of clear terminology. In particular, it enables us to distinguish between axiological and normative gaps, on the one hand, and between axiological gaps and other axiological (i. e. political, moral, etc.) defects of a legal system, on the other hand.

We have already noted that not every axiologically inadequate solution is called a "gap" by the jurists. When the legislator has considered all the relevant (in the prescriptive sense) circumstances of the case and then has given it a bad (unjust) solution, the result is an axiological defect of the system but not a gap. Before we can speak of axiological gaps, there must be a discrepancy between the thesis of relevance of the system and the hypothesis of relevance (for the UA in question). But, of course, the mere fact that the thesis and the hypothesis of relevance coincide (i. e. the fact that the legislator has taken into account all those properties which ought to be relevant) does not guarantee that all the solutions of the system are axiologically adequate. The solutions may be unjust even though all the relevant distinctions have been considered. But in such cases there are no axiological gaps in our sense of the term.

Nevertheless, the discrepancy between the thesis and the hypothesis of relevance is only a necessary, not a sufficient condition for the existence of axiological gaps. This sort of discrepancy may derive from three types of situation which we shall examine separately.

Situation I

The set of properties identified by the thesis of relevance is properly included in that of the hypothesis of relevance. This means that there is at least one property such that it ought to be relevant but is not relevant for the system in question. It also implies that the Universe of Cases corresponding to the hypothesis of relevance — $UC(hyp)$ — is finer than the UCR.

In this situation there is at least one case of axiological gap. (Later on we shall examine some examples of gaps of this kind.)

Situation II

The set of properties identified by the hypothesis of relevance is included in that of the thesis. This means that there is at least one relevant property which ought not to be so and that the UCR is finer than the $UC(hyp)$. Here the legislator has made too many distinctions. The consequence is that there are some solutions which are unjust (according to the hypothesis of relevance), but there are no axiological gaps.

We may take as an example system S_1 of ch. I. Suppose that according to some hypothesis of relevance the good faith of the transferor ought to be irrelevant for the obligation to restore real estate. In such situation, the solution given by the system S_1 to the case 2 (cf. table I-3, ch. I, sect. 5) is unjust, for the solution should be the same as in the case 1, viz. FR. Nevertheless, this situation is not an axiological gap either according to our definition or according to prevailing linguistic usage.

Situation III

The respective sets of properties identified according to the hypothesis of relevance and the thesis of relevance are different, but not comparable regarding inclusion. This means that there are some relevant properties which ought not to be relevant and some irrelevant properties which ought to be relevant. (In this situation the UCR and the $UC(hyp)$ are not comparable.)

This situation is of no special interest, as it is merely combination of the two preceding ones. Therefore, in this third situation there may be axiological gaps and also cases whose solutions are axiologically inadequate but involve no axiological gap.

As an example, we may suppose an hypothesis of relevance (for the model of ch. I) according to which the good faith of the transferor ought not to be relevant, but the inscription of the estate in some sort of Register of Real Estates ought to be relevant (this is more or less equivalent to DASSEN's proposals in his paper quoted in ch. I, sect. 6). If we accept this hypothesis of relevance, then the systems S_1 to S_4 have axiological gaps, as they do not take into account the property of being registered. But, there are also some solutions which are bad for different reasons: for example, because they have taken to be relevant the question whether the transferor acted in good or in bad faith.

6. *Axiological Gaps in Legal Theory*

There are two equally misleading tendencies in legal theory concerning the problem of axiological gaps. On the one hand, jurists tend to confuse axiological and normative gaps; on the other hand, they often fail to distinguish clearly between axiological gaps and other kinds of evaluative disagreements.

The confusion between axiological and normative gaps arises, to a large extent, from the indiscriminate and unfortunate use of the term "gap" (in combination with the previously mentioned ambiguity of the term "relevant"), especially in Continental legal doctrine. Unfortunately, the confusion is not merely terminological, but conceptual. We shall give some examples taken from German legal doctrine.

Nearly all legal writers insist upon the necessity of distinguishing between a moral or political defect in a law and a gap, which seems to reflect a desire to separate value problems from purely logical questions. Nevertheless, the same authors very frequently use criteria of value to define the concept of a legal gap, thus blurring the intended distinction. An excellent example of this tendency is provided by the well known legal philosopher KARL ENGISCH. Even in his earliest approach to the problem of legal gaps we find the basic ambiguity: ENGISCH says that a gap is an "unsatisfactory incompleteness in a whole" (unbefriedigende Unvollständigkeit inner-halb eines Ganzen)[1].

It would seem inadvisable to speak of an unsatisfactory incom-pleteness without taking the preliminary step of defining incom-pleteness. Whether or not an incompleteness (i. e. the lack of a solu-tion) is unsatisfactory is a value question which presupposes knowl-edge of what an incompleteness is. But the question of the existence or non-existence of a solution has nothing to do with values. ENGISCH, who does not distinguish between these two different prob-lems, fails to find a satisfactory criterion for the distinction be-tween normative and axiological gaps, in spite of his intention and his efforts in this direction. Thus he says, speaking of a solution given by positive law: "If we do not agree with this solution, we can speak of a 'legal-political gap' (rechtspolitische Lücke), of a crit-ical gap (kritische Lücke), of a non-genuine gap (unechte Lücke), i. e. of a gap from a point of view of a future and better law *(de lege ferenda),* but not of a true and genuine gap, that is, a gap in valid law *(de lege lata)*."[2] Two lines below ENGISCH expresses his intention of limiting his definition of the concept of a gap to what he calls gaps *de lege lata* only. Thus his definition seems to eluci-date the concept of what we call a normative gap: "Gaps are incom-pletenesses in positive law (enacted law or customary law) which we perceive as the absence of legal provisions for certain states of affairs where such provisions are expected to exist, and whose elimination requires and admits a judicial decision complementary to the law. The gaps make their appearance where neither the enacted law, nor the customary law provides an immediate answer to a legal question."[3]

However, the example which is quoted by ENGISCH as a typical case of a genuine gap and which is intended to illustrate the above definition is a clear case of an axiological gap (presence of an un-satisfactory solution) and not of a normative gap (absence of a solu-tion). It is a well known decision of the *Reichsgerichtshof* of 11. 3. 1927 concerning the termination of pregnancy by medical prescrip-tion.

---

1 K. ENGISCH, Einführung in das juristische Denken, Stuttgart, 1956, p. 135.

2 ENGISCH, op. cit., p. 138.

3 ENGISCH, op. cit., pp. 136—137.

The Penal Code which was in force in Germany at that time punished abortion generally without making any distinctions (§ 218). In the case that the *Reichsgerichtshof* had to judge, a physician procured an abortion in order to save the life of a woman who had suicidal tendencies as a consequence of the pregnancy, a fact that was confirmed by a psychiatric expert. The physician was acquitted by the Court on the ground that there was a gap in the Penal Code, a gap which the Court subsequently filled by an extended application of § 54 of the same Code, referring to the so-called *Notstand* (state of necessity). Clearly, this § 54 was inapplicable to the case, since it merely provided that an action is not punishable when there is actual danger for its author or a relative of his. In the case that concerns us there was no danger for the physician, nor was the woman a relative of his.

ENGISCH admits that this case clearly comes under the prescription of § 218 (referring to abortion), but goes on to assert emphatically that it is a typical case of a legal gap. This contradicts his own definition of "gap", according to which there is a gap when the law provides no answer to a legal question. But in our case there is an answer, although it is one that ENGISCH and the *Reichsgerichtshof* apparently dislike: they find it unsatisfactory (unjust). And the solution provided by the Code is unjust precisely because it does not take into account a circumstance that ENGISCH (and the Court) regard as relevant: the circumstance that the abortion was procured by a physician with the intention of saving the woman's life. In other words, there is a conflict between the hypothesis of relevance of the Court and the thesis of relevance of the Code. This is a conflict concerning values. It is therefore a typical instance of what we have called an axiological gap.

The same oscillation between logical and axiological problems occurs in other writers such as BIERLING[4], BINDER[5], SAUER[6],

---

4 E. R. BIERLING, Juristische Prinzipienlehre, vol. IV, 1911, p. 383: "We can speak of gaps in law only when existing legal norms (statutory, contractual or customary norms) do not completely satisfy the intention of certain legal relations or groups of legal relations."

5 J. BINDER, Philosophie des Rechts, 1925, p. 984: "There is gap in law when an exigency, objectively founded in given social and economical circumstances is not satisfied by the law."

6 W. SAUER, Juristische Methodenlehre, 1940, p. 283: There is a gap when the law is silent "where a legal norm is expected for a case ..."

LARENZ[7], BARTHOLOMEJCZIK[8]. etc. ESSER says openly: "The very question (which is decisive) whether we have to admit the existence of a 'gap' in a law is a value judgment and a decision of the will."[9] If the existence of a gap depends on a decision, then rational discussion of the problem is no longer possible.

The very fact that these jurists resort to such vague — if not completely empty — expressions as *Rechtsgefühl* (feeling for the law), *übergesetzliche Grundsätze* (supra-legal principles), *Richtigkeitsgedanke* (the idea of correctness), *Rechtsidee* (the idea of law), *Natur der Sache* (nature of things)[10] and so on, is a clear indication that we are in the presence of a basic perplexity.

In view of this rather deplorable situation it is scarcely surprising that other authors should choose to cut the Gordian knot by

---

And a norm is "expected" when it makes possible a decision that is in accordance with the "basic law", i. e. the idea of law.

7 K. LARENZ, Methodenlehre der Rechtswissenschaft, Berlin, 1960: "The dividing line between a 'gap in the regulations' and a merely political 'defect' *(de lege ferenda)* can be drawn only by asking whether there is 'incompleteness' with regard to the purpose immanent in the law or merely form the point of view of an independent and critical position. In both cases — as has been correctly emphazised by HECK and BINDER — it is a question of value and not merely of logico-formal verification. The statement that a law lacks a regulation which it *ought to* contain (either because it would accord with its intrinsic aim and purpose, or because of a political or ethical demand) is a value judgment. Now, the difference between a 'gap' and a defect derives from a difference in the criteria of value that are used: in the first case this criterion is based on the law itself as a whole of meaning that aspires to be complete and materially harmonious regulation; in the second case it is based on extra-legal principles of valuation. There is a gap where the law lacks a rule whose existence may be expected according to the fundamental ideas and the immanent teleology of legal regulation."

8 H. BARTHOLOMEJCZIK, Die Kunst der Gesetzesauslegung, Frankfurt am Main, 1960, p. 82.

9 J. ESSER, Grundsatz und Norm in der richterlichen Fortbildung des Privatrechts, Tübingen, 1956.

10 Cf. E. GARZÓN VALDÉS, Derecho y "naturaleza de las cosas", Córdoba, 1970. Curiously enough, even those writers who distinguish between a normative gap (absence of a solution) and an axiological gap (presence of an unsatisfactory solution) frequently do not believe it necessary to give a rigorous definition of the first concept. Cf. e. g. ENNECCERUS-NIPPERDEY, Allgemeiner Teil des bürgerlichen Rechts, Tübingen,

denying the existence of normative gaps and maintaining that they are a mere fiction habitually resorted to by jurists (especially judges) when they wish to conceal the fact that their real purpose is to modify the existing law. The pseudo-scientific claim that they are instead performing the task of filling gaps serves to veil the true nature of their activity — the modification of the law on political or moral grounds. The most conspicuous representative of this line of thought is undoubtedly HANS KELSEN[11].

But the fact that the term "gap" has been abused in legal language does not prove that there are no normative gaps; and, in any case, before talking of the existence or non-existence of gaps it is essential to define the concept. If we do not know what kind of entity this term refers to we cannot decide whether or not there are such entities.

The thesis that all legal orders are necessarily complete will be analyzed in ch. VII. But it is important to point out here that KELSEN does not distinguish between axiological gaps and other kinds of value problems. This, it may be remembered, is the second of the two tendencies mentioned at the beginning of this section. Kelsen's theory is incapable of giving an account of a very widespread usage of the term "gap", which we have tried to reconstruct under the name "axiological gap".

In German legal doctrine another distinction which arises from the same conceptual confusion is frequently made. This is the distinction between primary and secondary gaps. Primary gaps are

---

1959, § 58, pp. 336 ff.; H. NAWIASKY, Allgemeine Rechtslehre — System der rechtlichen Grundbegriffe, 1948, p. 142 ff.

KLUG critizes these conceptions in "Rechtslücke und Rechtsgeltung" (Festschrift für Hans Carl Nipperdey, München—Berlin, 1965, pp. 76—77) but his own definition of a legal gap is equally unsatisfactory. For KLUG there is a gap when a case has no solution and there is a norm to the effect that this case should have a solution. This restricts the meaning of the term to such an extent that it becomes practically useless.

A very interesting discussion of the concept of normative completeness may be found in H. FIEDLER, Juristische Logik in mathematischer Sicht, Archiv für Rechts- und Sozialphilosophie 52, 93—116 (1966). FIEDLER's conception of what he calls "combinatory completeness" is very close to ours, and his examples may be readily adapted to our terminology. Unfortunately, FIEDLER did not develop his interesting ideas at any length.

11 ZITTELMANN was the first to adopt this position (Lücken im Recht, 1902), but it is KELSEN who has developed it to its fullest extent.

supposed to exist from the very moment when a legal order is created; the secondary gaps make their appearance afterwards — either as a consequence of a change in the factual situation (e. g. by technical progress) or because of a change in valuations [12].

How can a legal order which is complete at a given moment become incomplete? This question is not difficult to answer. As the system's completeness is relative to a *UC* and a *US*, a change in one of these Universes may give rise to a normative gap (when we choose a less fine *UC* or a finer *US*). There is no mystery about this.

However, in most cases where legal philosophers talk of secondary gaps they do not mean normative gaps at all; what they are referring to — though somewhat obscurely — are axiological gaps, or perhaps, gaps of recognition. In order to illustrate this assertion we shall consider a well known example of a secondary gap which was discussed by ZITTELMANN in his famous paper "Lücken im Recht" (1902).

The German Commercial Code regulated in two different ways the making of contracts between present and absent parties respectively. The invention of the telephone created a problem: what provisions should be applied to contracts made by telephone? This is usually regarded as a typical case of a secondary gap, created by a technical invention. Yet it is clear that in this case there is no normative gap at all. The invention of the telephone can create two kinds of problem, neither of which can be attributed to a normative gap. The first problem is how to classify contracts made by telephone. Are they contracts between present or between absent parties? This is the kind of problem we have called a *gap of recognition*. (Cf. ch. II, sect. 4). Here we know that the case has a solution (because the classification of contracts into contracts between present and between absent parties is exhaustive); but we do not know what this solution is because we do not know to which of the two jointly exhaustive and mutually exclusive categories our case belongs.

This question of classification would be easy to decide (it seems obvios that a contract made by telephone is a contract between absent parties), where it not for a complication that raises difficulties

---

12 Cf. K. ENGISCH, Der Begriff der Rechtslücke, Sauer-Festschrift, 1949, pp. 85 ff.; K. LARENZ, op. cit., and U. KLUG, Observations sur le problème des lacunes en droit, Logique et Analyse 10, 98—115 (1967).

of another kind. Suppose that we were to decide that contracts made by telephone were contracts between absent parties. Then it would be reasonable to make a distinction between two kinds of contracts made between absent parties — contracts made by mail and contracts made by telephone — in order to treat them differently. For since in contracts made by telephone the offer and its acceptance occur simultaneously it is much more reasonable to apply to them the rules governing contracts between parties that are present than those governing contracts between absent parties. Here we are confronted by a typical case of an axiological gap. What has happened is that the invention of the telephone has produced a need to modify the law by taking into account a circumstance that has not been, and until now could not have been, considered by the law: it is a conflict between a hypothesis of relevance and the thesis of relevance of the German Commercial Code (of that time). But there was never a normative gap either before or after the invention of the telephone.

There is no doubt that a new property can come into existence as a result of advances in technology, but its occurrence can create a problem only when this property is evaluated as (prescriptively) relevant. This shows that the so-called secondary gaps are really axiological gaps; they do not arise, as alleged, in two different ways[13], but in one way: through changes in valuations. Changes in the facts can give rise to axiological gaps only when they are accompanied by new valuations.

VII. The Problem of Closure

1. Closed and Open Systems

The definitions of the concepts of completeness and incompleteness (gap) of normative systems which have been elaborated in the first part of this book have shown the relational structure of these concepts. Completeness, as a property of normative systems, is relative to a set of circumstances or cases (a *UC*) and a set of deontically qualified actions (a *US*).

Our investigations may seem disappointingly inconclusive to those who expected a categorical answer to the question whether there are or not any gaps in law or in some other normative system.

---

13 Cf. LARENZ and ENGISCH, op. cit.

So far nothing has been said about whether or not such gaps actually occur. Obviously, however, the task of elucidating a concept is prior to that of deciding whether in fact there is an object that corresponds to that concept; before deciding whether an object exists, we must agree what it is. So the conceptual problem of the definition must precede the factual problem of existence.

Now, if the completeness of a normative system is relative to a certain *UC* and a certain *US*, then it is clear that the existence of gaps is a contingent matter of fact; the question whether there are any gaps can only be decided in each particular situation, for a particular system, in relation to a definite Universe of Cases and a definite Universe of Solutions. Nothing can be said about it in a general account like ours, which is not concerned with any particular system as such.

This does not mean, however, that the question of normative completeness, i. e. the question of the existence of normative gaps, could not be raised at a purely conceptual level. Suppose, for instance, that we could prove that there are normative systems which are necessarily complete in the sense that they provide solutions for every possible case and for every possible action, i. e. that their completeness is not relative to any particular *UC* or any particular *UA*. Then the question whether normative gaps exist would be answered in the negative (at least for this type of system), and there would be no need for further research.

The idea of a *closed* normative system, i. e. a system which is necessarily complete, as opposed to an open system, has been frequently discussed in legal philosophy and also in deontic logic. Many legal theorists believe that all legal systems are closed in this sense and in any case nearly *all* share the view that there are *some* closed legal systems as, for instance, a system of penal law which contains the rule "nullum crimen, nulla poena sine lege".

As a starting point for the discussion of the problem of closure we shall adopt the definition of closedness given by VON WRIGHT[1]:

(I) "A normative system is closed when every action is deontically determined in this system ... A system which is not closed will be called *open*".

---

1 G. H. VON WRIGHT, An Essay in Deontic Logic and the General Theory of Action, Acta Philosophica Fennica, Fasc. XXI, Helsinki — Amsterdam, 1968, p. 83.

In VON WRIGHT's terminology an action is deontically determined in a system S, "when it is either permitted or forbidden in this system".

The above definition seems to be suitable only for categorical normative systems, as it fails to take into account the fact that an action may occur in different circumstances or cases. But VON WRIGHT himself gives a more general definition of closedness in terms of what he calls the *dyadic calculus:*

(II) "Any system S of norms is therefore *closed,* of which it holds true that, for all values of the variables, either a norm to the effect that $P(p/q)$ or a norm to the effect that $O(\sim p/q)$ belongs to this system." [2]

The definition (II) may readily be adapted to our terminology; we have only to stipulate that the range of values of the variable p are actions (either all possible actions or actions belonging to a certain class of actions) and that the range of values of the variable q are cases. This would mean that a closed normative system is such that in it every action is deontically determined in every possible case. (As we shall see later, the reference to "all possible cases" is subject to important qualifications; cf. *infra,* sect. 6.)

Those systems which are not closed will be called *open.* An open system may be complete, but its completeness is "essentially dependent" on the choice of the Universe of Cases and the Universe of Actions.

The possibility of closed normative systems, i. e. the problem of closure, will be analyzed in three steps.

In the first place, we shall examine the thesis that all normative systems are closed systems on purely conceptual grounds (sects. 2 and 3). This thesis has been maintained by some (deontic) logicians. In the second place, we shall discuss the thesis that all *legal* systems are necessarily closed (sects. 4 and 5). This doctrine — which is fairly prevalent among legal philosophers — has been supported on various grounds. Most of the arguments advanced by legal philosophers are identical with those discussed in sects. 2 and 3. This is demonstrated in sect. 5. Other types of argument — especially those concerning judicial decisions — will be examined in the next chapter. In sect. 6 we shall be concerned with the possibility

---

2 G. H. VON WRIGHT, op. cit., p. 84.

of closed normative systems and closure by means of special rules, which we shall call "rules of closure". This discussion seeks to produce a more refined concept of closedness, and to show the importance of the notion of relevance which was elaborated in the preceding chapter. The part played by the well known rule "nullum crimen sine lege" in legal contexts is analyzed in the final sect. (7).

2. Closure Based on the Interdefinability of "Permitted" and "Prohibited"

Nearly all the arguments of those writers who maintain that all normative systems are necessarily closed are based on the so-called Principle of Prohibition[1], which may be formulated as "Everything which is not prohibited is permitted" or "Everything is either permitted or prohibited". (We shall regard these two formulations as strictly equivalent.)

If the Principle of Prohibition expresses a necessary truth, then every action (or state of affairs) has a normative character (as permitted or prohibited) in every system and hence all normative systems are closed (i. e., they can have no gaps). Now, if "permitted" and "prohibited" are interdefinable, that is, if "permitted" means "not prohibited", and "prohibited" means "not permitted" — which seems plausible — then the Principle of Prohibition is necessarily true, because it is analytic. Therefore, if we accept the contention that the deontic characters P and O are interdefinable with the aid of the negation, then all normative systems become trivially closed, for every system characterizes deontically all possible actions or states of affairs. This is the conclusion VON WRIGHT draws in his latest book: An Essay in Deontic Logic and the General Theory of Action[2].

---

1 We adopt this rather unusual name in order to distinguish the Principle of Prohibition from what VON WRIGHT calls the Principle of Permission and from the rule *nullum crimen sine lege,* both of which will be discussed later.

2 G. H. VON WRIGHT, An Essay in Deontic Logic and the General Theory of Action, Acta Philosophica Fennica, Fasc. XXI, Helsinki — Amsterdam, 1968, p. 82 ff.; cf. especially p. 85: "Thus, if we regard the two deontic characters of permission and obligation (prohibition) as being interdefinable, it follows from the above answer to question b) that every normative system is, trivially, a *closed* system."

Of course, VON WRIGHT is not satisfied with this result, since it is obvious that in some sense there may be incomplete normative systems (i. e., systems with gaps). And it is precisely in order to avoid such conclusion, that he rejects in *Norm and Action* the interdefinability of "permitted" and "prohibited" and takes P ("permitted") to be autonomous deontic character[3].

Nevertheless, it seems to be quite clear that at least in some sense "permitted" means the same as "not prohibited" and this may be the reason why VON WRIGHT is somewhat hesitant on this point. In his latest book, mentioned above, he changes his opinion once more and accepts the interdefinability thesis, but distinguishes six different concepts of permission (P_1—P_6) and six corresponding concepts of prohibition or obligation (O_1—O_6), so that his new conception allows for the existence of open systems. All that is needed for this is that the concepts of permission and prohibition which occur in the Principle of Prohibition should not be the "corresponding" ones, because only the corresponding concepts of permission and prohibition are interdefinable (e. g. P_1 and O_1, P_2 and O_2, etc.), but if the concepts are not corresponding (if the concept of permission is, say, P_1 and the concept of prohibition O_2), then they are no longer interdefinable.

The main source of VON WRIGHT's difficulties lies — in our opinion — in his acceptance of the thesis that the interdefinability of "permitted" and "prohibited" entails that all normative systems are necessarily closed. We shall instead maintain that these two propositions are logically independent, and that it is perfectly possible to accept the thesis of interdefinability and at the same time reject the thesis of closure. We shall try to argue that the so-called Principle of Prohibition is misleading as it admits of two different interpretations. On one interpretation it is analytically true but does not close any system (and therefore does not exclude the possibility of normative gaps). On the other interpretation the Principle is contingent and presupposes for its truth the very statement which it purports to prove, *i. e.*, that all normative systems are closed. Its claims to the dual function, traditionally assigned to it, are spurious; it cannot simultaneously be a necessary truth and close all normative systems.

---

3 Norm and Action, p. 85 ff.

In order to demonstrate the ambiguity of the Principle we must begin by drawing an important and well known distinction between *norms* and *normative propositions*[4].

Norms are prescriptive sentences, used to enjoin, to permit or to prohibit certain actions (*i. e.*, sentences which say that certain actions ought to be done, may be done or must not be done).

Normative propositions are expressed by descriptive sentences, used to convey information about norms or about the obligations, permissions or prohibitions issued by norms.

The interdefinability of the three deontic characters O, P and *Ph* means that the *norms* "Permitted p", "Not obligatory not p" and "Not prohibited p" are logically equivalent and mean the same. So are the norms "Prohibited p", "Not permitted p" and "Obligatory not p".

But the situation becomes radically different when we turn from norms to normative propositions.

By saying that p is prohibited by the system α we are not issuing a norm, but stating a normative proposition; the proposition in question belongs to a different linguistic level from the sentences of the system. It is a metalinguistic proposition in relation to the language of the system α. To say that p is prohibited by α is to say that the norm that prohibits p belongs to or is a consequence of the system α. Therefore the metasystematic sentence "p is prohibited by α" is true if and only if among the consequences of α there is a norm which prohibits p. This norm may have the form of "Prohibited p", "Not permitted p" or "Obligatory not p". As *norms* all these sentences are equivalent.

When a norm that permits p is a consequence of the system α, we say that p is permitted by α. This norm may have the form of "Permitted p", or "Not prohibited p", etc. As norms these sentences are likewise equivalent.

These considerations allow us to define two new concepts of permission and prohibition, which we shall call *strong permission* and *strong prohibition*.

---

4 Norm and Action, pp. 104—106. Similar, though not identical distinctions are to be found in KELSEN, Reine Rechtslehre, 2nd ed., Wien, 1960, p. 73 ff.; General Theory of Law and State, New York, 1941, p. 45, and in ALF ROSS, On Law and Justice, London, 1958, pp. 8—11. On differences between KELSEN and ROSS see H. L. A. HART, Kelsen visited, UCLA Law Review, vol. 10, No. 4, 1963, pp. 709—728.

Definition of strong permission: To say that p is strongly permitted in the case q by the system α means that a norm to the effect that p is permitted in q is a consequence of α.

Definition of strong prohibition: To say that p is strongly prohibited in the case q by the system α means that a norm to the effect that p is prohibited in q is a consequence of α [6].

These definitions are not circular because the terms "permitted" and "prohibited" have different meaning in the *definiendum* and in the *definiens*. In the *definiens* the expressions "permitted" and "prohibited" refer to deontic characters which are elements of the norms (in the same sense as other elements such as content, subject, conditions of application, etc.[7]). But in the *definiendum* these expressions do not refer to characters of norms, but to characters of actions which are qualified by norms. Being strongly permitted and strongly prohibited are not characters of norms but *characters of actions* and as such they are elements of normative propositions in the same sense in which norm-characters are elements of norms [8].

The characters of actions ("strongly permitted" and "strongly prohibited") are defined in terms of the norm-characters because an action has a certain normative character relative to a certain normative system α if and only if there is a norm in α to the effect that this action is permitted or prohibited. In this sense the characters of actions may be said to be dependent on the norm-characters [9].

---

6 A concept of strong obligation could be defined in a similar way, but we omit it for the sake of brevity.

7 Cf. von WRIGHT, Norm and Action, ch. V: The Analysis of Norms, p. 70 ff.

8 A systematical presentation of the logic of these notions is to be found in C. E. ALCHOURRON, Logic of Norms and Logic of Normative Propositions, Logique et Analyse 12 (1969), 242—268.

9 This is a typical case of what CARNAP calls the *transposed mode of speech* (The Logical Syntax of Language, London, 1955, p. 80). CARNAP even gives an example taken from law: "According to the ordinary use of language, an action a of a certain person is called *legal crime* if the penal law of the country in which that person lives places the description of a kind of action to which a belongs in the list of crimes." (Op. cit. p. 308.)

In the same sense, to say that an action is (strongly) prohibited in the system α is to use the transposed mode of speech, for the action has the character of strongly prohibited if and only if the norm that prohibits it belongs to α.

The distinction between the characters of norms and the characters of actions is very important; as we shall see later, the confusion of these two concepts is the main source of difficulties in the interpretation of what we have called the Principle of Prohibition.

"Permitted" and "prohibited" as characters of norms are contradictory; "permitted" means the same as "not prohibited" and "prohibited" means "not permitted". But when these expressions refer to characters of actions (meaning strong permission and strong prohibition), they are not contradictory and not even contrary. It is perfectly possible that neither the permission nor the pohibition of p is a consequence of α: this is the case when α does not contain any norm permitting p or prohibiting p. The sentences "The norm that permits p is a consequence of α" and "The norm that prohibits p is a consequence of α" may both be false. Moreover, both of them may be true: a system may contain a norm that permits p *and* a norm that prohibits p. In this case, p is at the same time strongly permitted and strongly prohibited by the same system. This is surely not an impossibility. It only implies that the system in question is inconsistent, because the norms "Permitted p" and "Prohibited p" are, of course, contradictory. But the fact that a system is inconsistent, *i. e.*, that it contains two contradictory norms, does not imply that the normative propositions by means of which this system is described should be inconsistent as well. There is nothing paradoxical about a consistent description of an inconsistent normative system.

Another interesting feature of normative propositions is the possibility of two types of negation. Consider the following two sentences (expressing normative propositions): "p is permitted by α" and "p is not permitted by α". If the second sentence means that p is prohibited by α, then it is not a negation of the first sentence: what is negated is not the normative proposition but the norm referred to by it. The sentences refer (indirectly) to two different norms, of which one is the negation of the other. This reference may be made explicit if the sentences are reformulated as follows: "The norm that permits p is a consequence of α" and "The norm that does not permit (= prohibits) p is a consequence of α".

This type of negation of normative propositions, in which what is negated is not the proposition itself, but the norm referred to by it, may be conveniently called *internal negation*. But there is another type of negation, which is the negation of the normative proposition itself. We shall call it *external negation*.

An external negation of the sentence "The norm that permits p is a consequence of α" is the sentence "The norm that permits p is not a consequence of α". It is easy to see that a normative proposition is incompatible with (contradictory to) its external negation, but is not incompatible with its internal negation. (The difference between internal and external negation is often concealed in ordinary language because sentences like "p is not permitted by α" are misleadingly ambiguous: does it mean that there is no norm permitting p or that there is a norm prohibiting p?)

The internal negation of the strong prohibition is a strong permission: to say that the norm that does not prohibit p ($=$ permits p) is a consequence of α is the same as to say that p is strongly permitted by α. But the external negation of a sentence that states the strong prohibition of p does not mean that p is strongly permitted. All that such a sentence says is that a certain norm (the prohibition of p) is not a consequence of the system, but it leaves open the question whether among the consequences of α there is some other norm which refers to p, or no norm referring to p at all. It may well be the case that p is strongly permitted in α (if there is a norm in α which permits p) or that it is not (if p is not permitted by any norm belonging to the system).

Nevertheless, it is quite usual to say that an action is permitted by virtue of the mere fact that there is no prohibition of it. But then the term "permitted" has a quite different meaning. In order to characterize this meaning we shall introduce the notion of *weak permission*.

Definition of weak permission: To say that p is weakly permitted in the case q by the system α means that among the consequences of α there is no norm which prohibits ($=$ does not permit) p in the case q.

Weak permission is, like strong permission, a character of actions, not of norms [10]. But weak permission differs from strong permission in an important way: strong permission expresses a positive fact (the existence of a permissive norm), whereas weak permission refers to a negative fact: the non-existence of a prohibitive norm.

---

10 In a similar way the concept of weak prohibition could be defined as the absence (in α) of a norm that permits p. But this concept is rarely used, if at all.

Unfortunately, in ordinary language and even in technical juristic parlance the same term "permitted" is used to express all three of the different concepts of permission (permission as norm-character, strong and weak permissions as characters of actions). This fact leads to many confusions. Needless to say, we are not anxious to correct the ordinary usage; all we wish to do is to stress some conceptual distinctions which are blurred in ordinary language.

3. Analysis of the Principle of Prohibition

We are now in a position to discuss the Principle of Prohibition with the help of conceptual distinctions we made in the preceding section.

The Principle of Prohibition may be explicitly formulated as a metasystematic proposition, *i. e.*, as a proposition about normative systems: For all systems α, for all actions p and for all cases q, if p is not prohibited in q by α, then p is permitted in q by α.

What do the expressions "prohibited" and "permitted" mean here? If we accept the contention (which seems reasonable) that the Principle is not a norm, but a normative proposition, then these expressions cannot signify characters of norms. Hence "prohibited" must refer to strong prohibition. But the expression "permitted" is still ambiguous for it can mean strong or weak permission. We shall distinguish therefore two versions of the Principle of Prohibition, which we shall call respectively the weak and the strong version, according to the meaning assigned to "permitted" (weak or strong permission).

In the weak version, the Principle of Prohibition is analytic and therefore necessarily true. On this interpretation the Principle states that if the prohibition of p in q is not a consequence of α, then the prohibition of p in q is not a consequence of α, and this is just a particular case of the Principle of Identity. To prove it we only need to substitute for "prohibited" and "permitted" the corresponding definitions of strong prohibition and weak permission, given in the preceding section. Then the weak version of the Principle of Prohibition ("Everything which is not strongly prohibited, is weakly permitted") becomes clearly tautological. If the Principle of Prohibition is given a disjunctive form ("Everything is either strongly prohibited or weakly permitted"), then the substitution yields a proposition which is an instantiation of the Principle of Excluded Middle.

Though the Principle of Prohibition becomes, on what we call the "weak" interpretation, necessarily true, its truth is compatible with the existence of normative gaps, for it does not close any normative system and hence does not exclude the possibility of incomplete systems. This can be easily shown: a gap is a case which is not correlated by the system with any solution. Hence, it is not correlated with a solution of the form "Prohibited p", and since it is not so correlated, p is not prohibited in the system. But if p is not prohibited, then it is permitted in the weak sense. We may conclude that a gap is a case in which there is an action p such that it is weakly permitted (and is not strongly permitted) by the system. This shows that weak permission is not only compatible with the existence of a gap, but is even entailed by it, though not vice versa. (That is to say, the existence of a gap logically implies that the case is weakly permitted; but weak permission does not imply that there is a gap.)

It is, of course, possible to define the concept of a gap as a case which is neither prohibited, nor weakly permitted. But this is too easy a way of dealing with the problem. Such a definition would simply define the gaps out of existence, as it would follow trivially that there can be no gaps. This device (which is what HART calls a "definitional stop"[1]) is, in spite of its triviality, often used by legal philosophers. Needless to say that to define the concept of a gap in such a way that gaps become logically impossible is quite pointless. Such a concept is void of any interest. A more promising undertaking is to provide a definition that makes it possible to give an account of problems jurists have in mind when they speak of legal gaps. To show that there is such a concept and that it is fruitful in dealing with concrete problems of legal science is one of the aims of this book.

Let us now look at the *strong version* of the Principle of Prohibition. On this interpretation the Principle states: "Everything that is not strongly prohibited, is strongly permitted". This we may expand in the following way: "For every system α, for every action p and for every case q, if the prohibition of p in q is not a consequence of α, then the permission of p in q is a consequence of α."

---

1 H. L. A. HART, Punishment and Responsibility, Oxford, 1968, p. 5 ff.

It is not difficult to see that in its strong version the Principle of Prohibition, far from being necessary, is a contingent proposition. This proposition would be true if and only if all normative systems were absolutely closed, *i. e.*, complete in relation to every *UC* and every *US*. For from the mere fact that a certain norm (the norm to the effect that *p* is prohibited in *q*) does not belong to a certain system, it does not follow that another, different norm (namely, the norm to the effect that *p* is permitted in *q*) belongs to this system. Therefore the Principle of Prohibition in its strong version, is not necessarily true.

In any case, if the strong version of the Principle of Prohibition presupposes (for its truth) that all normative systems are closed, it cannot be put forward as an argument to prove that all normative systems are closed. Such an argument would be clearly circular[2].

4. The Postulate of the Necessary Completeness of the Law

Our next task will be the discussion of the thesis that all *legal* systems are closed. We shall call this thesis the Postulate of the Necessary Completeness of the Law (some writers use the term "hermetic plenitude") or for short, the Postulate of Completeness.

Before examining the arguments different writers have advanced in support of this Postulate, we must clarify its meaning in order to determine what exactly this Postulate says. For by no means all those jurists or legal philosophers who claim that the law is complete do in fact deny the existence of legal gaps. Let us see a few examples.

a) Some writers understand by "completeness of the law" the requirement or demand that all legal systems should be complete.

---

2 Nor can the formula "$Pp \vee P \sim p$" which VON WRIGHT calls *Principle of Permission* be adduced in support of the claim that all normative systems are closed. This formula, which may be read as "Any given act is either itself permitted or its negation is permitted", is a theorem of VON WRIGHT's system of deontic logic (Deontic Logic, Mind, 60, 1—15 [1951]; reprinted in Logical Studies, London, 1957, 58—74), but is not a theorem of the logic of normative propositions, as it is not necessary either in its strong interpretation (where "permitted" means strongly permitted), or in the weak one ("permitted" = weakly permitted). Cf. C. E. ALCHOURRON, Logic of Norms and Logic of Normative Propositions, Logique et Analyse 12 (1969), 242—268.

For instance, CARNELUTTI says: "By the term 'completeness' we understand the demand that in the legal order there should be a mandate which would apply to or provide a solution of any conflict of interest that might arise in any society regulated by law."[1] "The perfection of the legal order should not be understood as a property of this order in the sense that gaps do not exist, but in the sense that there is a demand that these gaps should be eliminated . . ."[2].

We quite agree with CARNELUTTI; in fact we shall argue later (chapter IX) that what he calls demand of completeness is a rational ideal. But this is *not* the thesis we are interested in discussing here. By the Postulate of Completeness we shall understand the assertion that all legal systems *are*, as a matter of fact, complete and, moreover, that this is a necessary fact, but not the demand that they should be complete.

b) Nor are we interested in analyzing the position of those writers who admit the existence of legal gaps, but maintain that the law is always complete in the sense that it provides the necessary means to eliminate those gaps. This appears to be the position of DEL VECCHIO[3] and presumably also of RECASÉNS SICHES (we say "presumably" because his exposition is not exceedingly clear on this point)[4].

Whatever the truth value of this thesis, it is evident that the possibility of eliminating the gaps does not entail that they do not exist. On the contrary: to speak of eliminating gaps only makes sense if there are or may be gaps. This is what some authors apparently fail to see. Thus, in a well known textbook it is maintained that:

> "The impression that there are gaps arises from considering in abstract form the content of general norms only. But it must not be forgotten that the legal order contains not only general norms, but also individual norms . . . Insofar as the legal order delegates to an authority (*e. g.* a judge) the determination of the

---

1 F. CARNELUTTI, Teoria Generale del Diritto, 1940, Spanish translation: Teoría General del Derecho, Madrid, 1955, p. 107.

2 Op. cit., p. 116.

3 G. DEL VECCHIO, Filosofía del Derecho (Spanish translation, Barcelona, 1947, 5th ed., p. 339).

4 L. RECASENS SICHES, Tratado General de Filosofía del Derecho, Mexico, 1959, pp. 323—325.

individual norm which gives the precise legal sense of the individual conduct in question, it is clear that it contains provisions for every possible individual case ... In *all* cases the legal order provides — by means of an individual norm issued by the judge — a solution for the case in question and therefore the legal order is complete and free from gaps. In other terms: there are no gaps, because there are judges." [5]

This is just like saying that trousers can have no holes because there are always tailors to patch them! The interesting question is whether the judge can decide the case according to existing norms [6], that is, whether or not the legal system provides a solution for the case. To say that the case has a solution because the judge has given it a solution is simply trivial.

c) There is another thesis worth mentioning, based on the distinction between Law (Recht, Derecho, Droit) and legal rules (Gesetze, leyes, lois). According to this thesis there are no gaps in Law (Rechtslücken, lagunas del Derecho), though there may be gaps in the set of legal rules (Gesetzeslücken, lagunas de la ley).

It is far from clear what exactly is meant by this distinction and the whole doctrine appears to be rather ambiguous. Some writers who explicitly maintain this doctrine seem to say no more than the courts can eliminate or "fill" the gaps. Thus the well known Spanish legal philosopher LEGAZ Y LACAMBRA says: "The legal rules (leyes) provide no solution, but the judge must give a solution. Or, what amounts to the same thing, the enacted law and the customary law have gaps; the legal order cannot have them; where legislator and custom do not provide a solution, a judicial decision, as a source of law, must give a solution." [7]

This appears to be the position which we have already considered in b).

On another interpretation the doctrine means that the set of legal sentences that constitute the positive law (statutes, customs, etc.) may be incomplete; but there is a set such that if it is added to the positive law, the resulting system (legal order) becomes com-

---

5 E. R. AFTALION, F. GARCIA OLANO, J. VILANOVA, Introducción al Derecho, 5th ed., Buenos Aires, 1956, vol. I, p. 257.

6 Cf. H. KELSEN, Reine Rechtslehre, 2nd ed., Wien, 1960, p. 251.

7 L. LEGAZ Y LACAMBRA, Filosofía del Derecho, Barcelona, 1953, p. 396.

plete. The whole problem would then be the choice of the basis of
the system. If the basis is sufficiently broad, *i. e.,* if it includes the
natural law, then the legal system is closed. This amounts to saying that all legal orders (when conveniently integrated with the
natural law) are complete, which is the Postulate of Completeness
in a slightly modified form.

To sum up, the Postulate of the Necessary Completeness of the
Law, as we understand it here, is the assertion that all legal systems
are complete in relation to any possible Universe of Cases and any
Universe of Solutions. In the next section we shall discuss some of
the arguments advanced in support of this contention.

5. Analysis of the Postulate of Completeness

The contention that all legal systems are necessarily complete is
usually based on some version of the Principle of Prohibition which
we have already discussed (sect. 3). In legal philosophy this Principle has been supported by a variety of arguments; sometimes it is
given a logical basis, sometimes an ontological one.

We shall not examine all the theories which have been advanced
by legal philosophers in support of the Postulate of Completeness,
but a few typical examples will be considered in order to show how
our analysis of the Principle of Prohibition applies to legal theory.

a) HANS KELSEN's doctrine may be taken as a typical case of
what may be called the *logical version* of the Principle of Prohibition.

Regarding the problem of legal gaps two different states may be
distinguished in KELSEN's thought.

In the first edition of his *Reine Rechtslehre* (1934) the contention that there are no gaps in law is based on the fact that the law
guarantees the freedom of doing what is not prohibited, for it prohibits interference with those actions which are not prohibited. Thus
every action which is not prohibited by the law, is permitted by it
in the strong sense[1]. For it is clear that a normative system can

---

1 H. KELSEN, Reine Rechtslehre, 1st ed., Wien, 1934, p. 100: "Denn
indem [die Rechtsordnung] die Menschen zu einem ganz bestimmten Verhalten verpflichtet, gewährleistet sie jenseits dieser Rechtspflichten die Freiheit. Gegenüber demjenigen, der ein durch die geltende Ordnung nicht
statuiertes Verhalten von einem anderen beansprucht, hat dieser ein durch
die Rechtsordnung eingeräumtes 'Recht' auf Unterlassung dieses Verhal-
tens. 'Recht' im Sinne von rechtlich gewährleisteter Freiheit."

guarantee the freedom of doing what is not prohibited in KELSEN's sense, only if it contains a norm to this effect, *i. e.,* a norm which makes it illegal to interfere with the non-prohibited actions of other people, by means of establishing a sanction for such acts of interference. But it is difficult to see (and KELSEN gives no reason for it) why such a norm should be present in every possible legal order. On the contrary, such a guarantee — if it exists at all — can only be contingent, unless there are necessary legal norms. But this, as a positivist, KELSEN cannot admit. In other words, as we have already shown (cf. sect. 3), if "permitted" is taken in its strong sense, then the Principle of Prohibition is a contingent proposition and cannot support the claim that all law is necessarily complete.

KELSEN himself has subsequently acknowledged this fact and this acknowledgement has forced him to introduce a substantial change into his doctrine of legal gaps [2].

Thus in the second edition of the Reine Rechtslehre (1960), KELSEN modifies his interpretation of the Principle of Prohibition and now takes the term "permitted" in its weak sense of being not prohibited. But then the Principle becomes completely harmless, as it does not exclude the existence of legal gaps. KELSEN himself seems to admit it when he says that there may be a conflict of interests which is not solved by legal order, because no legal order can solve all possible conflicts of interests [3].

Nevertheless KELSEN insists in his thesis that there are no gaps in law, though he has to pay a very high prize for it. For what he says about legal gaps in the second edition amounts to an implicit change of his definition of "gap". In the first edition, a gap is defined as a case that has no solution because there is no law applicable to it [4]. Consequently, KELSEN's main effort was to show that for all cases there is always some relevant norm: in those cases for

---

2 Cf. H. Kelsen, Reine Rechtslehre, 2nd ed., Wien, 1960, pp. 247—255.

3 Reine Rechtslehre, 2nd ed. (1960), p. 249: "Dann liegt, wie schon hervorgehoben, ein Interessenkonflikt vor, dem die Rechtsordnung nicht vorbeugt; und keine Rechtsordnung kann allen möglichen Interessenkonflikten vorbeugen."

4 Reine Rechtslehre, 1st ed. (1934), p. 100: "Allein, echte Lücken in dem Sinne, daß ein Rechtsstreit gemäß den geltenden Normen nicht entscheidbar wäre, weil das Gesetz — wie man sagt — mangels einer auf diesen Fall beziehenden Vorschrift nicht angewendet werden kann, gibt es nicht ..."

which there is no specific norm, the general negative norm (what is not prohibited, is permitted) is applied. This negative norm — which on this doctrine belongs to all legal orders — precluded the existence of legal gaps.

But in the second edition, KELSEN abandons (with good reasons) this position and no longer claims that a certain norm should have the mysterious property of belonging to all legal orders. When there is no norm which refers to a case, then the judge cannot (in KELSEN's new view) apply any particular norm, but he can still apply something, viz., the whole legal order[5].

It is far from clear what we are to understand by the application of the whole order, which is not an application of any of its norms. But even if we disregard this difficulty, KELSEN's argument would be plausible only if by "gap" we no longer understood a case to which no norm is applicable, but instead took it to mean a case to which "it is logically impossible to apply the legal order".

Now, for KELSEN the legal order may always be applied because if there is no particular norm applicable to the case, then the judge can apply the whole order. And this is possible, as KELSEN explains it, because every action which is not prohibited is, *ipso facto,* permitted. This permission does not require any more the presence of a norm that guarantees the freedom of doing what is not prohibited; it only means that there is no prohibition.

Thus it becomes clear that the Principle of Prohibition changes its meaning in the second edition of Reine Rechtslehre. What this Principle states now is that every action which is not prohibited by the system is weakly permitted. This is, of course, trivially true (given the definition of weak permission), but it does not exclude — as we have already seen in sect. 3 — the possibility of normative gaps.

KELSEN seems to have explored both possible ways of interpreting the Principle of Prohibition. In the first edition his thesis is based on the strong version of the Principle; in the second edition

---

5 Reine Rechtslehre, 2nd ed. (1960), p. 251: "Die Anwendung der geltenden Rechtsordnung ist in dem Fall, in dem die traditionelle Theorie eine Lücke annimmt, nicht logisch unmöglich. Zwar ist in diesem Falle die Anwendung einer einzelnen Rechtsnorm nicht möglich, aber die Anwendung der Rechtsordnung, und auch das ist Rechtsanwendung, ist möglich. Rechtsanwendung ist nicht logisch ausgeschlossen."

it is based on its weak version. Both fail in the task KELSEN assigns to them.

b) An example of "ontological foundation" of the Principle of Prohibition is to be found in the works of CARLOS COSSIO. As a matter of fact, COSSIO gives various arguments in order to reject the possibility of legal gaps, some of which we have already discussed[6]. Here we shall limit ourselves to what he calls the ontological principle.

According to COSSIO's theory all human actions have a deontic character, for the deontic property "permitted" is intrinsic to the very notion of action. (It should be observed that we are partly using our own terminology in restating Cossio's doctrine.)

By virtue of his peculiar ontological structure, man is metaphysically free, and this means that all his actions are "ontologically" permitted. The law (which according to COSSIO means positive law, as there is no natural law) proceeds to impose restrictions on this metaphysical freedom of man, by prohibiting some of his actions. From the "ontological axiom of freedom" it follows that permission is prior to prohibition: for an action to be prohibited there must be a (positive) norm, but for its being permitted no norm is needed. Every action carries with it a permission which is the expression of human freedom. Therefore, the Principle that everything that is not prohibited is permitted is not an analytic but a synthetic proposition, but at the same time it is necessary. "Permitted" is not to be taken here either in its strong, or in its weak sense; it refers to the ontological structure of human conduct. (This is, of course, a very rough summary of Cossio's doctrine, but it is sufficient for our purposes.)

This theory is based on metaphysical assumptions that hardly admit of any verification. Its analysis would certainly go beyond the scope of the present book. Fortunately we can spare ourselves this task without detriment to our discussion of the problem that concerns us.

Remember that our problem was to determine whether all legal orders are complete (and, moreover, closed) in the sense that they provide solutions for all possible cases. This we called the Postulate

---

6 Cf. ch. VI, sect. 7. For the ontological foundation of COSSIO's theory see his La Teoría Egológica del Derecho y el Concepto Jurídico de la Libertad, 2nd ed., Buenos Aires, 1964.

of the Necessary Completeness of the Law. But the question whether human conduct as such has some intrinsic normative character is quite irrelevant to our problem.

When a certain action has not been deontically determined by a normative system, and this means in our terminology that from this system no solution can be inferred for a particular case, then we say that this case is a gap in this system and that the system is incomplete. The question whether or not this same case is solved by some other system or even whether it has some intrinsic deontic property is outside the scope of our discussion. What we want to know is not whether a certain action is prohibited or permitted by *some* system (or by some metaphysical postulate), but whether it is permitted or prohibited by a certain (definite) system of norms[7]. In other words, we are interested in the question of completeness of normative systems and the claim that human action has some normative character based on its ontological structure is quite irrelevant to this question.

Therefore, even if it were true that there is something like a metaphysical freedom of man, in virtue of which all human action would have some deontic character, Cossio's ontological axiom could not be advanced in support of the view that all legal systems are closed.

6. Rules of Closure

We shall postpone until the next chapter the discussion of some other arguments which have been used to support the postulate of the necessary completeness of the law (arguments based on the judicial function) and deal now with a different though related question. Instead of asking whether all normative systems are necessarily closed (i. e. whether closedness is part of their concept) — a question which we have already answered in the negative — we shall ask whether closed normative systems are possible and if so, how they are possible. In other words, we are inquiring how the closure of a normative system may be achieved.

---

7 Even if it could be proved that all actions are deontically determined (by some system), it would not follow that all systems are such that all actions are determined by them. And it is the second of these theses, not the first, that is embodied in the Postulate of Completeness.

One way of making a system complete is to correlate each and every one of the cases with a maximal solution. This procedure may be called *closure by cases*. But to speak of *all* the cases presupposes the existence of a limited set of cases (a *UC*), and to speak about maximal solutions presupposes the existence of a limited set of solutions (a *US*max). But there is no guarantee that a system that is complete in relation to the chosen *UC* and the *US*max will also be complete in relation to other universes. How can completeness be made a constant feature of the system in spite of the variations of the *UC* and the *US*max, that is needed to qualify it as closed?

It would seem that the only solution is to make use of some type of rule of closure, that is, a rule that would qualify deontically all actions not already qualified by the system in question. Let us see how a rule of closure of this kind will function and what are its limitations.

A rule of closure must satisfy the following conditions of adequacy: (a) it must close the system, i. e., make it complete in relation to any *UC* and any *UA*, and (b) it must preserve the consistency of the system, that is, introduce no inconsistencies, so that if the original system is consistent, the new system resulting from the addition of the rule of closure must also be consistent. (Both these requirements seem reasonable enough, but, as we shall see, they are not always compatible, and in certain situations it becomes necessary to sacrifice one or other of them.)

The rule of closure allows us, starting from a set of sentences α, to identify another set of sentences (normally larger than α) which we shall call the *closure* of α. The adequacy conditions mentioned above require that the closure of α should be complete (even if α is not complete) and consistent (if α is consistent).

The rules of closure are analogous to the rules of inference in this sense: just as the rules of inference allow us, starting from a set of sentences α, to identify another set of sentences that we call the consequences of α $[Cn(\alpha)]$, so the rules of closure allow us to pass from a given set of sentences (α) to another set (closure of α). However, the rule of closure differs from logical rules in two important respects: (i) the rule of closure is *contingent*, and (ii) it is *normative*, in the sense that it allows to infer new normative consequences (which could not be inferred from the original set).

Like the ordinary rules of inference, the rule of closure belongs to the system in a different sense from its other components (sentences). It is a rule of second level that refers to the sentences of the system (which constitute the first level), but not to itself (self-reference of the rule of closure would lead to some familiar paradoxes). But unlike the ordinary rules of inference, the rule of closure has a supplementary character: it can be used only when it has been established that no solution can be inferred for the case in question by means of the ordinary rules of inference. This supplementary character gives rise to certain difficulties which render the functioning of the rule of closure rather problematic.

Indeed, resort to the rule of closure (since it may occur only when the deontic character of an action cannot be inferred from the system) presupposes the existence of a decision procedure to identify the normative consequences of the system. However, even in a moderately complicated logic, such as the functional calculus of the first order, there is no effective procedure for proving that a certain sentence is *not* a theorem of the system. If one seeks to prove that a sentence is a theorem, but fails to construct the proof, this may mean either of two things: (a) the proof does not exist, and the sentence in question is not a theorem, or (b) the proof has not been found, but nonetheless it exists. Because of this second possibility, failure to find a proof is never conclusive; there is always the possibility that it exists to be found at some later stage.

If it is agreed that the rule of closure must be applied only in cases where there is no solution and not in cases where a particular person fails to find a solution, it is doubtful whether it may ever be applied at all, because of the sheer difficulty of determining when the appropriate occasion arises.

Having given this general characterization of the rules of closure, let us now see what form a rule of this kind must take in order to perform satisfactorily the function assigned to it. To do this we shall first discuss the functioning of the rules of closure in a *categorical normative system*. (Theorists have concentrated almost exclusively on problems of closure in relation to categorical systems[1]; the closure of hypothetical systems has rarely, if ever, been the object of their scrutiny.)

Let us recall that in categorical systems the solutions that may be inferred from the system are the same for all cases. This allows us to ignore cases and refer only to solutions.

---

1 Cf. von Wright, Norm and Action, pp. 87 ff.

We shall consider two types of rule of closure, one that is relative to a UA and another that is absolute (for any UA) The first might be stated as follows:

(C1) If from a normative system α the prohibition of an action p (being a deontic content of a given UA) cannot be inferred, then the permission of p may be inferred.

Consequently, the closure of α (relative to the UA) is the set of all the sentences belonging to the consequences of α plus the sentences permitting all the actions (deontic contents) corresponding to the UA in question which are not prohibited by α. The rule $C1$ satisfies the requirements imposed by the criteria of adequacy: it makes a system complete and preserves its consistency.

It is a simple matter to generalize this rule so that it becomes independent of a given UA:

(C2) If from a normative system α the prohibition of a deontic content p (corresponding to any UA), cannot be inferred then the permission of p may be inferred.

A categorical normative system containing a rule of closure of the type $C2$ is closed in the sense of the definition (I) given in sect. 1, since any action (of any UA) is deontically determined in that system.

The problem of closure of *hypothetical normative systems* is more complicated. A rule analogous to $C1$ would have the following form:

(C3) If from a normative system α the prohibition of a deontic content p (corresponding to a UA_i) cannot be inferred for a case q (of any UC), then the permission of p in case q may be inferred.

However, rule $C3$ does not satisfy the criteria of adequacy that we have stipulated for the rules of closure, since, as we shall show, it does not preserve the consistency of the system.

Let us suppose that for a UA composed of only one action R ($UA = \{R\}$), the system α correlates the case "$p \cdot q$" with the maximal solution "PhR" and the case "$p \cdot {\sim}q$" with "FR" (that is, the conditional sentences "${\sim}PR \cdot P{\sim}R/p \cdot q$" and "$PR \cdot P{\sim}R/p \cdot {\sim}q$" are consequences of α). Both cases have a complete solution; neither is a gap in the system α. Let us moreover suppose that α is consistent and that the Universe of Cases characterized by p and q — i. e. $UC\,(pq)$ — is the Universe of Relevant Cases (UCR) for α in the given UA. Now, let us take case "p" which belongs to a UC less fine than UCR. What solution can be inferred from α as regards

"R" for case "p"? It is obvious that there is none, since the case is correlated neither with "PR" nor with "$\sim PR$". If we applied rule $C3$, we should infer the permission of R for the case p ("PR/p"). But then case "$p \cdot q$" would be correlated with two incompatible solutions: "PR" and "PhR". Rule $C3$ would in this case introduce a contradiction into a system which was, originally, consistent.

To avoid these disastrous results it is necessary to introduce a restriction, forbidding the application of the rule of closure to the cases belonging to Universes of Cases that are less fine than the UCR of the system. Then, since the solution of the cases of the UCR automatically resolves all cases of all UCs finer than the UCR, we can limit the field of application of the rule of closure to the UCR of the system. So we obtain

($C4$) If from a normative system α the prohibition of a deontic content p (corresponding to a UA_i) cannot be inferred for a case q of the UCR of α, then the permission of p in case q may be inferred.

Rule $C4$ preserves the consistency of the system, but the closure is relative not only to the chosen UA, but also to the UCR of the system. This last limitation is unavoidable if the rule of closure is to preserve the consistency of the system. All we can do is to generalize the closure as regards the Universe of Actions.

($C5$) If from a normative system α the prohibition of any deontic content p (corresponding to any UA) cannot be inferred for a case q of the UCR of α, then the permission of p in case q may be inferred[2].

Rule $C5$ is the most general rule of closure which may be formulated for hypothetical normative systems if consistency is to be preserved. However, it is not an absolute closure, but relative to the UCR of the system; a system containing rule $C5$ is not complete in relation to any UC, but only in relation to the UCR and is incomplete in relation to UCs less fine than the UCR.

Since, therefore, the absolute closure of a hypothetical normative system would be incompatible with the important requirement that the consistency of the system should be preserved, it must be dis-

---

2 As the notion of a UCR has been defined in terms of the UA (cf. ch. VI, sect. 4), the UCR to which rule $C5$ refers must be understood as being the UCR of the largest possible UA, that is, the UA embracing all the basic actions that may be expressed in the language in question.

missed as an impossibility; all that can be achieved so far as non-categorical systems are concerned is a closure relative to the *UCR*.

On the other hand, this agrees with what jurists intuitively understand by a rule of closure, e. g. the rule "nullum crimen" in penal law. The failure of a system that is closed in this sense to solve the cases of a *UC* less fine than the *UCR* would normally be attributed not to deficiencies in the system, but to a lack of information about the properties of the case, that is, it would be regarded not as a normative gap, but as a gap of knowledge or a gap of recognition.

Our discussion of the problem of closure has shown the importance of a concept which was elaborated with a very different aim in a very different context. This is the notion of relevance and the Universe of Relevant Cases (*UCR*) which has been used in ch. VI to characterize the concept of an axiological gap. The fact that we have had to reintroduce this concept to explain the rules of closure shows its fruitfulness.

VON WRIGHT[3] has raised the question whether the rule of closure must necessarily be permissive, in the sense of permitting all actions not prohibited by a system, or whether other deontic characters may also be used to close a system.

If consistency is to be preserved, it seems that the rule of closure must be permissive, since permission is the only deontic character which may qualify an action and its negation without inconsistency. A prohibitive rule of closure ("any action not qualified by a system is prohibited") would lead to inconsistencies in cases where p and $\sim p$ are not deontically qualified, since "Php" and "$Ph\sim p$" are incompatible. The same would happen with a rule of closure of character O ("all that is not permitted is obligatory") and there would also be a contradiction in the case where the permission of p can be inferred, but nothing can be inferred as regards $\sim p$, since "Pp" and "$O\sim p$" are incompatible.

VON WRIGHT proposes the following rules of closure as possible alternatives: "Any act, the doing of which is not permitted, is forbidden" and "Any forbearance which is not permitted is forbidden". However, these rules — although they prevent the inconsistencies mentioned above — do not close the system. The former does not solve the case where the negation of (forbearance from) a permitted act is not qualified by the system, and the latter does not solve the

---

3 Norm and Action, pp. 87—88.

case where an act the negation of which (forbearance from which) is permitted, is not qualified.

What emerges from these considerations is that, if consistency is to be preserved, rules of closure forbidding or enjoining actions not qualified by a system are not possible. In this sense, character P occupies a privileged position[4]. Naturally, nothing prevents us from formulating complex rules of closure forbidding (or enjoining) some actions, while permitting others[5].

In the following section we shall examine the well known rule "nullum crimen" which we have used as a pre-analytical basis (explicandum) for the explication of the rules of closure.

7. The Rule "Nullum Crimen Sine Lege"

The best known example of a rule of closure in the field of law is the famous rule "nullum crimen sine lege". This rule appears in almost modern legal orders, but it is not easy to determine its content and to elucidate the way it functions. There are two main reasons for this difficulty. In the first place, the rule seems to have several different functions; in the second place, there is a series of

---

4 Nevertheless, there is a case in which even a permissive rule of closure may result in inconsistency. Let us suppose that it can be inferred from the system α that p is not facultative (not optional) in case q, i. e. "$\sim Fp/q$" is a consequence of α. As p is not forbidden, we may infer by means of the rule of closure that p is permitted. But as $\sim p$ is not forbidden either, the permission of $\sim p$ may also be inferred. However, the joint permission of p and $\sim p$ is incompatible with $\sim Fp$, so that the rule of closure has introduced an inconsistency.

In practice, it would be most unusual to find a norm that confined itself to the bare statement that an action is not facultative. We may therefore disregard this case for all practical purposes. But the theoretical difficulty remains.

5 The following might serve as an example of a complexe rule of closure: "If neither 'Pp' nor '$P \sim p$' can be inferred from α, then 'Fp' may be inferred; but if 'Pp' can be inferred, but nothing can be inferred about $\sim p$, then 'Op' may be inferred." It would certainly be difficult to justify axiologically a rule of this type, which appears to be completely arbitrary; but from a purely theoretical point of view no objection could be made, since the rule satisfies both conditions of adequacy: the closure of the system and the preservation of consistency.

complementary rules which are closely bound up with the rule "nullum crimen", so that it is not always easy to draw a dividing line among all these rules.

Without claiming to make an exhaustive analysis, we shall try to point out the main features and functions of the rule "nullum crimen" in order to determine how it can be interpreted as a rule of closure.

(a) The rule may be regarded as a *directive given to the legislator* in the sense that it stipulates that he must not create crimes *ex post facto,* that is, he must not punish actions performed before the statute forbidding them was enacted. To emphasize this function of the rule, it may be formulated as "nullum crimen, nulla poena sine praevia lege", with a special stress on the word "praevia".

An almost indispensable complement of the rule "nullum crimen, nulla poena sine previa lege" when understood as a directive to the legislator, is the requirement that penal offenses should be defined as precisely as possible. This requirement is to be found in Continental legal doctrine in the theory of *Tatbestand* and is also well known in American constitutional law as the "void-for-vagueness rule". This rule means that a criminal statute violates due process and is constitutionally defective if it is not reasonably specific in defining the nature of the proscribed conduct, because the law should convey to the individuals a reasonably clear directive wherever an act is declared to be punishable[1].

The rule "nullum crimen, nulla poena sine praevia lege" expresses a standard of justice, that is, it indicates the requirements that penal legislation must satisfy if it is not to violate this standard.

b) Another way of interpreting the rule "nullum crimen" is to regard it as a *directive given to judges,* in the sense that it stipulates that judges must not decree penal sanctions (and indeed must acquit

---

1 Cf. Sherwin v. People, 100 N. Y. 351, 3 N. E. 465, 469 (1885): "The multiplication of offenses by construction of penal statutes is in conflict with the general policy of the law, and a statutory crime can only be created by phraseology which is clear, direct, and unquestionable as to its intention." Com. v. Slome, 321 Mass. 713, 75 N. E. 2nd 517, 519 (1947): "A statute creating a crime must be sufficiently definite in specifying the conduct that is commanded or inhibited ... It must fix with a reasonable degree of definiteness what it requires or prohibits." See also United States v. Cohen Grocery Co., 255 U. S. 81 (1921).

the accused) if the charge against him concerns an act which occurred at a time when there was no norm in existence qualifying the act as a criminal offense. It might be adequately formulated as "nulla poena sine lege"[2].

The rule "nulla poena" requires as a complement the prohibition of the analogical or extensive interpretation of penal law, since it might otherwise easily be disregarded. These two rules are so closely related that it is not clear whether they are in reality two different rules or simply two faces of the same coin.

Other rules completing and, above all, facilitating the application of the rule "nulla poena" are the presumption of the innocence of the defendant and the principle "in dubio pro reo". We say that these rules facilitate the application of the rule "nulla poena" because they provide the means of overcoming the theoretical difficulty referred to in sect. 6, by reversing the onus of proof (onus probandi). If it has not been proved that the defendant has committed a crime, the judge must acquit him. And so there are none of the problems that would arise if the defendant were required to prove a negative (i. e. that his behaviour is not criminal), since it is the prosecution that must prove its criminal character, that is, prove that prohibition of the behaviour in question can be inferred from the system.

The rule "nulla poena", when seen as a directive to judges, typifies the expression in penal law of a political ideology. A liberal penal law may be characterized as one that contains this rule, together with the complementary principles we have mentioned.

c) The rule "nullum crimen sine lege" may also be understood as a rule of closure permitting all the actions not prohibited by penal law, i. e. authorizing the inference of the permission of any action (in a given case), if from the system no prohibition for that action can be inferred.

On this interpretation the effect of the rule is to make the system a closed one (in relation to the UCR). But we should bear in mind that the rule "nullum crimen" — in the three interpretations we have examined — is usually restricted to penal law. Even in cases where it is formulated in broad general terms without expressly referring to penal law (as in the Argentinian Constitution,

---

2 Cf. G. H. VON WRIGHT, Norm and Action, op. cit., p. 87.

§ 19), we find that in practice it is not applied in civil law. The rule of closure may therefore be stated in this way: "All that is not penally prohibited, is penally permitted." The fact that an action is penally permitted means that it does not incur penal sanctions, but this does not exclude the possibility that it may be prohibited by some other norm (e. g. a police edict, a norm of civil law, etc.).

On this last interpretation (as a rule of closure) the rule "nullum crimen" is not necessarily the expression of a political ideology or of a certain ideal of justice. It might equally be introduced for purely "technical" reasons, that is, in order to produce a complete normative system, capable of providing an answer to every question. As we shall argue later, the ideal of completeness is not a political, but a rational ideal.

We make no claim that the three interpretations of the rule "nullum crimen" that we have considered are exhaustive; still less do we maintain that they are incompatible. It is more than likely that this rule fulfils all these functions simultaneously (and even others as well). Our aim has been merely to give an outline of some conceptual differences, which have not always been clearly distinguished.

Summarizing the results of this chapter, we may state:

(i) The notion of an absolute closure, as reflected in definition (II) (sect. 1) is not applicable to non-categorical normative systems, since it would not preserve their consistency. As legal systems are hypothetical, it follows that no legal system can be absolutely closed. It is only categorical systems that can be closed in the sense of definition (I) (sect. 1).

(ii) The restricted concept of closure as relative to a UCR seems to be a good reconstruction of the concept of closure that is used by jurists (even though they rarely, if ever, use this term). In particular the *nullum crimen* rule of penal law, taken as a rule of closure, seems to lack the scope of rule $C3$ (absolute closure), but to exercise the more limited function of rules $C4$ or $C5$ (closure relative to the UCR).

(iii) In spite of this restriction, it is important to insist on the distinction between completeness and closedness, and, consequently, between open and (relatively) closed systems. An open system may be complete in relation to a particular UC and a particular UA but incomplete in relation to others. A (relatively) closed system is necessarily complete in relation to the *UCR* (and any *UC* finer than the *UCR*) and — by rule *C5* — complete in relation to any *UA*. Consequently, closedness is much stronger concept than mere completeness.

VIII. Judical Decisions and the Problem of Legal Gaps

In this chapter we shall analyze some of the questions arising in relation to the problem of legal gaps at the level of judicial decisions. These problems are peculiar to normative systems in which there are judges with compulsory jurisdiction, that is, functionaries that are specially charged with resolving disagreements arising from the application of general norms to individual cases. In fact, such an institution will be found only in the sphere of law.

But we are not going to discuss here all the problems that the occurence of legal gaps creates for judges; neither shall we deal with the techniques employed by judges to remove or "fill" the gaps. We prefer to limit ourselves to the examination of a doctrine — widely spread among jurists — which seeks to deny the existence of normative gaps or, at least, to minimize their importance, on the basis of certain arguments relating to the function of the judge. Two versions of this doctrine may be distinguished: the stronger one maintains that, although there are gaps for the subject of the law, there are none for the judge, who always has a duty to perform, either the duty of finding against the defendant, or else that of rejecting the petition. In its weaker version, the doctrine maintains that the judge *can* (though he need not) resolve all cases by application of the existing law, that is, without "filling" the gaps.

We consider this doctrine to be untenable. Both versions — the stronger and the weaker — are based on fallacious arguments which are analyzed in sects. 5, 6 and 7. But in order to analyze them we have been obliged to give some account — admittedly a sketchy and incomplete one — of the phenomenon of jurisdiction (sect. 1) and to discuss the function of the different types of judicial decisions (sect. 2). In sect. 3 the norms regulating the judge's conduct are studied. These norms give rise to what we call the secondary system or system of the judge, in contradistinction to the system of the subject or primary system. The two systems are related through the grounding of the decision; the concept of grounding is analyzed in sect. 4. The last three sections (5, 6 and 7) are devoted to the analysis of the problems that the occurrence of normative gaps creates for the judge.

1. The Function of Jurisdiction

A legal system, like other normative systems, qualifies deontically certain types of behaviour (in certain circumstances) and thus regulates the actions of the individuals belonging to a certain social group, contributing to their peaceful co-existence by prescribing in advance how any conflicts of interest that may arise are to be solved.

Solving conflicts of interest is, obviously, one of the fundamental aims of the law. But, as history shows, this aim can hardly be attained — except in small communities with great social cohesion, e. g. based on a religion or an ideology — by the mere existence of a "primary" legal system made up of general norms which solve generic cases. Such a system would not be very effective[1]; the difficulties that make for the ineffectiveness of the law — considered as a system of general norms — arise from factors of two kinds: (A) Doubt or ignorance concerning the solution that corresponds to an individual case, and (B) transgression of the norms or lack of obedience to them.

(A) may be characterized as a situation where there is a *lack of knowledge* about the normative qualification of a certain action (in a given case). The problem created by this situation is, therefore, a *problem of knowledge.*

Lack of knowledge (doubt or ignorance) about the legal status of an action may have different origins. In the first place, it may be caused by a *defect in the system,* which, in turn, may be the lack of a solution (a case of normative gap), or else the existence of several and incompatible solutions (a case of inconsistency). In such cases *the* solution cannot be known because there is no solution or else there is no single solution.

In the second place, ignorance of the solution corresponding to a case may arise from the fact that the system solves generic cases, whereas it is also necessary to know the solution for individual cases. The *subsumtion* of individual cases under generic cases creates

---

1 Cf. H. L. A. HART, The Concept of Law, p. 113 ff.

problems that we have examined briefly in ch. II. Here the case (even the individual case) has its solution, but the solution is not known, either because there is not enough information about some relevant fact (gap of knowledge), or because the (individual) case falls into the zone of vagueness (zone of penumbra) of some relevant concept (gap of recognition).

Situation (B) is not a problem of knowledge of the law, but of cases in which an individual transgresses (voluntarily or involuntarily) the norms of the system by failing to fulfil an obligation or by performing a forbidden act. In these cases the law provides for the imposition of sanctions and/or the obligation of compensating for the damage caused by the nonfulfilment of the obligation.

The following table summarizes what has been said about the difficulties and problems concerning the effectiveness of the law:

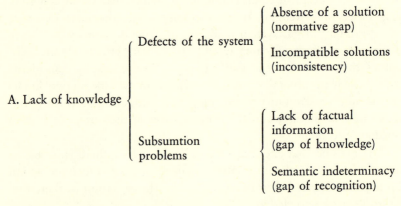

A. Lack of knowledge
- Defects of the system
  - Absence of a solution (normative gap)
  - Incompatible solutions (inconsistency)
- Subsumtion problems
  - Lack of factual information (gap of knowledge)
  - Semantic indeterminacy (gap of recognition)

B. Disobedience (transgression)

One of the remedies for these defects and difficulties is the institution of *compulsory jurisdiction*. This consists in giving to certain state officials (judges) the task of deciding how the individual in each individual case must behave in order to conform to the law and of imposing obligations and sanctions upon all those who do not behave in the way prescribed by the law. Jurisdiction is compulsory in two senses: the defendant cannot elude the suit and his agreement is not necessary for the process; it is also compulsory in the sense that the obligations and sanctions ordered by the judge are imposed coercively, i. e. through the application of force if they are resisted.

The jurisdictional function of the judges and other jurisdictional organs[2] consists primarily in solving conflicts of interest, which may be classified in two main groups: (a) those where the controversy concerns the classification of an individual case, that is, those in which it is disputed whether or not a certain individual case belongs to a certain generic case; (b) those dealing with the deontic qualification of a certain action. Here the question is what ought to or may or must not be done by a certain individual (more precisely: a subject of the law) in an individual case. Consequently, the questions the judge must answer belong to two main types: (a) questions of classification, referring to the subsumption of an individual case under a generic case; and (b) normative questions, referring to the deontic qualification of an action in an individual case. (The problems judges have to solve always concern individual cases, for they have to resolve concrete conflicts and must not make "abstract declarations").

The function of jurisdiction consists, therefore, in answering the questions the judge is asked, and, as the questions are of two types, so also are the possible answers.

To give an adequate answer to a question about the classification of an individual case, the judge must decide whether this case is, or is not, an instance of a certain generic case, that is, whether or not it possesses the defining property of the generic case. This activity is predominantly cognitive, for the judge has to know the facts and find out the meaning of the expressions in which the generic case is defined. But this activity is not exclusively cognitive, since sometimes the judge must *give* a meaning to certain terms[3].

The adequate answer to a normative question consists in saying what a certain person ought to or may or must not do on certain occasions and in certain circumstances. In order to do this the judge

---

2 We speak of "jurisdictional" and not of "judicial" function because there may be non-judicial organs having jurisdictional functions (for instance, some administrative organs). On the other hand, judges also sometimes fulfil other functions which are not strictly jurisdictional.

3 On this problem see ALF ROSS, On Law and Justice, pp. 119—123 and 135 ff.; H. L. A. HART, Positivism and the Separation of Law and Morals, 71 Harvard Law Review, 1958, pp. 593—629; G. R. CARRIÓ, Notas sobre Derecho y Lenguaje, Buenos Aires, 1965, pp. 45—47, and CH. PERELMAN, Avoir un sens et donner un sens, Logique et Analyse 5 (1962).

must issue a norm imposing an obligation or granting a permission (authorization). This is a *normative* activity.

The centralization of the function of jurisdiction in the hands of specialized officials gives rise to the existence of two normative systems, parallel but interdependent: the system of norms regulating the behaviour of the subjects of the law, which we shall call the *primary system* or *subject system,* and the system of norms regulating the behaviour of the judges and other jurisdictional organs, which we shall call the *secondary system* or *judge system.* Later we shall examine the nature of the norms that compose the latter system and determine how the two systems are interrelated.

2. *Judicial Decision*

The activity of the judge in the process culminates in the decision which puts an end to the controversy and by means of which the judge gives an answer to the question that has been posed.

We shall distinguish between two types of decision: *declarative decisions* and *normative decisions.* It is the nature of the problem itself that determines the nature of the decision; declarative decisions correspond to controversies arising from a problem of classification, whereas normative decisions resolve normative problems. In other words: declarative decisions are those which put an end to a process dealing with a problem of classification; we shall call this the declarative process. Normative problems bring about normative processes: normative decisions belong to these.

Declarative processes — which may be controversial or voluntary — may be regarded as questions of the form "Does the individual case i belong to the generic case q?" The only adequate answers to this kind of question are the statements "i does not belong to q" or "i belongs to q". Therefore, declarative decisions contain a statement of the form: "The individual case i belongs to the generic case q" or its denial.

In *normative processes* — which are always controversial — there is a disagreement about the normative status of a certain action of the defendant. The plaintiff asserts that the defendant has the obligation to perform an action (or to refrain from it) and asks the judge to order the defendant to perform (or to refrain from) this action. The defendant maintains he has no such obligation and asks the judge to reject the petition. (In a penal process there is a similar situation: the prosecution maintains that the accused has performed an action classified as delict and asks for a sanction to be applied to him. This analogy will allow us to omit from now on any reference to penal processes.)

Consequently, in normative processes questions of the form "Is p obligatory?" are asked, and the only adequate answers are norms or solutions of the form "Op" or "$\sim Op$" (that is "$P\sim p$"). Both in the question and in the answer the operation of the legal system is presupposed; therefore, normative decisions do not contain normative propositions *about* the system (their function is not to give information about the solution given by the law to a certain case; this function belongs to legal science), but *norms* or *solutions* derived from the system.

(It would be wrong to think that these two types of process exclude each other; in fact, questions of classification and normative questions may be mixed in the same process. For instance, in a bankruptcy suit the judge states that a person is bankrupt [classification] and orders the closing of the premises, interception of the mail, etc. But nothing prevents us from distinguishing conceptually between normative questions and classification questions.)

Declarative decisions are statements of the form "the individual case i belongs to the generic case q" or "i does not belong to q". These decisions contain no norms. But this does not mean that they may not have a normative effect. We must distinguish between two kinds of normative effect that a decision may have: (a) when a decision contains a norm (qualifying an action as obligatory, prohibited or permitted) we shall say that is has *primary normative effects*. These effects originate in the decision itself. (b) When a norm that does not occur in the decision connects to the latter certain normative consequences, we shall say that the decision has *secondary normative effects*. The secondary effects do not arise from the decision itself which functions purely as a fact conditioning certain effects (which are normative by virtue of some other norm).

Declarative decisions sometimes have secondary effects, but as they contain no norms, they lack primary normative effects. As typical examples of declarative decisions we may mention those that declare a divorce or the validity of a will or the nullity of a contract, the prescription of an obligation, etc.

While the contents of declarative decisions are statements which admit (assert) or reject (deny) a certain classification of an individual case, *normative decisions* contain *norms* regulating what ought to or may be done in the case in question. Therefore, normative decisions have primary normative effects, apart from their secondary ones.

Legal writers costumarily classify decisions into three categories: merely declarative, condemnatory and constitutive decisions[1]. This classification may be objected to for several reasons. First, the criterion on which the classification is based is far from being clear. If it is the same criterion that we have adopted, that is, the logical character of the decision (statement vs. norm), then the third category is superfluous, because constitutive decisions differ from other declarative decisions only because of their secondary normative effects. On the other hand, it would be wrong to identify normative decisions with condemnatory decisions. Indeed, there is no justification for confining the term "normative" to decisions in which the judge admits the claim imposing an obligation on the defendant. The declarative or normative character of a decision depends on the nature of the question posed and not on the resolution adopted by the judge (accepting or rejecting the claim).

When it is a problem of classification that has to be resolved, the adequate answer of the judge is always a statement. If the plaintiff asks the judge to declare that the individual case i belongs to the generic case q and the judge thinks that this is so, he will admit the claim and will declare that i is q. If he reaches the opposite conclusion, he will reject the claim declaring that i is not q.

When what must be resolved is a problem requiring a normative decision because what is disputed is whether something ought to or may be done in an individual case, both the decision admitting the claim and that rejecting it must be normative ones. If the decision admits the claim, its conclusion will be the norm asked for by the plaintiff, e. g. "Op" (where p is a certain action of the defendant). If the decision rejects the demand, its conclusion will be a norm incompatible with that requested by the plaintiff. If what the plaintiff claims is that the defendant should perform the action p, the decision rejecting it will contain as a conclusion a norm implying the permission of the negation of p ("$P{\sim}p$"): e. g. the

---

1 Cf., for example, E. J. COUTURE, Fundamentos de Derecho Procesal Civil, Buenos Aires, 1942, pp. 174 ff.; G. CHIOVENDA, Principii di diritto processuale civile (1913), §§ 6—8.

norm "$\sim Op$". (As we have seen in ch. VII, insofar as they are norms, expressions of the form "$\sim Op$" and "$P \sim p$" are equivalent.) In both cases the normative decision contains a norm (and moreover an individual norm). Therefore it is not true to say that only condemnatory decisions are normative and that all negative decisions are declarative[2]. Each may be declarative or normative, according to the nature of the question posed.

3. The Secondary System

We have given the name of secondary system or judge system to the set of norms regulating the actions of judges as such. These norms may be divided into two groups: (i) those that determine in what conditions the judges may judge and what types of question they may resolve (norms of competence); and (ii) those that establish obligations and prohibitions for the judges.

(i) *Norms of competence:* Following traditional terminology, we shall call norms of competence the norms conferring jurisdictional powers on the judge, that is, the power to judge. Such norms establish that certain persons can (are competent to) deal with certain kinds of cases and issue certain kinds of decisions, observing certain formalities.

Norms of competence are norms of conduct for the judges, if we regard them as permissive norms establishing the permission to perform certain acts in certain circumstances[1]. At the same time they are *constitutive* of judicial authority; nobody becomes a judge except on account of a norm of competence and to the degree and extent that this norm specifies. This is so because the concept of judge is usually defined in terms of the norms of competence and, therefore, these norms are part of the meaning of the term "judge".

It is important to stress the difference between the norms of competence (which are permissive) and those which impose obligations and prohibitions on judges, which also are norms of conduct. If we define the concept of judge in terms of (or in reference to) norms of competence, then only the latter will be necessary for the existence of judges; on the other hand, the norms imposing obliga-

---

2 G. CHIOVENDA, op. cit., § 7.

1 Cf. G. H. VON WRIGHT, Norm and Action, p. 192 ff.

tions, including the obligation to decide the case, would be merely contingent ones[2].

(ii) *Norms of obligation:* In modern legal orders there are usually, apart from the norms of competence, norms establishing obligations and prohibitions for the judges. The aim of these norms is to regulate the behaviour of the judges in the exercise of their jurisdictional activity. Therefore, these norms are also a part of the system of the judge.

Among the obligations of the judges there are two which bear directly upon the problem of legal gaps.

1) First, judges have the *obligation to decide the case,* that is, to give a decision which resolves the controversy that has come before them. This generic obligation to decide involves a series of specific obligations, which are related to different parts of the suit, for example, the hearing of evidence, etc., and is *relative* to the judge's competence. If the case is not within his competence, not only has the judge no obligation to resolve it, but he is also normally forbidden to do so.

2) Judges also have the *obligation to ground their decisions on the law.* The obligation to ground, i. e. to justify the decision may have two meanings. In its stronger meaning, a decision is grounded or justified when it has a ground and this ground is stated in the decision. In its weaker meaning, a decision is grounded when it may be justified, even if, in fact, its ground has not been stated (for example, if it is considered too obvious).

The obligation to justify the decision, i. e. to state its reasons or grounds, is usually found in most procedural codes and even constitutions. And even if there are some decisions which are not explicitly grounded (e. g. some orders of the Supreme Court of the United States), they surely do not lack grounds, for if it were so they would be arbitrary. We may therefore conclude that the requirement that the decisions should be grounded in the strong sense applies to most of the decisions, and in its weaker sense, to

2 It has been maintained by CARLOS COSSIO (La Plenitud del Ordenamiento Jurídico, 2nd ed., Buenos Aires, 1947, p. 59) that the judge always has an obligation to decide the case not because there is a legal norm imposing this obligation, but because it is an "ontological necessity" (sic). But he gives no reasons in support of this theory.

all judicial decisions. On the other hand, it is only with respect to decisions which are grounded (in either of the two senses) that problems derived from the existence of legal gaps may arise.

The obligation to ground the decision is very important because it is the bridge between the two systems, the primary and the secondary system. To see how this "bridge" functions we have to examine the notion of justification.

4. The Justification of the Decision

The obligation to ground a decision on the law has two different meanings according to the type of decision.

If it is a declarative decision, the problem consists in showing that the indiviual case i has (or lacks) the defining property of a generic case q. Here the justification of the decision involves problems that are fundamentally semantic, since the main difficulty lies in identifying the property referred to by the expressions found in legal discourse. The obligation to ground the decision on the law means here that the judge must not give legal terms and expressions an arbitrary meaning, but must make use, as far as possible, of the meanings they already have. (To determine these meanings is certainly no easy task, but we shall not attempt to discuss these problems here. See ALF ROSS, On Law and Justice, ch. 4.)

The difficulties involved in this task arise from two sources: lack of sufficient information about the facts of the case and semantic indeterminacy (vagueness) in the relevant concepts, that is, gaps of knowledge and gaps of recognition. On the other hand, the eventual normative gaps do not create, in principle, any problem at all in these contexts. This is obvious enough: if what is in dispute is whether an individual case belongs to a generic case, the fact that the latter has no solution is quite irrelevant.

When it is a normative controversy that has to be resolved, the judge has to *give* a solution (in the technical sense in which we are using this term, i. e. he has to issue a deontic sentence of the form "Op" or "Pp", etc.). But as it is an individual case that he has to resolve, the solution which occurs in the conclusion of a normative decision must be an individual solution[1].

---

1 On the difference between generic and individual solutions see ch. III, sect. 1.

The justification (grounding) of an individual solution consists in showing that it is derivable from a generic solution. Therefore, the justification of a normative decision is its derivation from a normative system (a system correlating generic cases with generic solutions). The process of justification contains several steps: (i) Classification or subsumption of the individual case under a generic case. (This shows that the problems of classification and, hence, the possibility of gaps of knowledge and gaps of recognition arise also in the justification of normative decisions.) (ii) Identification of the (generic) solution that the normative system correlates with the generic case. And (iii) derivation of the solution for the individual case by means of the rules of inference of the system[2].

From this account it is clear that the presence of normative gaps in the normative system used to justify a normative decision may prove to be the cause of serious difficulties in step (ii). We shall deal with these difficulties in subsequent sections of this chapter.

The obligation to ground on the law a normative decision is the obligation to use — in order to justify the decision — the subject system or primary system. In this sense the system of the judge is *secondary* compared with the system of the subject, since it presupposes the existence of the latter. It is precisely because judges are obliged in resolving conflicts of interest to ground their decisions on the primary system that the norms of the judge system refer — directly or indirectly — to other norms and are, consequently, second level norms.

The fact that judges ought to decide cases in accordance with what is prescribed by the primary system does not, of course, imply

---

2 Therefore it is somewhat misleading to speak in this context of the creation of an individual norm or solution by the judge, as KELSEN and other authors do. To say that the judge creates an individual norm when he gives a decision is, to say the least, an exaggeration, provided the latter is the mere application of the general norm that resolves the generic case. This means that the individual solution is a logical consequence of the description and subsumption of the individual case and of the norm that resolves que corresponding generic case. It is possible to speak about a true normative creation by the judge only when he — as is often the case in normative or axiological gaps — modifies the system, adding to it a new general norm. On this subject cf. E. BULYGIN, Sentenza giudiziaria e creazione di diritto, Rivista Internazionale di Filosofia del Diritto, 44, 164—180 (1967).

that they always do so. (It should be borne in mind that our purpose here is to describe not what judges in fact do, but what they ought to do according to the law, i. e. the judge system.) The possibility of discrepancies between the prescriptions of the primary system and the decision of the judge gives rise to interesting and complicated problems. Note that the discrepancy can appear not only when the judge makes a mistake thinking that the system says something different from what it really says, or when the judge deliberately puts aside the solution given by the primary system (either because he considers it is unfair or for other, less honourable, reasons), but also when one of the parties fails to prove the facts on which his case depends. Thus, for example, a person who has paid a dept has no longer an obligation in accordance with the primary system (as the obligation has been discharged by the payment), but if an action is brought against him by the ex-creditor and the defendant cannot prove the fact that he has paid, then he is ordered to pay again. Or when Sempronius who really has the right to a loan from Ticius but is not able to present his proof in time, loses his rights and his claim is rejected, though it was perfectly justified in accordance with the prescriptions of the primary system.

We shall not attempt to analyze these problems since they are not directly linked with our subject, but it is convenient to have them in mind, so as to avoid exaggerations typical of some writers with tendencies towards legal realism who from the fact that judicial decisions are not, sometimes, in agreement with the prescriptions of the primary system would infer either that the latter does not matter at all or that its norms "say what the judges say that they say" [3].

5. The Situation of the Judge in the Case of a Normative Gap

Let us now see how normative gaps in the primary system will affect the situation of the judge who has to resolve an individual case by applying this system. In this context we are only to take into account normative decisions, for — as we have already seen —

---

3 For a perceptive criticism of legal realism see H. L. A. HART, The Concept of Law, ch. VII, especially p. 138 ff.

the problem of the solution is irrelevant to declarative decisions, which only decide questions about the classification of individual cases. Consequently, in this section and in the two that follow we shall deal exclusively with normative decisions.

The generic obligation of the judge to ground his decision on the primary system brings about several *specific obligations,* according to the normative status that the action of the defendant which is under dispute has in the primary system. As this action can be qualified deontically in different ways, the judge will have different obligations, that is to say, he will have to resolve the case in different ways. We shall examine the types of case which may occur.

(i) *First Case.*

From the primary system it can be inferred that the defendant has an *obligation* to perform the action under dispute (and this action has therefore the character O). In this case, the judge has the *obligation to find against* the defendant. In so doing he also fulfils his generic obligation to decide the case.

(ii) *Second Case.*

From the primary system it can be inferred that the defendant is *permitted* to refrain from doing what the plaintiff claims he has to do. In this case the judge has the *obligation to reject* the petition. In so doing he also fulfils his obligation to decide the case. (The situation is similar when the defendant is forbidden to perform the action which the plaintiff wants him to perform. For if the action is forbidden, its omission is obligatory; and as in our terminology "obligatory" implies "permitted", it follows that the non-performance of the action is permitted.

(iii) Third Case.

From the primary system it cannot be inferred that the defendant has the obligation to perform the action in question, but neither can it be inferred that he is permitted to refrain from performing it. In other words, the action of the defendant is not deontically determined by the system. Hence we are in the presence of a normative gap. (Note that it may be either a total or a partial gap, as the situation does not change when the performance of the action is permitted provided that there is no norm permitting the defendant to refrain from it.)

When there is a gap, what ought the judge to do? Should he find against the defendant or reject the petition? The answer is clear:

if the primary system says nothing at all about the action under dispute, *the judge has no specific obligation* either to find against the defendant or to reject the suit. He has only the generic obligation to decide the case and he fulfils this obligation by deciding it in one of two possible ways: finding against the defendant or rejecting the petition (provided that these are the only two ways of deciding it). In other words, the judge has the obligation to decide, that is, to admit or to reject the suit, but he has neither an obligation to admit it nor an obligation to reject it. This may look paradoxical, but in fact there is no paradox here. Similar situations are often found in law: jurists deal with them under the heading of "alternative obligations". There is e. g. the well known case of Sempronius who has the obligation to give a cow or a horse to Ticius, but he has not the obligation to give Ticius a cow nor has he the obligation to give him a horse. He can fulfil his obligation by giving either of the two things, since he must give one of the two, but he is not obliged to give either in particular. The situation of the judge in the case of a normative gap is exactly the same. He too has no obligation to perform a particular action; he has only the obligation to, alternatively, admit *or* reject the suit. In short: the content of his obligation in the disjunction of two acts, but neither of the acts taken separately is obligatory.

It is important to bear this result in mind, since sometimes a fallacious argument based on the obligation to decide the case has been used to prove the non-existence of gaps in the law. The argument can be outlined thus: the judge is always obliged to give a decision, that is, he is obliged to admit or to reject the suit. If the defendant is obliged to behave in the way that the plaintiff demands, the judge is obliged to find against him; if the defendant is not obliged to do so, then the judge is not obliged to admit the suit and if he is not obliged to admit the suit, then he is obliged to reject it. Therefore — this is the conclusion reached by this argument — the judge is obliged to reject the suit in all cases in which he is not obliged to find against the defendant.

This argument presents an apparent analogy to a valid form of reasoning (the so-called disjunctive syllogism), in which from a disjunctive proposition and the negation of a disjunct the other disjunct is inferred. The validity of this form of argument is based on the incompatibility of the disjunction with the negation of both disjuncts. But in our case, the disjunctive sentence is normative, since it is modalized by the deontic operator O; hence it has the form "$O(p \lor q)$" ("It is obligatory to admit or to reject the suit"). And it is important not to confuse the obligation of performing a disjunctive act with the disjunction of two obligations, since the operator O is not distributive as regard the disjunction: "$O(p \lor q)$" does not imply "$Op \lor Oq$". Hence the norm "$O(p \lor q)$" is compatible with "$\sim Op$" and "$\sim Oq$". What is obligatory is the disjunction, not the disjuncts.

The intuitive plausibility of the argument we are criticizing derives partly from the fact that in some languages one and the same expression can be used to express a prohibition and also a mere absence of obligation. Thus, for instance, the Spanish term "no debe" can mean "need not" or "is not obliged" (absence of an obligation), but it can also mean "ought not" (i. e. a prohibition)[1]. Of course, if there would be a prohibition to admit the suit, then we could validly infer that the judge is obliged to reject it (provided he has the obligation to do one of the two things). But in our example there is no such prohibition, but the mere absence of a norm obligating the judge to find against the defendant. And from the obligation to decide the case and the absence of an obligation to admit the suit, an obligation to reject it cannot in any way be inferred. This shows that case (iii) — case of a normative gap — is very different from the other two cases. The characteristic feature of a case of gap is precisely the absence of any specific obligation for the judge[2].

6. Can the Judge Resolve a Case where there is a Normative Gap without Modifying the Law?

We have reached the conclusion that where gaps occur the judge has no specific obligation, but if he is forbidden to refrain from deciding the case, he must do one of two things, either find against the defendant or reject the suit. By doing one of these two things he

1 We understand that there is no such ambiguity in English, since "ought not" means always a prohibition and not a mere absence of obligation. Nevertheless, VON WRIGHT maintains that "ought not" admits of two interpretations: as expressing a prohibition or a permission (i. e. absence of an obligation). Cf. G. H. VON WRIGHT, Norm and Action, p. 136.

2 Case (iii) can, of course, only occur if the system is an open one, since a closed system has no gaps.

will perform his generic obligation to decide the case. But, how can he fulfil his obligation to ground his decision on the primary system?

It is clear that if the primary system does not say anything about the deontic status of the defendant's action, the judge cannot fulfil his obligation to ground his decision on this system, no matter which decision he arrives at. The most he can do in this situation is first modify the system, filling the gap, and then ground his decision on the new system. But in order to do this the judge must be authorized to modify the law — something that is at odds with the theory that the judge applies but does not create the law. It is true that some legal orders authorize the judge to behave as if he were a legislator[1]. Then the problem is easily solved: the judge first modifies the system, integrating into it a new norm which solves the gap case, and then, having removed the gap, proceeds in accordance with what the new system prescribes. But the fact that the judge is authorized to modify the law does not prove, of course, that normative gaps do not exist. On the contrary, only if we admit that there may be gaps, can we see any sense in a clause such as that in art. 1 of the Swiss Civil Code.

But if the judge is forbidden to modify the primary system, his situation is insoluble: he will necessarily let one of the obligations go unfulfilled. Indeed, if he resolves the individual case without at the same time resolving the corresponding generic case (that is to say, without modifying the system, since *ex hypothesis* the generic case has no solution), then his decision is not grounded on the primary system and therefore he violates his duty to judge only in accordance with the law. If he resolves the generic case, he modifies the system and as he is forbidden to do so, he performs a forbidden act. And finally, if he refrains from resolving the case, he violates his duty to judge. This shows that the three requirements are incompatible if normative gaps occur, as they can co-exist only if the system is complete. In the next chapter we shall deal with this problem again, but now we want to discuss the position of those writers who will not admit that the situation we have described as insoluble is really so.

The argument put forward to maintain that judges can resolve all the cases presented to them — including cases not resolved by

---

1 Swiss Civil Code, art. 1: "A défaut d'une disposition applicable, le juge prononce selon le droit coutumier, et a défaut d'une coutume, selon règles qu'il etablirait s'il avait a faire acte de legislateur."

any norm of the system — by applying the existing law without any need to modify it, is based on a supposed difference between decisions that admit the suit (positive decisions) and decisions that reject it (negative decisions). To find against the defendant the judge must quote a norm establishing the obligation to behave as the plaintiff demands; if such a norm does not exist (e. g. where there is a gap), then the judge has to "fill" the gap creating a norm, so as to be able to use it to justify his decision. But the situation is supposed to be radically different if the judge decides to reject the suit. Then there is no need — according to the doctrine we are examining — to introduce new norms into the system; it is enough to say that there is no norm imposing on the defendant the obligation to behave in the way the plaintiff claims. This negative fact (the non-existence of a norm) would be a good reason for a negative decision, which would thus be grounded on the prevailing law. Consequently, it is maintained that the judge can — in the sense of a logical and even empirical possibility — resolve all the cases for which there is no relevant norm without modifying the law.

HANS KELSEN is a typical exponent of this doctrine. Already in his *General Theory of Law and State*[2] he draws a distinction between the four following cases: (1) There is a general norm violated by the defendant; the judge has the duty to impose the sanction laid down by this norm. (2) There is no general norm which may be applied to the case, but there is a (permissive) rule of closure; the judge has the duty to reject the suit. (3) There is no norm which may be applied to the case and no rule of closure; if the judge decides to find against the defendant he must modify the existing law. (4) There is no norm applicable to the case and no rule of closure; the judge can decide to reject the suit on the ground that "no norm exists which obligates the defendant to the behaviour claimed by the plaintiff"[3]. In this case, the judge applies "the negative rule that nobody must be forced to observe conduct to which he is not obliged by law"[4]. In his *Reine Rechtslehre* (1960), KELSEN omits this last sentence in order to maintain — as we have seen in ch. VII, sect. 5 — that the judge applies the whole legal order[5].

---

2 H. KELSEN, General Theory of Law and State, Cambridge, Mass., 1945, p. 144—149.

3 Op. cit., p. 147.

4 Op. cit., p. 147.

5 H. KELSEN, Reine Rechtslehre, 2nd ed., Wien, 1960, p. 251.

We have to distinguish here between two different theses:
(1) The judge can resolve a case, even if there is no relevant norm,
and his decision, provided that it is a negative one, will be grounded
on the preexisting law; and (2) there are no gaps in law. Thesis (2)
purports to be based on thesis (1).

Thesis (2) has been already discussed in ch. VII, sect. 5, where
we reached the conclusion that KELSEN only apparently justifies (2)
by changing the meaning of the term "gap". We shall discuss now
the thesis (1).

Thesis (1) implies that the mere statement that the defendant
does not have the obligation attributed to him by the plaintiff is
sufficient to justify a negative decision. This thesis appears to be
plausible enough, and the majority of jurists would probably consider it to be quite cogent. Nevertheless, it is mistaken.

The mistake is based on the confusion between norms (solutions) and normative propositions, confusion encouraged by the
systematic ambiguity of such expressions as "p is not obligatory".
As expression of a norm, this sentence is equivalent to "$P\sim p$"
which implies the strong permission of "$\sim p$"; as a metalinguistic
proposition about the system, the sentence says that there is no
norm (in the system) of the form "Op", that is, it asserts the weak
permission of "$\sim p$". This is, therefore, the same ambiguity we have
discussed in ch. VII (sect. 2).

As we have already seen (sect. 2) a decision that resolves a normative question must have as its conclusion an individual norm
(solution) of the form "I order that p" (when the judge admits the
suit) or "I permit that $\sim p$" (when he rejects it). That is to say, the
judge does not give an information *about* the solution that corresponds to the case, but *gives* a solution, issuing an individual
norm. And this happens in a positive decision (that admits the suit)
as well as in a negative one (that rejects it). Therefore, if the latter
must be grounded on the law and must not be arbitrary, its ground
must be a general *norm* of the form "$\sim Op/q$" (which is equivalent
to "$P\sim p/q$") and not a mere proposition that p is not obligatory
in case q, since from a normative proposition no solution can be
derived.

In other words: the solution of an individual case is justified
only if it is grounded on the primary system, that is, if it is the
same solution that this system correlates with the corresponding

generic case. Therefore, the permission of $\sim p$ in the individual case (which is implied in the decision that rejects the suit) is justified only if the corresponding generic case is correlated by the system with the permission of $\sim p$ and this happens if and only if the system contains a norm which permits $\sim p$ in case q. This norm may be expressed by "$P\sim p/q$" or "$\sim Op/q$" or "$\sim Ph\sim p/q$", etc.[6] But where there is a gap no such norm exists (a gap is precisely a generic case which is not correlated with any solution), and therefore the judge cannot reject the suit without first modifying the system. Otherwise his decision will not be justified, i. e. it will not be grounded on the primary system.

We can thus conclude that there is no difference, in this respect, between a positive and a negative decision; in both cases the judge has first to fill the gap. If he fills it with a norm imposing an obligation on the defendant, he must find against him; if the new norm allows the defendant to refrain from doing what the plaintiff demands, then he must reject the suit. If he does not fill the gap and rejects the suit his decision is as far from being justified (grounded) as if he had admitted it. The mere fact that there is no norm imposing an obligation on the defendant does not justify the rejection of the suit.

Let us see an example. We can use for this purpose the model given in ch. I. Let us suppose that the judge is confronted with an individual case corresponding to the generic case 1 (ch. I, sect. 2); the plaintiff has proved that he is the lawful owner of a house and is now demanding its recovery; the defendant, in his turn, proves that he is a bona fide possessor and has purchased the house from another bona fide possessor by means of a contract of sale with consideration. Consequently he refuses to give back the house. Furthermore, let us suppose that the judge has only two norms similar to those of art. 2777 and 2778 (Argentine Civil Code), that is, his system is S_4. The judge finds that case 1 is not resolved by the system; there is a gap. What ought he to do?

We could imagine the plaintiff maintaining the following: "There is no norm referring to the case; this implies that there is no norm which allows the defendant to keep the house, therefore he must give it back." The defendant replies: "There is no norm obliging me to give back the house, therefore the suit must be rejected."

---

6   Cf. ch. VII, sect. 2.

Obviously, there is no reason to give preference to the defendant's position; his arguments are as convincing (or as little convincing) as those of the plaintiff. And if there is no norm obliging the refendant to give back the house, the judge has no obligation to find against him; but at the same time he is not obliged to reject the suit, for there is no norm which permits the defendant to keep the house.

To resolve the case in such a way that his decision would be grounded on the primary law, the judge must first resolve the generic case correlating it with a solution. If he correlates it with solution OR, he must admit the suit; if he correlates it with $\sim OR$, he must reject it. What he cannot do, unless his decision is to be arbitrary, is to reject the suit without resolving the generic case, for such a rejection would mean permitting the failure to return the house in this individual case. And to permit the failure to return something in an individual case is justified only if this is also permitted in analogous cases, that is, in the generic case (which is the class of all the individual cases which have the defining properties F, G and H).

It is noteworthy fact that all those writers who maintain that there is no gap in the Argentine Civil Code in case 1 argue that the case is solved by some norm, even if it is not solved by art. 2777 and 2778[7]. This involves an admission — tacit at least — on their part of our contention that the mere absence of a norm is not enough to justify a normative decision. If the system does not contain a norm that resolves the generic case, the rejection of a suit is as little justified as its admission. In fact, judges always try to solve the generic case, either by the analogous application of an existing norm or by creating a new norm.

Our contention is of course based on the belief that rejecting a suit implies permitting the defendant not to perform the action that the plaintiff demands of him, and to make this clear let us consider the following situation. Suppose a legal system with a gap; there is no norm relevant to the action p in case q. In other words, case q is not correlated by the system with any solution in terms of p. Furthermore, let us suppose that from a certain moment, judges invariable reject all suits in which the plaintiff claims that the defendant has the obligation to perform p in the circumstances q.

---

7 Cf. ch. I., sect. 6.

Would it not be correct to say that the system has been modified, that a new norm has appeared to the effect that p is not obligatory in q? And if we admit that there is a new norm (created by judges) to the effect that p is not obligatory in q, then $\sim p$ is strongly permitted, since the solutions "$\sim O p$" and "$P \sim p$" are equivalent.

We may therefore conclude that KELSEN's thesis (1) is false, and that judges cannot solve individual cases corresponding to a generic case that has no solution without first solving that generic case, or if they do not, their decision will be arbitrary. The alleged asymmetry between positive and negative decisions proves to be an illusion.

7. *Argumentum e contrario*

Another interesting attempt to minimize the importance of normative gaps at the level of judicial decisions, but without denying the possibility that they may occur, belongs to AMEDEO G. CONTE[1]. CONTE uses the term "closure" to refer to the alleged fact that a (primary) legal system makes it possible for a judge in resolving any dispute to ground his decision on this system without first modifying it, even if the system is not complete. Hence his thesis that all legal systems are closed (in his sense of the term), in spite of the fact that they may have gaps.

In CONTE's view, the possibility of reaching a decision in every case is based on the *argumentum e contrario*. He admits that this argument is logically invalid, but nonetheless he insists on saying that the decision of the judge is justified by it, provided that the totality of norms is used as the premiss of the argument.

There are several objections that may be made against this thesis, but we shall mention only a few of them. In the first place, if the *argumentum e contrario* is not logically valid, it is not clear how it can justify a decision. Unless the term "justify" is used in a rather peculiar way (in which case its meaning should be explained) the premisses of a logically invalid argument do not justify the conclusion.

---

1 A. G. CONTE, Décision complétude, clôture. A propos des lacunes en droit, Logique et Analyse 9, 1—18 (1966); Completezza e chiusura, Studi in memoria di Widar Cesarini Sforza, Milano, 1968, and Saggio sulla completezza degli ordinamenti giuridici, Torino, 1962.

In the second place, it would be convenient to limit the scope of the expression "the totality of norms" to the norms that constitute a certain set (e. g., the norms of a statute or a code, relevant to a certain problem). But even so, it is not clear how the *argumentum e contrario* is to operate if its premiss is the conjunction of *all* the norms in the set.

Let us consider the following example. Suppose that a system is composed of the two following norms:

N_1: "In circumstances A and B, p is obligatory."

N_2: "In circumstances non-A and non-B, p ist not obligatory."

We ask now: What is the deontic status of p (in this system) in the case where the circumstances are A and non-B?

The *argumentum e contrario* allows us to infer two incompatible conclusions, according to which of the two norms is adopted as a premiss. Starting from N_1, we may infer that p is not obligatory (because it is not the case that A and B). Starting from N_2, we may infer that p is obligatory, because it is not the case that non-A and non-B. Hence we arrive at contradictory results using the same formal scheme and starting from two norms that are not contradictory. (This is hardly surprising, since we have agreed that the argument used is not valid.) A harder question to answer is this: How can an *argumentum e contrario* proceed starting from the whole system, i. e., taking as its premiss both norms N_1 and N_2? What would be the conclusion of such an argument? Unless we can answer this question, CONTE's thesis must be rejected.

IX. Completeness as a Rational Ideal

1. Introduction

We have now reached a stage where it is appropriate to pause and cast a retrospective glance at the road we have travelled. What positive results have our discussions of normative systems achieved? Are the definitions of normative completeness and the correlative concept of a gap elaborated in this book really useful?

We can imagine a critic arguing: "You have defined a concept of completeness and given this a central position in your work with the discussions of all or nearly all the other problems you have considered revolving around it. But why should we prefer the concept as you define it to other possible definitions of 'completeness' or 'gap'? Definitions cannot be said to be true or false; they are only useful or useless for the task assigned to them. What task do you expect your concept of gap to perform? If your definition is not arbitrary the concept as you define it must reflect some important and typical use of the term 'gap'. That is, it must be a reconstruction of a concept actually used by those who deal with legal norms, but you have made no effort to show that your definition reflects a concept actually used by lawyers, judges or legal theorists. If it is a reconstruction it must be a reconstruction of something. What is this 'something' which your definition claims to reconstruct?"

Thus our imaginary critic. His questions are perfectly legitimate and they are not easy to answer. Like many authors harassed by critics, we might claim that we have been misunderstood and defend ourselves by alleging misinterpretation. Yet even though an answer of this kind seems evasive at first sight, it may perhaps — if adequately expanded — be the only appropriate one.

Our intention — we would reply — has been not to reconstruct an actual usage among jurists, but simply to make explicit something that is in the nature of an ideal that is shared by jurists with all other scientists. We might call it the ideal of completeness; it consists in a demand that all scientific systems — empirical, formal or normative — should be complete. This ideal of completeness is actual in the sense that it constitutes a prerequisite of all scientific inquiry. It is also a prerequisite of the activity pursued by jurists, if their work is to deserve the name of science. It is of fundamental importance to stress the fact that it is in no sense a political ideal arising from a particular ideology, but a purely rational ideal.

In this last chapter we shall try to adduce some of the grounds for this answer. We shall maintain in particular that the requirement of completeness in normative systems is an ideal rule, intrinsically bound up with a central function of the latter: making possible the ascription of normative characters to human action (sects. 2 and 3). The ideal of completeness — in contrast to other ideals which normative systems are also supposed to satisfy — is a rational ideal. In both the empirical sciences and the formal sciences we also find ideals that are analogous to that of normative completeness; all of which are only different manifestations of the Principle of Sufficient Reason (sects. 4 and 5).

But the ideal that we have endeavoured to make explicit must not be confused with the reality. From the requirement that normative systems should be complete, it cannot be inferred that they in fact are complete. Such an inference is based on a well known fallacy. Nevertheless, the belief that all legal systems are complete is not only shared by many legal theorists, but is also embodied in many positive legal orders. Indeed, it may be shown that the demands that such orders impose on judges presuppose that the completeness of a legal order is not simply an ideal, but a fact. In contrast to the ideal of completeness — which has a purely rational basis — this postulate of the completeness of the law fulfils a political function; it is a fiction that serves to conceal the inconsistency of certain political ideals that are deeply rooted in legal thought.

2. The Ideal of Normative Completeness

In ch. VII, when we dealt with the Postulate of the Necessary Completeness (hermetic plenitude) of the Law, we distinguished between the assertion that every legal order is complete and the demand that every legal order should be complete. This distinction has been very clearly formulated by CARNELUTTI, whom we quoted in this context (ch. VII, sect. 4). We have tried to show that the postulate of completeness when taken as an assertion that every legal system is necessarily complete (i. e. closed) is not justified. But it does not follow from this that the demand for completeness is not justified: to assert that completeness is a fact is one thing; to say that normative systems should be complete quite another. It is with this last proposition that we are now concerned.

What status has this demand? It seems clear that it is not a proposition of the kind that describes some actual state of affairs and therefore may be true or false. Nor is it a norm of conduct, since it does not establish any obligation, prohibition or permission; it short, it does not prescribe any behaviour. It seems reasonable to regard it as an *ideal rule* in VON WRIGHT's sense of this term[1]. It lays down what a normative system should be, that is, what properties or characteristics it must have in order to be a *good* normative system. Establishing as it does a standard or criterion for evaluating normative systems, this rule states an ideal: the ideal of normative completeness.

---

1 Cf. G. H. VON WRIGHT, Norm and Action, ch. 1.

In opposition to the opinion of many legal philosophers[2], we shall defend the view that this ideal is quite independent of political, moral or philosophical considerations. It is a purely rational ideal, being closely linked with explaining, with the giving of grounds or reasons, which is the rational activity *par excellence*. We shall now give a brief account of this activity.

3. Normative Justification

The most characteristic feature of scientific activity is its concern with rational explanation. To say that the central task of any science consists in providing a rational account of phenomena of a particular kind would hardly be an exaggeration.

"To explain the phenomena in the world of our experience, to answer the question 'why?' rather than only the question 'what?', is one of the foremost objectives of all rational inquiry; and especially, scientific research in its various branches strives to go beyond a mere description of its subject matter by providing an explanation of the phenomena it investigates."[1]

Scientific investigation assumes different forms with the different types of sciences: formal, empirical and normative.

In the *formal sciences* rational explanation appears as formal proof or derivation. To prove a theorem (logical or mathematical) is to deduce it from other theorems by means of the rules of inference.

In the *empirical sciences* explanation — often called causal explanation — consists in showing that the phenomenon to be explained is a particular case of a general law. (This phenomenon may be a particular fact or a general law.) Causal explanation involves the use of two types of sentences: those of the first type point to certain conditions existing before or simultaneously with the phenomenon to be explained. These are the antecedent conditions. Those of the second type express certain general laws. The phenomenon is explained if its description can be deduced from

---

2 Cf. N. Bobbio, Lacune del Diritto, Novissimo Digesto Italiano, vol. IX, pp. 419—424.

1 C. G. Hempel and P. Oppenheim, The Logic of Explanation, Philosophy of Science, 15 (1948), reprinted in H. Feigl and M. Brodbeck (editors), Readings in the Philosophy of Science, New York, 1953, p. 319 ff.

general laws and antecedent conditions. In other words: to explain a phenomenon is to show that its occurrence is in accordance with certain laws and in consequence of certain specific antecedent conditions[2].

When the subject of our inquiry is human behaviour, the question "why?" can take two different forms. In the first place, we might ask why a certain action took place or was performed by a certain agent. An appropriate answer to the question "Why did x do A?" would indicate the motives, that is, the facts that causally determine x's behaviour, and the measure of its adequacy would be the extent to which it gave a full causal explanation of the action. Sciences concerned with the causal explanation of human actions and activities are empirical (psychology, sociology, history, etc.).

But equally we might ask "why?" in relation to the deontic qualification that has been given to an action. In this case, we are concerned with explaining not the fact of the action, but its normative *status* according to some normative system. We are asking not why x did A, but why x *ought to* or *must not* or *may* do A. The appropriate answer to this type of question is not a causal explanation of the facts, but an account of our reasons for saying that the action is obligatory or prohibited or permitted. This is a special type of rational explanation that we shall call *normative justification*. It is *normative science,* such as the science of law (and perhaps ethics) which deals with normative justification.

Justifying the deontic qualification of an action by means of a normative system consists in showing that the obligation, the prohibition or the permission of this action can be inferred from (i. e. is a consequence of) this system. This qualification is seldom categorical, but almost always conditional upon the occurrence of certain facts or circumstances. So we can say that the deontic qualification (as obligatory, prohibited or permitted) of an action p in circumstances q is justified by a normative system if and only if this system correlates the case q with a solution whose deontic content is p.

Strictly speaking, what a normative system justifies is not the action, but the solution, that is, the deontic qualification of the action. It is only by an extension of the correct usage that we some-

---

2 We follow here the account given by HEMPEL and OPPENHEIM in the paper quoted above.

times talk of the justification of actions; but we must bear in mind
that the assertion that an action is justified by a normative system
means that from this system a deontic qualification of this action,
i. e. a solution, can be inferred[3].

Just as a causal explanation can be concerned as much with
particular facts as with general laws, so a normative justification can
refer as much to particular actions (individual solutions) as to generic actions (generic solutions).

There is a marked analogy between the logical structure of normative justification and that of causal explanation. In both cases
explaining (or justifying) consists in showing that the description
of a certain phenomenon (a solution) can be deduced from a scientific (normative) system that contains essentially general laws (general norms) and from certain sentences descriptive of the antecedent
conditions (or a case).

Just as a causal explanation can be used for different purposes,
e. g. for predicting future phenomena or explaining past facts, so
also can a normative justification be put to different uses. It can,
for example, serve as a guide for actions in the future or as a justification (in a more restricted sense) for actions in the past. The
logical structure of the operation is the same in both cases. Both
activities, causal explanation and normative justification, arise,
moreover, from one and the same need in man — his need, as
a rational being, to give a rational account of things, whether it is
an explanation of the phenomena of the world or a justification of
his own actions.

4. The Requirement of Completeness as a Rational Ideal

The ideal of completeness is not something that is peculiar to the
normative sciences; we also demand that scientific (empirical)
systems should be complete, in the sense of giving explanations for
all the phenomena in a certain field. In the field of empirical sciences this requirement seems such an obvious one that nobody would

---

3 To speak about the justification of actions leads to certain linguistic difficulties in the case of prohibition. It looks odd to say that p
is justified by the system α because the prohibition of p is a consequence
of α (in such a case we would rather say that it is the omission of p that
is justified). This difficulty does not arise if we bear in mind that what
is justified here is the solution, i. e. a deontic qualification of p.

question it: a theory that left unexplained some phenomena belonging to the class of those it purported to explain would be regarded as defective and in need of replacement by another, more complete, theory.

This requirement makes sense only in relation to explicable phenomena, that is, those which, in principle, *can* be explained. It would be absurd to expect a scientific system to explain phenomena that were not explicable, that is, phenomena which could not be explained. On the other hand, the very notion of a phenomenon which cannot be explained seems absurd; such a phenomenon would be essentially irrational, and human reason is loath to admit such a possibility. In fact, there are undoubtedly many phenomena which science cannot account for; but the fact that a phenomenon has not been explained does not in any way prove that it cannot be explained. Failure to find an explanation is no proof of the impossibility of explaining the phenomenon: it shows only that we have not yet found the appropriate theory. Scientific inquiry presupposes that all phenomena under investigation are, in principle, explicable, and this presupposition is the basis of the demand for completeness in scientific systems.

This presupposition, which in (the philosophy of) the empirical sciences is known as the Principle of Determinism or Law of Universal Causation, may be regarded as a particular version of a still more general principle according to which everything has a ground or reason: *nihil est sine ratione*. This is the Principle of Sufficient Reason which according to LEIBNIZ is one of the two great principles that govern our thought and on which all our reasoning is based (the other is the Principle of Contradiction, to which we shall refer later).

Similarly, the ideal of normative completeness, that is, the requirement that all normative systems should be complete in the sense that they must be able to solve all possible cases, presupposes that all cases can be solved. (Our analyses have shown that this presupposes the existence of a Universe of Cases and a Universe of Solutions.) To say that all cases can be solved means that for each case it is possible to construct a normative system such that it will correlate this case with a solution. We must reject as irrational, for it is as intolerable to reason as the notion of inexplicable (i. e., uncaused) phenomena, the hypothesis that there are insoluble cases, that is, situations where there is no ground (and, moreover, can be none) for preferring any particular line of action — in other words, situations in which any choice is essentially arbitrary.

The presupposition that all cases can be solved is a particular version (we might call it the *normative version*) of the same Principle of Sufficient Reason which — as we have pointed out is the basis of the requirement of completeness in scientific systems. When we asserted that the ideal of normative completeness was a purely rational ideal, we meant precisely that this ideal is grounded on the Principle of Sufficient Reason and is independent of any political or philosophical ideology.

5. *Its Scope and Limits*

The requirement of completeness is not the only standard by which we evaluate normative systems. There is the ideal of consistency which requires that no case should have two or more incompatible solutions. This ideal is grounded on the Principle of Contradiction, which has been already mentioned as one of LEIBNIZ' two basic principles of reason.

The rational character of the ideal of consistency has never seriously been questioned; to link the requirement of consistency with any religious or political position seems quite absurd. With the ideal of completeness the situation is different, as it is frequently assumed to be bound up with particular ideologies: positivism, liberalism, etc. This assumption is, however, a mistaken one that is based, among other things, on the failure to draw a clear distinction between the ideal of completeness and what we have called the postulate of completeness, i. e. between the requirement that normative systems should be complete and the assertion that some or all of them are in fact complete. In order to avoid this confusion it would be advisable to determine the scope and the limits of this ideal.

In the two preceding sections we have stressed the analogy between the ideal of normative completeness and the corresponding ideal in the empirical science, based on the analogy between normative justification and causal explanation. But analogy does not mean identity; it is therefore essential to point out the differences as well as the similarities. Over and above the differences in the subject matter of the explanation (empirical facts vs. solutions) and in the character of the general laws (descriptive vs. normative), which we have already mentioned, we must indicate two further differences, the second of which is especially important.

(a) In the so-called causal explanation, antecedent conditions are often (though not always) regarded as being the cause of the phenomenon to be explained, which is the corresponding effect. The nature of this causal relation is far from clear, for, as RUSSELL says: "... the word 'cause' is so inextricably bound up with misleading associations as to make its complete extrusion from philosophical vocabulary desirable." [1] (We have used the term "causal explanation" for reasons of pure convenience and without implying commitment to any of the theories about causality.) But whatever the meaning of the term "cause", it is still true that the situation in normative sciences is radically different: the case is never a "cause" of the solution.

(b) The second and more important difference concerns the conditions that the sentences of the system must satisfy. In a scientific explanation the sentences of the system used to explain a phenomenon must be *true*. This is part of what HEMPEL and OPPENHEIM call "empirical conditions of adequacy" [2]. Now, the selection of the sentences for the construction of a normative system is certainly not arbitrary. But truth is not a criterion for identifying the sentences that may occur in a normative system, since normative sentences are neither true nor false. The term that is usually applied to the sentences of a normative system is "valid" and the criteria for determining which sentences are valid vary according to the type of sentences. For the justification of deontic qualifications of actions (i. e. solutions) different types of normative sentences can be used. According to context, we have recourse to legal, moral, religious norms, to the rules of a game, etc. Consequently, we must distinguish between justifications that are legal, moral, religious and so on.

The criteria for determining the validity of legal sentences are certainly not identical with those used to establish the validity of moral rules or the rules of a game. But normative justification always presupposes the existence of a set of sentences that are regarded as valid, and in this sense it is *relative* to a criterion of validity.

---

1 B. RUSSELL, On the Notion of Cause, with Applications to the Free-Will Problem, Misticism and Logic (1918), reprinted in H. FEIGL and M. BRODBECK (editors), Readings in the Philosophy of Science, New York, 1953, pp. 387—407.

2 Op. cit., p. 322.

The fact that normative justification is relative in this way allows us to qualify the corresponding sciences as *dogmatic;* so we speak of legal dogmatics, religious dogmatics and so on.

Perhaps the most important difference between the empirical sciences and causal explanation on the one hand, and the normative sciences and justification on the other, lies in the difference between validity and truth. We shall make no attempt to give an exhaustive characterization of this difference. *One* of the differential features is the following: the criteria of (empirical) truth are not conventional; whether an empirical sentence is true or not is quite independent of our conventions. The criteria of validity, on the other hand, may (though they need not) be *conventional*. There is a considerable variation in the extent to which the validity of normative sentences is a matter of convention. The rules of a game like chess which are purely conventional are at one end of the scale; positive legal norms are also conventional, though to a lesser degree, in the sense that the validity of legal norms depends on certain basic conventions that are much less easy to modify than the rules of a game. The degree of "conventionality" varies in positive morals: it is higher in the rules refering to sexual morality, and lower where other questions are concerned. At the other end of the scale we find the norms of absolute (the so-called rational) morality and natural law; here the conventional character is non-existent, but the difference with regard to truth also vanishes; why cannot we say — granted that they exist — that the norms of rational morality or natural law are true?

It is because of this conventional element in the criteria of validity that normative systems may be "created" by man in a sense that is completely inapplicable to scientific systems. (The idea of a scientific legislator is quite absurd.)

The fact that normative justification is relative to a normative system does not mean that we cannot ask for a justification of the normative system itself. We are then confronted by a second level justification. Justification at a higher level is, in turn, relative to a set of sentences which may belong to the same type as the sentences of the first system or to a different type. Thus, for example, a legal system may be justified by reference to another legal system (as for instance, a provincial system may be justified by a federal system) or by means of a moral criterion or an ideal of justice. In fact, what is customarily required of a legal system is that it should satisfy not only the rational ideals of consistency and completeness, but also some ideal of justice, which may be bound up with philosophical conceptions, religious beliefs or political ideologies. It can also happen that the ideal of completeness is sacrificed to considerations of value. A legislator may leave gaps in a system, i. e. he may leave certain cases without solution, because he believes that any solution he provides may result in injustice. In such situations, the legislator usually delegates to another (administrative or judicial) authority the office of filling the gap. But this by no means implies that the ideal of completeness has been abandoned: the incomplete system as such is defective and must be made complete by another organ. The requirement of completeness is still in force.

6. A Rationalist Illusion

To say that the completeness of normative systems is an ideal and that this ideal presupposes that all cases are soluble is quite different from saying that the ideal has been realized in a particular system and that all the possible cases are really resolved in that system. We find it necessary to insist on this distinction, which may seem obvious, because many legal philosophers and scientists maintain not merely that one legal system or another is complete (which may well be true), but that all legal systems are complete. This last contention — which has been already discussed under the heading of "Postulate of Completeness" — really amounts to a confusion between ideal and reality. To believe that all legal systems are complete because they ought to be so is an illusion; to deduce the existence of completeness from the demand for completeness is a fallacy. And though the demand is rational, reason cannot justify the inference. So if by "rationalism" is meant the tendency to ascribe to reason faculties greater than those it really possesses, then we may well call the belief in the necessary completeness of legal systems a rationalist illusion.

Nevertheless, this belief has not only been shared by a great number of legal theorists; it is also presupposed in many positive legal orders, where certain demands made upon judges simply assume that the legal order is complete and that the Postulate of the Completeness of the Law is, accordingly, true.

These demands take the form of three principles which seem perfectly reasonable if we consider them separately, but which are inconsistent when taken together, as they presuppose something that is not in fact always present: the completeness of the law.

These three principles are:

(A) *Principle of unavoidability:* Judges must resolve all the cases submitted to them within the sphere of their competence.

This requirement often appears in positive law in the form of a prohibition against declining to judge (cf. ch. VIII, sect. 4), and even though each judge is obliged to resolve only the cases within his competence, it is supposed that the competence of all the judges, taken together, is exhaustive. So it is assumed that for each and every possible case there is a judge with competence and the obligation to provide a solution.

(B) *Principle of justification:* A judicial decision requires a ground or reason and judges must state the reasons for their decisions.

Not only is it the unavoidable duty of a judge to resolve all cases submitted to him within the limits of his competence; it is also required of him that his decision should not be arbitrary and that he should give the reasons justifying the solution he adopts. The purpose of this principle is to eliminate one of the possible sources of the injustice, which might infect judicial decisions if judges were free to choose one or another solution without sufficient reasons.

This requirement is also almost universally embodied in positive law in the form of obligations imposed upon judges by rules (or codes) of procedure.

(C) *Principle of legality:* Judicial decisions must be grounded on legal norms.

This principle is complementary to the previous one: it is held that every decision requires not merely grounds, but grounds of a special kind: they must be legal. The judge must not go beyond the sphere of law, by appealing to non-legal (e. g. moral) norms, except in cases where the law itself authorizes him to do so. And even in these cases the ultimate ground for the decision will obviously be a legal norm.

This principle imposes a restriction on the selection of grounds, limiting the range of sentences which may appear as acceptable grounds.

We can summarize the three principles mentioned above by saying:

(D) Judges must resolve all cases submitted to them within the limits of their competence by means of decisions grounded on legal norms.

Now, it seems reasonable to believe that nobody can be obliged to do what it is impossible for him to do: *ultra posse nemo obligatur*. This idea frequently appears in the philosophical tradition associated with the name of KANT, as the principle that ought implies can.

(E) Every obligation implies the possibility of performing the obligatory action.

It would seem virtually unthinkable to reject this principle, as its negation would imply that there could be an obligation to perform an action which it was impossible to perform, and this seems to make no sense, or at least to be incompatible with the concept of obligation. Since, when a duty is imposed, the intention is that the duty should be performed, the impossibility of performing the required action makes nonsense of the act of imposing the obligation.

In this sense it seems reasonable to assume that if a positive legal order imposes on judges the obligation expressed in (D), then it is presumed to be within their power to fulfil this obligation. In other words, from (D) and (E) the following proposition can be inferred:

(F) Judges *can* resolve all cases submitted to them within the limits of their competence by means of decisions grounded on legal norms.

But (F) implies the following proposition:

(G) The set of all legal norms contains normative grounds for the solution of any case submitted to a judge.

Proposition (G) is purely and simply the Postulate of the Necessary Completeness (hermetic plenitude) of the Law, which we have already discussed. Indeed, (G) says that all legal orders resolve all possible cases, from which it may be inferred that they are complete, i. e. have no gaps.

It is clear, then, that from these three principles which are customarily accepted by jurists and embodied in positive law, the Postulate of Completeness can be deduced. This means that the requirements they express presuppose the truth of this postulate. But the postulate is true only in exceptional instances, that is, in relation to closed systems, such as penal law that contains the rule of closure *nullum crimen*. When applied to the majority of legal systems, the postulate, as we have already seen, is false. Hence it follows that the three principles (A, B and C) are jointly inconsistent.

7. The Ideological Function of the Postulate of Completeness

The Postulate of Completeness is a fiction designed to conceal the fact that the requirements embodied in the principles of unavoidability, justification and legality when taken together express inconsistent demands since they impose on judges obligations that are impossible to fulfil. But these principles are deeply rooted in legal thought and it is this fact which accounts for the extraordinary vitality of the Postulate of Completeness.

In order to understand why these principles are so dear to legal theorists, we shall examine them and their grounds in greater detail.

The principle of unavoidability is grounded on practical considerations which seem to be very reasonable. If the law is to be an effective tool for supporting the social order and making it possible for men to live together in society, it must supply the necessary means of resolving all the conflicts of interest that can arise as a natural consequence of the fact that the individuals who make up society as a whole have incompatible interests. To abandon this principle would mean permitting judges to leave certain conflicts without any solution, which would undoubtedly involve serious practical problems. This principle does not, therefore, represent any special political ideology.

Nor has the principle of justification ideological implications. This principle expresses the demand that judicial decisions should be *rational* and not arbitrary. Decisions are rational when they are grounded on (justified by) general norms.

We may add that this insistence on rationality entails that the reasons on which the decision is grounded cannot depend on the judge's own will; he cannot freely create these reasons, but must extract them from somewhere; otherwise the justification would be only apparent, and the decision arbitrary and irrational. This shows that the familiar doctrine that judges apply but do not create law has in it a kernel of truth. It may be reformulated in this way: if the judge's decisions must be rationally justified, then the grounds for the decision cannot be created by him; the judge "applies" but does not create these grounds. In this reformulation the doctrine loses its ideological and political connotations and limits itself to expressing a purely rational requirement[1].

Of the three principles the only one that has an ideological basis is the principle of legality. Indeed, this principle is bound up with the ideologies of Positivism and Liberalism. The expression "legal positivism" is notoriously ambiguous[2], but in *one* of its senses, positivism may be characterized as the conception of law as a set of norms issued by human (positive) legislator, i. e. norms that are formally established[3]. In this sense it is a doctrine about the sources of law[4]. In its more extreme form, which is represented by the French exegetic school of the early nineteenth century, it regards formal legislation as the sole source of law; accordingly, only enacted laws issued by the legislative power (statutes) are considered valid legal norms and, by virtue of the principle of legality, admissible for the justification of judicial decisions. Other less rigid versions of positivism admit as well as statutes other kinds of enacted law and even custom and precedent.

Positivism (in this sense) has had as its central feature the ideal of completeness[5]; in its beginnings it made great efforts to realize

---

1 BOBBIO associates the dogma of completeness with the liberal theory of State and, especially, with the doctrine of the separation of powers. Lacune del Diritto, Novissimo Digesto Italiano, vol. IX, 419—424. However, in our "deduction" of the Postulate of Completeness from the principles of positive law we had no need to have recourse to these doctrines. And even though the doctrine of the separation of powers is an expression of liberalism (that is, of an ideology), what is involved in the principle of justification is only the requirement that judicial decisions should be rational (which is also reflected in this doctrine) and not its ideological character.

2 Cf. H. L. A. HART, Positivism and the Separation of Law and Morals, Harvard Law Review 71, 606—612 (1958); ALF ROSS, Validity and the Conflict between Legal Positivism and Natural Law, Revista Juridica de Buenos Aires IV, p. 46—91 (1961); N. BOBBIO, El problema del positivismo jurídico, Buenos Aires, 1965.

3 Cf. ALF ROSS, On Law and Justice, London, 1958, p. 100—101.

4 J. SPIROPOULOS (Die allgemeinen Rechtsgrundsätze) characterizes this type of positivism as "Quellenpurismus" (quoted by N. BOBBIO in Principi Generali di Diritto, Novissimo Digesto Italiano).

5 Cf. N. BOBBIO, El problema del positivismo jurídico, Buenos Aires, 1965, p. 45.

this ideal — by means of codification — but it ended by confusing ideal with reality, dogmatically declaring that all positive legal orders are complete. This dogma is necessary to preserve the principle of legality, which, if taken in conjunction with the other two principles, leads — as we have seen — to consequences that are not easy to justify.

Curiously enough, this dogma of completeness is held not only by the supporters of positivism, but also by its opponents. Indeed, many an attack on positivism, from GÉNY to our days, has had as its sole aim widening the set of admissible (valid) norms by integrating it with customary law, moral principles, natural law, judicial precedents and the like. But the next step is to ascribe to the set that has been enlarged in this way the same characteristic that it had before — in the positivist conception — that of being closed. In this way certain opponents of positivism repeat at a different level the fallacy of confusing ideal with reality[6].

It is this same confusion which, at least in part, is responsible for the fact that some writers, after rejecting the Postulate of Completeness as a positivist dogma, go on to attribute, quite mistakenly, the ideal of completeness to the same ideological origin[7].

---

6 For example, R. DWORKIN, Is a Law a System of Rules? Essays in Legal Philosophy (F. SUMMERS, editor), Oxford, 1968.

7 N. BOBBIO, Lacune del Diritto, Novissimo Digesto Italiano, vol. IX, 419—424.

Appendix:
Some Definitions and Theorems

The main ideas contained in this book can be formulated more precisely as purely syntactical notions, referred to the syntactical structure of a language whose (main) function is to express norms regulating human behaviour.

In order to describe the structure of this normative (prescriptive) language (i. e. the object-language of our concern), we shall use the following symbols in our metalanguage: 'x', 'y', 'z', etc. as syntactical variables for individuals of the object-language; 'α', 'β', 'γ', etc. as variables for sets of individuals, and the usual symbols of the calculus of classes such as: '$\subset$' (inclusion), '$+$' (sum), '$\cdot$' (product), '$-$' (complement or difference), '$\wedge$' (emptly set), 'X' (Cartesian product), '$\in$' (membership), '$\notin$' (not-membership). The symbol '$\{x| -x-\}$' denotes the set of entities that satisfy the condition '$-x-$'.

The object-language contains two finite sets of primitive constants: $P_1, P_2 \ldots P_n$ and $A_1, A_2 \ldots A_m$. (In the intended interpretation the P-constants stand for the basic properties referred to in the text, and the A-constants stand for the basic actions.) It also contains as logical constants the negation, the conjunction and the deontic permissive operator, denoted in the metalanguage by '$-$', '$\cdot$' and 'P', respectively. Other truth-functional connectives such as disjunction and material implication and the deontic operator for obligation are defined in the usual way and denoted in the meta-language by 'v', '$\rightarrow$' and '0' ('0' being an abbreviation of '$-P-$').

Universe of Properties (UP):

D 1) Every non-empty subset of the set of the P-constants is a *UP*. $UP_1, UP_2 \ldots UP_{2^n-1}$ is the sequence of the *UPs* of the language. (Therefore $\{UP_1, UP_2 \ldots UP_{2^n-1}\} = \{\alpha | \alpha \subset \{P_1, P_2 \ldots P_n\}$ and $\alpha \neq \wedge\}$).

Universe of Actions (UA):

D 2) Every non-empty subset of the A-constants is a UA.

UA_1, $UA_2 \ldots UA_{2^m-1}$ is the sequence of the UAs of the language. (Therefore $\{UA_1,\ UA_2 \ldots UA_{2^m-1}\} = \{\alpha | \alpha \subset \{A_1,\ A_2. \ldots A_m\}$ and $\alpha \neq \wedge\}$).

In order to define the set of all meaningful expressions of the object-language we introduce the auxiliary notions of closure of a set [Clos (α)] and normative closure of a set [N Clos (α)].

D 3) Clos (α) is the smallest set β such that (1) $\alpha \subset \beta$ and (2) if $x, y \in \beta$, then $-x, (x.y) \in \beta$.

D 4) N Clos (α) is the smallest set β such that (1) for any x, if $x \in$ Clos (α), then $Px \in \beta$, and (2) for any x and y, if $x, y \in \beta$, then $-x, (x.y) \in \beta$.

Let M be the set of all well-formed (meaningful) expressions of the object-language.

D 5) $M = $ Clos $(\{P_1, P_2 .. P_n\} + N$ Clos $(\{A_1, A_2 .. A_m\})) + $ Clos $(\{A_1, A_2 .. A_m\})$.

Immediate consequences of this definition are the following theorems:

T 1) Clos $(\{P_1, P_2 \ldots P_n\}) \subset M$

T 2) N Clos $(\{A_1, A_2 \ldots A_m\}) \subset M$

T 3) Clos $(\{P_1, P_2 .. P_n\} + N$ Clos $(\{A_1, A_2 .. A_m\})) \subset M$

T 4) Clos $(\{A_1, A_2 .. A_m\}) \subset M$

T 5) N Clos $(\{P_1, P_2 .. P_n\}) \subset -M$

T 6) Clos $(\{P_1, P_2 .. P_n\} + \{A_1, A_2 \ldots A_m\}) \subset -M$

T 7) N Clos $(N$ Clos $(\{A_1, A_2 \ldots A_m\})) \subset -M$

T 2) and T 5) mean that whereas the deontic modalizations of A-expressions are meaningful, the modalizations of P-expressions are not. T 6) means that the truth-functional combinations of P- and A-expressions are not meaningful. T 7) excludes the possibility of iterated modalities.

Universe of Cases (UC):

To every UP_i $(1 \leq i \leq 2^n - 1)$ of the UP-sequence corresponds a unique set UC_i such that

D 6) $UC_i = \{x | (E\alpha) \ \alpha \subset UP_i$ and $x = (\underset{y \in \alpha}{\Pi y} . \underset{y \in (UP_i - \alpha)}{\Pi \bar{y}})\}$,

where $(\underset{y \in \alpha}{\Pi y})$ denotes the conjunction of all the elements of α, and $(\underset{y \in \alpha}{\Pi \bar{y}})$ denotes the conjunction of the negations of the elements of α.

In this way we get the following sequence of UCs:

$$\{UC_1, UC_2 \ldots UC_{2^n-1}\}$$

In a similar way we obtain for each UA_i a set of state-descriptions of actions DUA_i, according to the following definition:

D 7) $DUA_i = \{x \mid (E\alpha) \subset UA_i \text{ and } x = (\underset{y \in \alpha}{\Pi y} . \underset{y \in (UA_i - \alpha)}{\Pi \bar{y}})\}$

This gives rise to the following sequence of sets of state-descriptions: $DUA_1 \ DUA_2 \ldots DUA_{2^m-1}$.

For each DUA_i (and consequently for each UA_i) there is a set of maximal solutions $US \max_i$ and a set of minimal solutions $US \min_i$.

D 8) $US \max_i = \{x \mid (E\alpha) \ \alpha \subset DUA_i \text{ and } \alpha \neq \wedge \text{ and } x = (\underset{y \in \alpha}{\Pi P y} . \underset{y \in (DUA_i - \alpha)}{\Pi - P y})\}$

D 9) $US \min_i = \{x \mid (E\alpha) \ \alpha \subset DUA_i \text{ and } \alpha \neq DUA_i \text{ and }$
$\quad x = (\underset{y \in \alpha}{\Sigma P y} \vee \underset{y \in (DUA_i - \alpha)}{\Sigma - P y})\}$

(The symbol $\underset{y \in \alpha}{\Pi P y}$ denotes the conjunction of all P-modalizations of the elements of α; the symbol $\underset{y \in \alpha}{\Pi - P y}$ denotes the conjunction of all the negations of P-modalizations of the elements of α, and the symbols $\underset{y \in \alpha}{\Sigma P y}$ and $\underset{y \in \alpha}{\Sigma - P y}$ denote the corresponding disjunctions.)

Obvious consequences of the preceding definitions are:

T 8) $UC_i \subset \text{Clos} \ (UP_i)$

T 9) $US \max_i \subset N \ \text{Clos} \ (UA_i)$

T 10) $US \min_i \subset N \ \text{Clos} \ (UA_i)$

Let L be the set of all elements of M which express laws of logic. L includes the laws of the usual bivalent truth-functional logic and the specific deontic laws.

Definition of L:

Let L_0 be the set of all truth-functional valid elements of M. L is the smallest set β such that:

(1) $[O \ (x \to y) \to (O x \to O y)] \in \beta$, for every $x, y \in Cl \ (\{A_1 \ldots A_m\})$

(2) $L_0 \subset \beta$

(3) If $x \in L_0$, then $O x \in \beta$, where $x \in Cl \ (\{A_1 \ldots A_m\})$

(4) If $-x \in L_0$, then $-O x \in \beta$, where $x \in Cl \ (\{A_1 \ldots A_m\})$

(5) If $x, (x \to y) \in \beta$, then $y \in \beta$, for any x, y.

The following theorems express the main properties of UC, $US \max$ and $US \min$.

T 11) If $x \in US$ max$_i$ and $y \in N$ Clos (UA_i), then $(x \rightarrow y) \in L$ or $(x \rightarrow -y)$
$\in L$, for any x and any y.

T 12) If $x \in US$ min$_i$ and $y \in N$ Clos (UA_i), then $(y \rightarrow x) \in L$ or $(-y \rightarrow x)$
$\in L$, for any x and any y.

T 13) For any x, if $x \in UC_i$, then $-x \notin L$.

T 14) $(\underset{x \in UC_i}{\Sigma x}) \in L$

T 15) For any x, if $x \in US$ max$_i$, then $-x \notin L$.

T 16) $(\underset{x \in US \, \text{max}_i}{\Sigma x}) \in L$

T 17) For any x, if $x \in US$ min$_i$, then $x \notin L$.

T 18) $(\underset{x \in US \, \text{min}_i}{\Sigma -x}) \in L$

T 19) If $x \neq y$, then $(x \rightarrow -y) \in L$, for any x, $y \in UC_i$.

T 20) If $x \neq y$, then $(x \rightarrow -y) \in L$, for any x, $y \in US$ max$_i$.

T 21) If $x \neq y$, then $(-x \rightarrow y) \in L$, for any x, $y \in US$ min$_i$.

The importance of T 11) will become evident later, in connection with the notion of completeness (cf. T 39), whereas T 12) has a bearing on the notion of normative set (see below). The elements of each UC and each US max are jointly exhaustive (T 14 and T 16), mutually exclusive (T 19 and T 20) and not logically false (T 13 and T 15). To the exclusiveness of the elements of US max corresponds the property of being logically complementary of the elements of each US min (T 21).

Other notions that has been used in the text are that of cases, solutions and deontic contents. The corresponding definitions are:

D 10) *Case:* $Ca \, (UP_i) = \text{Clos} \, (UP_i) - (L + \{x| -x \in L\})$

D 11) Complex case: $CCa \, (UP_i) = Ca \, (UP_i) - UC_i$

The elementary cases corresponding to UP_i are the elements of UC_i.

D 12) *Deontic content:* $\text{Con} \, (UA_i) = \text{Clos} \, (UA_i) - (L + \{x| -x \in L\})$

D 13) *Solution:* $\text{Sol} \, (UA_i) = N \text{ Clos} \, (UA_i) - (L + \{x| -x \in L\})$

T 22) $UC_i \subset Ca \, (UP_i)$

T 23) $DUA_i \subset \text{Con} \, (UA_i)$

T 24) US max$_i \subset \text{Sol} \, (UA_i)$

T 25) US min$_i \subset \text{Sol} \, (UA_i)$

Every solution implies some minimal solution and is implied by some maximal solution:

T 26) If $x \in \text{Sol} \, (UA_i)$, then there is a $y \in US$ min$_i$ such that $(x \rightarrow y) \in L$.

T 27) If $x \in \text{Sol} \, (UA_i)$, then there is a $y \in US$ max$_i$ such that $(y \rightarrow x) \in L$.

As a generalization of the notions of UC and US max, we introduce the notion of a *division:*

D 14) $\mathrm{Div} = \{\alpha | (1)\ \alpha \subset M$

(2) α has at least two different elements,

(3) $(\underset{x \in \alpha}{\Sigma} x) \in L$

(4) for any x, y, if x, $y \in \alpha$ and $x \neq y$, then $(x \rightarrow -y) \in L$.

(5) for any x, if $x \in \alpha$, then $-x \notin L\}$.

T 28) $UC_i \in \mathrm{Div}$

T 29) $US\ \max_i \in \mathrm{Div}$

D 15) $\alpha \overset{d}{<} \beta$ (α is a *finer division* than β) if and only if:

(1) α, $\beta \in \mathrm{Div}$

(2) for every $x \in \alpha$, there is a $y \in \beta$, such that $(x \rightarrow y) \in L$.

(3) there is an $x \in \alpha$, such that there is no $y \in \beta$, for which it is true that $(y \rightarrow x) \in L$.

T 30) $UP_i \subset UP_j$ if and only if $UC_j \overset{d}{<} UC_i$ (for $i \neq j$).

T 31) $UA_i \subset UA_j$ if and only if $US\ \max_j \overset{d}{<} US\ \max_i$ (for $i \neq j$).

The notion of a consequence:

D 16) $Cn\ (\alpha)$ is the smallest set $\beta \subset M$, such that (1) $L \subset \beta$,

(2) $\alpha \subset \beta$, and

(3) for every x and every y, if x, $(x \rightarrow y) \in \beta$, then $y \in \beta$.

Deductive correlation established by a set of meaningful expressions:

D 17) $\overset{\alpha}{\rightarrow} = \{\langle x, y \rangle | y \in Cn\ (\alpha + \{x\})\}$

(The sign '$\langle x, y \rangle$' refers to the ordered pair of x and y, and $\{x\}$ denotes the class whose only element is x).

Deductive correlation with limited domain and counterdomain:

D 18) $\beta \overset{\alpha}{\rightarrow} \gamma = [\overset{\alpha}{\rightarrow} \cdot (\beta \times \gamma)]$

T 32) $Cn\ (\wedge) = L$

T 33) If $\alpha \subset M$, then $\alpha \subset Cn\ (\alpha)$

T 34) If $\alpha \subset M$, then $Cn\ (Cn\ (\alpha)) = Cn\ (\alpha)$

T 35) If $\alpha \subset M$, then $Cn\ (\alpha)$ is identical with the sum of the consequences of all finite subsets of α.

T 36) $x \overset{\alpha}{\rightarrow} y$ if and only if $y \in Cn\ (\alpha + \{x\})$, and also if and only if $(x \rightarrow y) \in Cn\ (\alpha)$.

(Here the symbol '$x \overset{\alpha}{\rightarrow} y$' is used as an alternative expression for '$\langle x, y \rangle \in \overset{\alpha}{\rightarrow}$').

Completeness (*Cm*):

D 19) $Cm\,(UC_i,\ US\ \max_j) = \{\alpha | UC_i \subset D'\ (UC_i \overset{\alpha}{\to} US\ \max_j)\}$
(where the symbol $D'R$ refers to the domain of the relation R.)

As to every *UP* corresponds one and only one *UC*, and to every *UA* corresponds one and only one *US* max, instead of saying that α is complete in relation to UC_i and *US* max$_j$, we can also speak of completeness in relation to UP_i and UA_j [$Cm\,(UP_i,\ UA_j)$]. Both expressions may be used to identify the same family of sets.

T 37) $\alpha \in Cm\,(UC_i,\ US\ \max_j)$ if and only if for every $x \in UC_i$ there is some $y \in US\ \max_j$ such that $x \overset{\alpha}{\to} y$.

T 38) $\alpha \in Cm\,(UP_i,\ UA_j)$ if and only if $(x \overset{\alpha}{\to} y)$ or $(x \overset{\alpha}{\to} -y)$, for every $x \in UC_i$ and every $y \in N$ Clos (UA_j).

T 39) $\alpha \in Cm\,(UP_i,\ UA_j)$ if and only if $(x \overset{\alpha}{\to} y)$ or $(x \overset{\alpha}{\to} -y)$, for every $x \in UC_i$ and every $y \in$ Sol (UA_j).

T 39) shows that a set α is complete when every possible solution is implied or excluded by α for each elementary case. This is perhaps the most interesting feature of the notion of completeness; therefore (T 39) could be taken as a definition of completeness instead of D 19).

T 40) If $\alpha \in Cm\,(UC_i,\ US\ \max_j)$ and $UC_k \overset{d}{<} UC_i$, then $\alpha \in Cm\,(UC_k,\ US\ \max_j)$.

T 41) If $\alpha \in Cm\,(UP_i,\ UA_j)$ and $UP_i \subset UP_k$, then $\alpha \in Cm\,(UP_k,\ UA_j)$ (from T 40 and T 30).

T 42) If $\alpha \in Cm\,(UC_i,\ US\ \max_j)$ and $US\ \max_j \overset{d}{<} US\ \max_k$, then $\alpha \in Cm\,(UC_i,\ US\ \max_k)$.

T 43) If $\alpha \in Cm\,(UP_i,\ UA_j)$ and $UA_k \subset UA_j$, then $\alpha \in Cm\,(UP_i,\ UA_k)$.

The theorems T 40—T 43 show the hereditary character of completeness regarding the relation of fineness between Universes of Cases and Universes of Maximal Solutions (and correspondingly, the relation of inclusion between Universes of Properties and Universes of Actions). Completeness is hereditary from less fine to finer *UCs* (T 40), and from finer to less fine *US* max's (T 42).

Consistency (*Ct*):

D 20) $Ct\,(UC_i,\ US\ \max_j)\ [=Ct\,(UP_i,\ UA_j)] = \{\alpha | (UC_i \overset{\alpha}{\to} US\ \max_j)$
$\in$ Fun$\}$ (where 'Fun' denotes the set of functions, i. e. many-one relations).

T 44) $\alpha \in Ct\,(UC_i,\ US\ \max_j)$ if and only if $x \overset{\alpha}{\to} y$ and $x \overset{\alpha}{\to} z$ imply $y=z$, for every $x \in UC_i$ and every $y,\ z \in US\ \max_j$.

T 45) $\alpha \in Ct\,(UC_i,\ US\ \max_j)$ if and only if for every $x \in UC_i$ there is a $y \in M$ such that $(x \to y) \notin Cn\,(\alpha)$.

This theorem shows that the notion of consistency is not dependent on a definite US max; the same idea is also, perhaps more explicitly, expressed in

T 46) $\alpha \in Ct$ $(UC_i, US \max_j)$ for some j $(1 \leq j \leq 2^m - 1)$ if and only if $\alpha \in Ct$ $(UC_i, US \max_j)$ for every j $(1 \leq j \leq 2^m - 1)$.

This allows us to define consistency in relation only to a UC:

D 21) Ct $(UC_i) = \{\alpha | Cn (\alpha + \{x\}) \neq M,$ for every $x \in UC_i\}$

[Instead of Ct (UC_i) we can also write Ct (UP_i)].

T 47) Ct $(UC_i) = \{\alpha | \alpha \in Ct$ $(UC_i, US \max_j)$ for some j $(1 \leq j \leq 2^m - 1)$.

T 48) If $\alpha \in Ct$ (UC_i) and $UC_i \overset{d}{<} UC_k$, then $\alpha \in Ct$ (UC_k).

T 49) If $\alpha \in Ct$ (UP_i) and $UP_k \subset UC_i$, then $\alpha \in Ct$ (UP_k).

(T 48) shows that consistency is hereditary from finer to less fine UCs.

T 50) If $UC_i \overset{d}{<} UC_k$, then Ct $(UC_i) \subset Ct$ (UC_k).

T 51) If $UP_k \subset UP_i$, then Ct $(UP_i) \subset Ct$ (UP_k).

Independence (Ind):

D 22) *Ind* $(UC_i, US \min_j)$ $[= Ind$ $(UP_i, UA_j)] = \{\alpha | $ for any $\beta \subset \alpha$ and $\beta \neq \alpha$, it is true that $(UC_i \overset{\beta}{\to} US \min_j) \neq (UC_i \overset{\alpha}{\to} US \min_j)$.

T 52) $\alpha \in Ind$ $(UC_i, US \min_j)$ if and only if for any $\beta \subset \alpha$ and $\beta \neq \alpha$, there is an $x \in UC_i$ and a $y \in US \min_j$, such that it is true that $(x \overset{\alpha}{\to} y)$, but not true that $(x \overset{\beta}{\to} y)$.

T 53) $\alpha \in Ind$ (UP_i, UA_j) if and only if for any $\beta \subset \alpha$ and $\beta \neq \alpha$, there is an $x \in Ca$ (UP_i) and a $y \in Sol$ (UA_j) such that it is true that $(x \overset{\alpha}{\to} y)$, but not true that $(x \overset{\beta}{\to} y)$.

Normative sets (N):

D 23) N $(UC_i, US \min_j)$ $[= N$ $(UP_i, UA_j)] = \{\alpha | (UC_i \overset{\alpha}{\to} US \min_j) \neq \wedge\}$

T 54) $\alpha \in N$ $(UC_i, US \min_j)$ if and only if $x \overset{\alpha}{\to} y$ is true for some $x \in UC_i$ and some $y \in US \min_j$.

T 55) $\alpha \in N$ (UP_i, UA_j) if and only if $x \overset{\alpha}{\to} y$ is true for some $x \in Ca$ (UP_i) and some $y \in Sol$ (UA_j).

This theorem says that normative sets are those sets that (deductively) correlate some case with some solution. This is the most obvious property that would be intuitively required in order to regard a set as normative.

Categorical normative sets (Cat):

D 24) $Cat\,(UC_i, US\,\min_j)\,[=Cat\,(UP_i, UA_j)]=\{\alpha\,|\,\mathsf{Q}'\,(UC_i\xrightarrow{\alpha}US\,\min_j)$
$\subset Cn\,(\alpha)\}$ (where the symbol $\mathsf{Q}'R$ refers to the counterdomain of the relation R).

T 56) $\alpha\in Cat\,(UC_i, US\,\min_j)$ if and only if there is some $x\in UC_i$ such that $x\xrightarrow{\alpha}y$ (if and) only if $y\in Cn\,(\alpha)$, for any $y\in US\,\min_j$.

T 57) $\alpha\in Cat\,(UP_i, UA_j)$ if and only if there is some $x\in Ca\,(UP_i)$ such that $x\xrightarrow{\alpha}y$ (if and) only if $y\in Cn\,(\alpha)$, for any $y\in Sol\,(UA_j)$.

T 58) $\alpha\in Cat\,(UC_i, US\,\min_j)$ for some i $(1\le i\le 2^n-1)$ if and only if for every i $(1\le i\le 2^n-1)$ $\alpha\in Cat\,(UC_i, US\,\min_j)$.

This theorem shows that the notion of a categorical normative set does not depend on any particular UC and is only relative to a US min.

D 25) $\alpha\in Cat\,(UA_j)=\{\alpha\,|\,\mathsf{Q}'[Ca\,(\{P_1\ldots P_n\})\xrightarrow{\alpha}US\,\min_j]\subset Cn\,(\alpha)\}$

T 59) $Cat\,(UA_j)=\{\alpha|\text{for some }i\ (1\le i\le 2^n-1)\ \alpha\in Cat\,(UC_i, US\,\min_j)\}$

T 60) $\alpha\in Cat\,(UA_j)$ if and only if for any $y\in US\,\min_j$ and for any UC_i if there is some $x\in UC_i$ and $x\xrightarrow{\alpha}y$, then for any $x\in UC_i$ it is true that $x\xrightarrow{\alpha}y$.

In the text (p. 57) T 60 occurs as a definition of categorical normative systems.

T 61) If $\alpha\in Cat\,(UA_j)$ and $US\,\min_j\overset{d}{<}US\,\min_k$, then $\alpha\in Cat\,(UA_k)$

T 62) If $US\,\min_j\overset{d}{<}US\,\min_k$, then $Cat\,(UA_j)\subset Cat\,(UA_k)$

T 63) If $UA_k\subset UA_j$, then $Cat\,(UA_j)\subset Cat\,(UA_k)$

The property of being a categorical normative set is hereditary from finer to less fine divisions.

Empirical (Emp) or factual and purely normative (PN) sets:

D 26) $Emp\,(UP_i)\,[=Emp\,(UC_i)]=\{\alpha\,|[Ca\,(UP_i)\,.\,Cn\,(\alpha)]\neq\wedge\}$

T 64) If $\alpha\notin Ct\,(UP_i)$, then $\alpha\in Emp\,(UP_i)$

T 64 shows that all inconsistent sets are empirical (factual).

D 27) $PN\,(UC_i, US\,\min_j)=[N\,(UC_i, US\,\min_j)-Emp\,(UC_i)]$

T 65) If $\alpha\in PN\,(UC_i, US\,\min_j)$, then $\alpha\in Ct\,(UC_i)$.

T 65 shows that all purely normative systems are consistent.

The notion of relevance:

Definition of the notion of a *complementary case* (Comp):

D 28) $Comp\,(z, UP_i)=\{\langle x, y\rangle|\text{there is a set }\alpha\text{ such that }\{z\}\subset\alpha\subset UP_i,$
and (1) $x=(\underset{y\in\alpha}{\Pi\,y}\,.\,\underset{y\in(UP_i-\alpha)}{\Pi\,\bar{y}}\ )$ and $y=(\underset{y\in(\alpha-\{z\})}{\Pi\,y}\ .\,\underset{y\in[UP_i-(\alpha-\{z\})]}{\Pi\,\bar{y}}\qquad)$
or (2) $y=(\underset{y\in\alpha}{\Pi\,y}\,.\,\underset{y\in(UP_i-\alpha)}{\Pi\,\bar{y}}\ )$ and $x=(\underset{y\in(\alpha-\{z\})}{\Pi\,y}\ .\,\underset{y\in[UP_i-(\alpha-\{z\})]}{\Pi\,\bar{y}}\qquad)\}$

T 66) If $[x \, Comp \, (z, UP_i) \, y]$, then $x, y \in UC_i$ and $x \neq y$.

T 67) If $[x \, Comp \, (z, UP_i) \, y]$, then $[y \, Comp \, (z, UP_i) \, x]$.

T 68) For any $x \in UC_i$ and for any $z \in UP_i$, there is a y such that $[x \, Comp \, (z, UP_i) \, y]$.

T 69) $Comp \, (z, UP_i) \in Fun$

Equal normative status:

D 29) $\underset{UA_i}{\overset{\alpha}{\sim}} = \{\langle x, y \rangle | \text{for any } z, \, x \, (\overset{\alpha}{\to} US \, min_j) \, z \text{ if and only if } y \, (\overset{\alpha}{\to}$

$US \, min_j) \, z\}$.

T 70) $x \underset{UA_i}{\overset{\alpha}{\sim}} y$ if and only if $[Cn \, (\alpha + \{x\}). \, Sol \, (UA_i)] = [Cn \, (\alpha + \{y\}) \, .$

$Sol \, (UA_i)]$.

Definition of "relevant in a case":

D 30) $Rel \, (\alpha, UA_j, UP_i, x) = \{z | x \in UC_i \text{ and } z \in UP_i \text{ and it is not true}$
that $Comp \, (z, UP_i)' \, x \underset{UA_j}{\overset{\alpha}{\sim}} x\}$. ('$Comp \, (z, UP_i)' \, x$' denotes the
complementary case of x relative to z in UP_i).

D 31) $Rel \, (\alpha, UA_j) = \{z | \text{there is an } i \, (1 \leq i \leq 2^n - 1) \text{ and there is an } x$
such that $z \in Rel \, (\alpha, UA_j, UP_i, x)\}$.

T 71) $Rel \, (\alpha, UA_j) \neq \wedge$ if and only if for some $i \, (1 \leq i \leq 2^n - 1)$ it is true
that $Rel \, (\alpha, UA_j) = UP_i$.

When there are relevant properties, the set of all the relevant properties is identical with *a* UP. This is the UPR (α, UA_j), i. e. the Universe of Relevant Properties. The Universe of Relevant Cases [UCR (α, UA_j)] is the corresponding UC. For the situation in which there are no relevant properties [i. e. $Rel \, (\alpha, UA_j) = \wedge$] we stipulate that UCR $(\alpha, UA_j) = \wedge$.

T 72) $Rel \, (\alpha, UA_j) = \wedge$ if and only if $\alpha \in Cat \, (UA_j)$.

T 72 shows that there are relevant properties for and only for normative non-categorical sets.

T 73) If $\alpha \notin N \, (UA_j)$, then $Rel \, (UA_j) = \wedge$.

T 74) Let α be such that $\alpha \in Cm \, (UC_i, US \, max_j)$ and $\alpha \in Ct \, (UC_k)$,
such that $UP_i \subset UP_k$, and $UP_i \neq UP_k$, then $(UP_k - UP_i) \subset -Rel$
(α, UA_j).

This theorem is referred to in the text as T 3 (cf. p. 100).

The Problem of Closure

In Chapter VII, Section 6 we have formulated several rules of closure, i. e. rules whose application to a given set α leads to another (larger) set β, such that β is complete. The purpose of (this kind of) closure is to achieve completeness and to preserve consistency. In the text, the closure of categorical and that of non-categorical normative systems have been dealt with separately. Here we give a more general account of the notion of closure.

The definition of closure Cl_1 (as the set resulting from the application of a rule of closure to a given set) given below (D 32) is analoguous to the rule $C\,1$, but whereas $C\,1$ is only applicable to categorical sets, here we drop this restriction. The result of it (reflected in T 76 and T 77) is that Cl_1 does not preserve consistency when applied to non-categorical systems. A general concept of closure that achieves completeness and preserves consistency is given in D 33 (Cl), which is a sort of amalgam of $C\,1$ and $C\,4$ of the text.

D 32) $Cl_1\,(\alpha,\,UA_j) = (\alpha + \{Py|y\in Con\,(UA_j)\text{ and }-Py\notin Cn\,(\alpha)\})$

T 75) $Cl_1\,(\alpha,\,UA_j)\in Cm\,(UP_i,\,UA_j)\;[=Cm\,(UC_i,\,US\,\max_j)]$

T 76) If $\alpha\in Cat\,(UP_i,\,UA_j)$ and $\alpha\in Ct\,(UP_i,\,UA_j)$, then $Cl_1\,(\alpha,\,UA_j)\in Ct\,(UP_i,\,UA_j)$.

T 77) If $\alpha\in Cat\,(UA_j)$ and $\alpha\in Ct\,(UP_i)$, then $Cl_1\,(\alpha,\,UA_j)\in Ct\,(UP_i)$.

T 75 shows that Cl_1 is complete regarding any $UP\,(UC)$. But it preserves consistency only if α is a categorical set (T 76, T 77).

D 33) $Cl\,(\alpha,\,UA_j) = [\alpha + \{x\rightarrow Py|(x\rightarrow -Py)\notin Cn\,(\alpha)$, where $x\in UCR\,(\alpha,\,UA_j)$ if $UCR\,(\alpha,\,UA_j)\neq\wedge$, and $x\in Ca\,(\{P_1\ldots P_n\})$ if $UCR\,(\alpha,\,UA_j) = \wedge$, and $y\in Con\,(UA_j)\}]$.

T 78) If $Rel\,(\alpha,\,UA_j)\neq\wedge$, then $Cl\,(\alpha,\,UA_j)\in Cm\,[UCR(\alpha,\,UA_j)$, $US\,\max_j]$.

T 79) If $Rel\,(\alpha,\,UA_j) = \wedge$, then $Cn\,[Cl_1\,(\alpha,\,UA_j)] = Cn\,[Cl\,(\alpha,\,UA_j)]$.

T 80) If $Rel\,(\alpha,\,UA_j) = \wedge$, then $Cl\,(\alpha,\,UA_j)\in Cm\,(UP_i,\,UA_j)$

In these theorems '$Rel\,(\alpha,\,UA_j) = \wedge$' can be replaced by '$\alpha\in Cat\,(UA_j)$' and '$Rel\,(\alpha,\,UA_j)\neq\wedge$' by '$\alpha\notin Cat\,(UA_j)$, which shows that the closure of categorical systems is complete for any UC, and that for non-categorical systems the closure is complete in UCR (T 78 and T 80). T 79 shows that for categorical normative systems both notions of closure (Cl_1 and Cl) are equivalent.

T 81) If $\alpha\in Ct\,(UP_i)$, then $Cl\,(\alpha,\,UA_j)\in Ct\,(UP_i)$.

This theorem shows that the closure Cl (D 33) preserves consistency both for categorical and non-categorical sets.

T 82) If $UA_j \subset UA_k$, then $Cl\ (\alpha, UA_j) \subset Cl\ (\alpha, UA_k)$.

A logic for normative propositions

The ideas developed in Sections 2 and 3 (Chapter VII) presuppose a logic of normative propositions (i. e. propositions *about* norms) which is analogous to but not identical with the (deontic) logic of the object-language. Here we formulate explicitly the main features of this logic[1].

The following symbols will be introduced in the meta-language: '$\sim$' for negation, '&' for conjunction, 'o' for non-exclusive disjunction, '$\supset$' for material implication, '$\equiv$' for material equivalence, and the usual signs for universal and existential quantifiers. We shall also stipulate that the variables 'x' stand for an element of the set $Ca\ (\{P_1 \ldots P_n\})$ and the variables 'y' for an element of $Con\ (\{A_1 \ldots \ldots A_m\})$.

A characteristic feature of the logic of normative propositions is the occurence of various concepts of permission and obligation, widely used in descriptive discourse (i. e. discourse about norms) and which should not be confused with the corresponding deontic operators.

Strong and weak operators, conditional and categorical:

Conditional strong obligation:

D 34) $\bigcirc s\ (y|x) = (x \rightarrow Oy) \in Cn\ (\alpha)\ [= x \overset{\alpha}{\rightarrow} Oy]$.

Conditional strong permission:

D 35) $\mathbb{P} s\ (y|x) = (x \rightarrow Py) \in Cn\ (\alpha)\ [= x \overset{\alpha}{\rightarrow} Py]$.

Conditional weak obligation:

D 36) $\bigcirc w\ (y|x) = (x \rightarrow P - y) \notin Cn\ (\alpha)\ [= \text{not}\ (x \overset{\alpha}{\rightarrow} P - y)]$

---

1 A more comprehensive account of the logic of normative propositions may be found in C. E. ALCHOURRÓN, Logic of norms and Logic of normative propositions, Logique et Analyse 12, 242—268 (1969), though the presentation is different. Here it is developed in a syntactical meta-language about the language to which the deontic logic belongs, whereas in the paper it is imbedded in the same language as the deontic logic.

Conditional weak permission:

D 37) $\mathbb{P} \underset{\alpha}{w} (y|x) = (x \to O - y) \notin Cn (\alpha) \ [= \text{not} (x \overset{\alpha}{\to} O - y)]$

Categorical strong obligation:

D 38) $\underset{\alpha}{O} s (y) = O y \in Cn (\alpha) \ [= \underset{\alpha}{O} s (y|x), \text{ for every } x]$

Categorical strong permission:

D 39) $\mathbb{P} \underset{\alpha}{s} (y) = P y \in Cn (\alpha) \ [= \mathbb{P} \underset{\alpha}{s} (y|x), \text{ for every } x]$

Categorical weak obligation:

D 40) $\underset{\alpha}{O} w (y) = P - y \notin Cn (\alpha) \ [= \underset{\alpha}{O} w (y|x), \text{ for some } x]$

Categorical weak permission:

D 41) $\mathbb{P} \underset{\alpha}{w} (y) = O - y \notin Cn (\alpha) \ [= \mathbb{P} \underset{\alpha}{w} (y|x), \text{ for some } x]$

External negation:

of conditional operators: of categorical operators:

T 83) $\sim \underset{\alpha}{O} s \ (y|x) \equiv \ \mathbb{P} \underset{\alpha}{w} (-y|x)$ T 83') $\sim \underset{\alpha}{O} s \ (y) \equiv \ \mathbb{P} \underset{\alpha}{w} (-y)$

T 84) $\sim \mathbb{P} \underset{\alpha}{s} \ (y|x) \equiv \ \underset{\alpha}{O} w \ (-y|x)$ T 84') $\sim \mathbb{P} \underset{\alpha}{s} \ (y) \equiv \ \underset{\alpha}{O} w \ (-y)$

T 85) $\sim \underset{\alpha}{O} w \ (y|x) \equiv \ \mathbb{P} \underset{\alpha}{s} \ (-y|x)$ T 85') $\sim \underset{\alpha}{O} w \ (y) \equiv \ \mathbb{P} \underset{\alpha}{s} \ (-y)$

T 86) $\sim \mathbb{P} \underset{\alpha}{w} \ (y|x) \equiv \ \underset{\alpha}{O} s \ (-y|x)$ T 86') $\sim \mathbb{P} \underset{\alpha}{w} \ (y) \equiv \ \underset{\alpha}{O} s \ (-y)$

T 87) $\underset{\alpha}{O} s \ (y|x) \equiv \sim \mathbb{P} \underset{\alpha}{w} \ (-y|x)$ T 87') $\underset{\alpha}{O} s \ (y) \equiv \sim \mathbb{P} \underset{\alpha}{w} \ (-y)$

T 88) $\mathbb{P} \underset{\alpha}{s} \ (y|x) \equiv \sim \underset{\alpha}{O} w \ (-y|x)$ T 88') $\mathbb{P} \underset{\alpha}{s} \ (y) \equiv \sim \underset{\alpha}{O} w \ (-y)$

T 89) $\underset{\alpha}{O} w \ (y|x) \equiv \sim \mathbb{P} \underset{\alpha}{s} \ (-y|x)$ T 89') $\underset{\alpha}{O} w \ (y) \equiv \sim \mathbb{P} \underset{\alpha}{s} \ (-y)$

T 90) $\mathbb{P} \underset{\alpha}{w} \ (y|x) \equiv \sim \underset{\alpha}{O} s \ (-y|x)$ T 90') $\mathbb{P} \underset{\alpha}{w} \ (y) \equiv \sim \underset{\alpha}{O} s \ (-y)$

Internal negation:

D 42) $] \underset{\alpha}{O} s \ (y|x) = (x \to - O y) \in Cn (\alpha)$

D 42') $] \underset{\alpha}{O} s \ (y) = - O y \in Cn (\alpha)$

D 43) $] \mathbb{P} \underset{\alpha}{s} \ (y|x) = (x \to - P y) \in Cn (\alpha)$

D 43') $] \mathbb{P} \underset{\alpha}{s} \ (y) = - P y \in Cn (\alpha)$

D 44) $] \underset{\alpha}{O} w \ (y|x) = (x \to - P - y) \notin Cn (\alpha)$

D 44') $] \underset{\alpha}{O} w \ (y) = - P - y \notin Cn (\alpha)$

D 45) $\;] \underset{\alpha}{\mathbb{P}}\, w\,(y|x) = (x \rightarrow -O-y) \notin Cn\,(\alpha)$

D 45') $\;] \underset{\alpha}{\mathbb{P}}\, w\,(y) = -O-y \notin Cn\,(\alpha)$

T 91) $\;] \underset{\alpha}{\mathbb{O}} s\,(y|x) \equiv \underset{\alpha}{\mathbb{P}} s\,(-y|x)$

T 91') $\;] \underset{\alpha}{\mathbb{O}} s\,(y) \equiv \underset{\alpha}{\mathbb{P}} s\,(-y)$

T 92) $\;] \underset{\alpha}{\mathbb{P}} s\,(y|x) \equiv \underset{\alpha}{\mathbb{O}} s\,(-y|x)$

T 92') $\;] \underset{\alpha}{\mathbb{P}} s\,(y) \equiv \underset{\alpha}{\mathbb{O}} s\,(-y)$

T 93) $\;] \underset{\alpha}{\mathbb{O}} w\,(y|x) \equiv \underset{\alpha}{\mathbb{P}} w\,(-y|x)$

T 93') $\;] \underset{\alpha}{\mathbb{O}} w\,(y) \equiv \underset{\alpha}{\mathbb{P}} w\,(-y)$

T 94) $\;] \underset{\alpha}{\mathbb{P}} w\,(y|x) \equiv \underset{\alpha}{\mathbb{O}} w\,(-y|x)$

T 94') $\;] \underset{\alpha}{\mathbb{P}} w\,(y) \equiv \underset{\alpha}{\mathbb{O}} w\,(-y)$

T 95) $\;\underset{\alpha}{\mathbb{O}} s\,(y|x) \equiv\,] \underset{\alpha}{\mathbb{P}} s\,(-y|x) \equiv\, \sim\,] \underset{\alpha}{\mathbb{O}} w\,(y|x)$

T 95') $\;\underset{\alpha}{\mathbb{O}} s\,(y) \equiv\,] \underset{\alpha}{\mathbb{P}} s\,(-y) \equiv\, \sim\,] \underset{\alpha}{\mathbb{O}} w\,(y)$

T 96) $\;\underset{\alpha}{\mathbb{P}} s\,(y|x) \equiv\,] \underset{\alpha}{\mathbb{O}} s\,(-y|x) \equiv\, \sim\,] \underset{\alpha}{\mathbb{P}} w\,(y|x)$

T 96') $\;\underset{\alpha}{\mathbb{P}} s\,(y) \equiv\,] \underset{\alpha}{\mathbb{O}} s\,(-y) \equiv\, \sim\,] \underset{\alpha}{\mathbb{P}} w\,(y)$

T 97) $\;\underset{\alpha}{\mathbb{O}} w\,(y|x) \equiv\,] \underset{\alpha}{\mathbb{P}} w\,(-y|x) \equiv\, \sim\,] \underset{\alpha}{\mathbb{O}} s\,(y|x)$

T 97') $\;\underset{\alpha}{\mathbb{O}} w\,(y) \equiv\,] \underset{\alpha}{\mathbb{P}} w\,(-y) \equiv\, \sim\,] \underset{\alpha}{\mathbb{O}} s\,(y)$

T 98) $\;\underset{\alpha}{\mathbb{P}} w\,(y|x) \equiv\,] \underset{\alpha}{\mathbb{O}} w\,(-y|x) \equiv\, \sim\,] \underset{\alpha}{\mathbb{P}} s\,(y|x)$

T 98') $\;\underset{\alpha}{\mathbb{P}} w\,(y) \equiv\,] \underset{\alpha}{\mathbb{O}} w\,(-y) \equiv\, \sim\,] \underset{\alpha}{\mathbb{P}} s\,(y)$

In general: $]] \underset{\alpha}{\chi} \equiv \underset{\alpha}{\chi} \equiv\, \sim\, \sim \underset{\alpha}{\chi}$ (where $\underset{\alpha}{\chi}$ is $\underset{\alpha}{\mathbb{O}} s$, $\underset{\alpha}{\mathbb{P}} s$, $\underset{\alpha}{\mathbb{O}} w$ or $\underset{\alpha}{\mathbb{P}} w$).

Laws of subalternation and distribution:

T 99) $\;\underset{\alpha}{\mathbb{O}} s\,(y|x) \supset \underset{\alpha}{\mathbb{P}} s\,(y|x)$

T 99') $\;\underset{\alpha}{\mathbb{O}} s\,(y) \supset \underset{\alpha}{\mathbb{P}} s\,(y)$

T 100) $\;\underset{\alpha}{\mathbb{O}} w\,(y|x) \supset \underset{\alpha}{\mathbb{P}} w\,(y|x)$

T 100') $\;\underset{\alpha}{\mathbb{O}} w\,(y) \supset \underset{\alpha}{\mathbb{P}} w\,(y)$

T 101) $\;\underset{\alpha}{\mathbb{O}} s\,(y_1.y_2|x) \equiv \underset{\alpha}{\mathbb{O}} s\,(y_1|x)\ \&\ \underset{\alpha}{\mathbb{O}} s\,(y_2|x)$

T 101') $\;\underset{\alpha}{\mathbb{O}} s\,(y_1.y_2) \equiv \underset{\alpha}{\mathbb{O}} s\,(y_1)\ \&\ \underset{\alpha}{\mathbb{O}} s\,(y_2)$

T 102) $\mathbb{P}\underset{\alpha}{w}\,(y_1 \vee y_2|x) \equiv \mathbb{P}\underset{\alpha}{w}\,(y_1|x)\;\text{o}\;\mathbb{P}\underset{\alpha}{w}\,(y_2|x)$

T 102') $\mathbb{P}\underset{\alpha}{w}\,(y_1.y_2) \equiv \mathbb{P}\underset{\alpha}{w}\,(y_1)\;\text{o}\;\mathbb{P}\underset{\alpha}{w}\,(y_2)$

T 103) $\mathbb{P}\underset{\alpha}{s}\,(y_1|x)\;\text{o}\;\mathbb{P}\underset{\alpha}{s}\,(y_2|x) \supset \mathbb{P}\underset{\alpha}{s}\,(y_1 \vee y_2|x)$

T 103') $\mathbb{P}\underset{\alpha}{s}\,(y_1)\;\text{o}\;\mathbb{P}\underset{\alpha}{s}\,(y_2) \supset \mathbb{P}\underset{\alpha}{s}\,(y_1 \vee y_2)$

T 104) $\bigcirc\underset{\alpha}{w}\,(y_1.y_2|x) \supset \bigcirc\underset{\alpha}{w}\,(y_1|x)\;\&\;\bigcirc\underset{\alpha}{w}\,(y_2|x)$

T 104') $\bigcirc\underset{\alpha}{w}\,(y_1.y_2) \supset \bigcirc\underset{\alpha}{w}\,(y_1)\;\&\;\bigcirc\underset{\alpha}{w}\,(y_2)$

T 105) $\underset{\alpha}{\chi}\,(y|x_1 \vee x_2) \equiv \underset{\alpha}{\chi}\,(y|x_1)\;\&\;\underset{\alpha}{\chi}\,(y|x_2)$ (χ is $\bigcirc\underset{\alpha}{s}$, $\mathbb{P}\underset{\alpha}{s}$, $\bigcirc\underset{\alpha}{w}$ or $\mathbb{P}\underset{\alpha}{w}$)

Normative determination and completeness:

T 106) $\rceil\mathbb{P}\underset{\alpha}{s}\,(y|x)\;\text{o}\;\mathbb{P}\underset{\alpha}{w}\,(y|x)$ T 106') $\rceil\mathbb{P}\underset{\alpha}{s}\,(y)\;\text{o}\;\mathbb{P}\underset{\alpha}{w}\,(y)$

Normative determination:

D 46) $Det\underset{\alpha}{}\,(y|x) = \rceil\mathbb{P}\underset{\alpha}{s}\,(y|x)\;\text{o}\;\mathbb{P}\underset{\alpha}{s}\,(y|x)$ (This formila can be read

(in a transposed mode of speech): Action y is normatively determined by α in case x when y is forbidden by α in case x (because the internal negation of a strong permission represents a sense of 'prohibition') or y is strongly permitted by α in case x.)

D 47) $Det\underset{\alpha}{}\,(y) = \rceil\mathbb{P}\underset{\alpha}{s}\,(y)\;\text{o}\;\mathbb{P}\underset{\alpha}{s}\,(y)$

T 107) $Det\underset{\alpha}{}\,(y) \supset Det\underset{\alpha}{}\,(y|x)$

T 108) $[Det\underset{\alpha}{}\,(y_1|x)\;\&\;Det\underset{\alpha}{}\,(y_2|x)] \supset [\mathbb{P}\underset{\alpha}{s}\,(y_1 \vee y_2|x) \equiv \mathbb{P}\underset{\alpha}{s}\,(y_1|x)\;\text{o}\;\mathbb{P}\underset{\alpha}{s}$
$(y_2|x)]$

T 108') $[Det\underset{\alpha}{}\,(y_1)\;\&\;Det\underset{\alpha}{}\,(y_2)] \supset [\mathbb{P}\underset{\alpha}{s}\,(y_1 \vee y_2) \equiv \mathbb{P}\underset{\alpha}{s}\,(y_1)\;\text{o}\;\mathbb{P}\underset{\alpha}{s}\,(y_2)]$

T 109) $[Det\underset{\alpha}{}\,(-y_1|x)\;\&\;Det\underset{\alpha}{}\,(-y_2|x)] \supset [\bigcirc\underset{\alpha}{w}\,(y_1.y_2|x) \equiv \bigcirc\underset{\alpha}{w}\,(y_1|x)$
$\&\;\bigcirc\underset{\alpha}{w}\,(y_2|x)]$

T 109') $[Det\underset{\alpha}{}\,(-y_1)\;\&\;Det\underset{\alpha}{}\,(-y_2)] \supset [\bigcirc\underset{\alpha}{w}\,(y_1.y_2) \equiv \bigcirc\underset{\alpha}{w}\,(y_1)\;\&$
$\bigcirc\underset{\alpha}{w}\,(y_2)]$

T 110) $Det\underset{\alpha}{}\,(y|x) \supset [\mathbb{P}\underset{\alpha}{w}\,(y|x) \supset \mathbb{P}\underset{\alpha}{s}\,(y|x)]$

T 110') $Det\underset{\alpha}{}\,(y) \supset [\mathbb{P}\underset{\alpha}{w}\,(y) \supset \mathbb{P}\underset{\alpha}{s}\,(y)]$

T 111) $Det\underset{\alpha}{}\,(-y|x) \supset [\bigcirc\underset{\alpha}{w}\,(y|x) \supset \bigcirc\underset{\alpha}{s}\,(y|x)]$

T 111') $Det\underset{\alpha}{}\,(-y) \supset [\bigcirc\underset{\alpha}{w}\,(y) \supset \bigcirc\underset{\alpha}{s}\,(y)]$

D 48) $Det\ (UA_j|x) = (y)\ [y \in Con\ (UA_j) \supset Det\ (y|x)]$
     α

D 48') $Det\ (UA_j) = (y)\ [y \in Con\ (UA_j) \supset Det\ (y)]$
     α

D 49) $Det\ (y|UC_i) = (x)\ [x \in UC_i \supset Det\ (y|x)]$
     α

D 50) $Det\ (UA_j|UC_i) = (x)\ (y)\ [x \in UC_i\ \&\ y \in Con\ (UA_j) \supset Det\ (y|x)]$
     α

T 112) $Det\ (UA_j|UC_i) \equiv \alpha \in Cm\ (UC_i,\ US\ max_j)$
     α

T 112') $Det\ (UA_j) \equiv \alpha \in Cm\ (UC_i,\ US\ max_j)$
     α

T 113) $Det\ (UA_j|x) \equiv (Ez)\ [z \in US\ max_j\ \&\ (x \to z) \in Cn\ (\alpha)] \equiv$
     α

$(US\ max_j . Cn\ [\alpha + \{x\}]) \neq \wedge .$

D 48—D 50 define the notions of normative determination of a
set of actions in a case (D 48), of an action in a set of cases (D 49) and
of a set of actions in a set of cases (D 50). T 112 shows that the normative determination of a set of actions in a set of cases by α is equivalent to the completeness of α in relation to the corresponding UC
and US max.

Consistency and normativeness:

T 114) $1 \mathbb{P} w\ (y|x)\ o\ \mathbb{P} s\ (y|x)$
     α α

T 114') $1 \mathbb{P} w\ (y)\ o\ \mathbb{P} s\ (y)$
     α α

T 115) $[1 \mathbb{P} w\ (y|x)\ o\ \mathbb{P} w\ (y|x)] \equiv \sim [1 \mathbb{P} s\ (y|x)\ \&\ \mathbb{P} s\ (y|x)]$
     α α α α

T 115') $[1 \mathbb{P} w\ (y)\ o\ \mathbb{P} w\ (y)] \equiv \sim [1 \mathbb{P} s\ (y)\ \&\ \mathbb{P} s\ (y)]$
     α α α α

T 116) $(Ey)\ [1 \mathbb{P} w\ (y|x)\ o\ \mathbb{P} w\ (y|x)] \equiv (y)\ [1 \mathbb{P} w\ (y|x)\ o\ \mathbb{P} w\ (y|x)]$
      α α α α

Definition of consistency (in a case):

D 51) $Ct\ (x) = (Ey)\ [1 \mathbb{P} w\ (y|x)\ o\ \mathbb{P} w\ (y|x)]$
     α α α

(A set α is consistent in a case when no action is forbidden and
permitted in this case. This reading results from the combination of
D 51 with T 115 and T 116. The formula D 51 has been chosen in
order to show the structural similarity of the concepts of determination and consistency; compare D 46 and D 51.)

T 117) $Ct\ (x) \supset [\mathbb{P} s\ (y|x) \supset \mathbb{P} w\ (y|x)]$
     α α α

T 118) $Ct\ (x) \supset [\mathbb{O} s\ (y|x) \supset \mathbb{O} w\ (y|x)]$
     α α α

D 52) $Ct\ (y) = [\mathbb{P} w\ (y)\ o\ 1 \mathbb{P} w\ (y)]$
     α α α

13*

T 119) $\underset{\alpha}{Ct}\ (y) \supset [\underset{\alpha}{\mathbb{P}s}\ (y) \supset \underset{\alpha}{\mathbb{P}w}\ (y)]$

T 120) $\underset{\alpha}{Ct}\ (y) \supset [\underset{\alpha}{\mathbb{O}s}\ (y) \supset \underset{\alpha}{\mathbb{O}w}\ (y)]$

T 121) $[\underset{\alpha}{Det}\ (y|x)\ \&\ \underset{\alpha}{Ct}\ (x)] \supset [\underset{\alpha}{\mathbb{P}s}\ (y|x) \equiv \underset{\alpha}{\mathbb{P}w}\ (y|x)]$

T 122) $[\underset{\alpha}{Det}\ (y|x)\ \&\ \underset{\alpha}{Ct}\ (x)] \supset [\underset{\alpha}{\mathbb{O}s}\ (y|x) \equiv \underset{\alpha}{\mathbb{O}w}\ (y|x)]$

T 123) $\alpha \in Ct\ (UC_i) \equiv (x)\ [x \in UC_i \supset \underset{\alpha}{Ct}\ (x)]$

Normativeness:

D 53) $\underset{\alpha}{N}\ (y|x) = [\underset{\alpha}{\mathbb{P}s}\ (y|x)\ \text{o}\ \underset{\alpha}{\mathbb{P}s}\ (-y|x)]$

(To be read: An action is normed by α in a case when this action or its negation is strongly permitted by α in that case.)

D 53') $\underset{\alpha}{N}\ (y) = [\underset{\alpha}{\mathbb{P}s}\ (y)\ \text{o}\ \underset{\alpha}{\mathbb{P}s}\ (-y)]$

T 124) $\underset{\alpha}{N}\ (y|x) \equiv \underset{\alpha}{Det}\ (y|x)\ \text{o}\ \underset{\alpha}{Det}\ (-y|x)$

T 124') $\underset{\alpha}{N}\ (y) \equiv [\underset{\alpha}{Det}\ (y)\ \text{o}\ \underset{\alpha}{Det}\ (-y)]$

T 125) $\alpha \in N\ (UC_i,\ US\ \text{min}_j) \equiv (Ex)\ (Ey)\ (x \in Ca\ [UP_i]\ \&\ y \in Con$
$(UA_j)\ \&\ \underset{\alpha}{N}\ (y|x)]$

(A set α is normative when it norms some action in some case.)

Bibliography

This bibliography has no claim to completeness. Its purpose is to suggest some further readings in Logic and Philosophy of Science (A) and to list some of the writings of jurists and legal philosophers relevant to the problems discussed in this book (B).

A. Logic and Philosophy of Science

ALCHOURRÓN, C. E., Logic of norms and logic of normative propositions, Logique et Analyse *12*, 1969, 242—268.

ANDERSON, A. R., The Formal Analysis of Normative Systems, in: N. RESCHER (editor), The Logic of Decision and Action, Pittsburgh, 1966, 147—213.

BETH, E. W., The Foundations of Mathematics (2nd ed.), Amsterdam, 1965.

BUNGE, M., Scientific Research, 2 volumes, New York, 1967.

BUNGE, M. (editor), The Critical Approach to Science and Philosophy, New York, 1964.

CARNAP, R., Logical Syntax of Language, London, 1937 (orig. 1934).

—, Testability and Meaning, Philosophy of Science *3*, 1936, and *4*, 1937.

—, Meaning and Necessity. A Study in Semantics and Modal Logic (2nd ed.), Chicago, 1956.

—, Introduction to Symbolic Logic and its Applications, New York, 1958.

—, Logical Foundations of Probability (2nd ed.), Chicago, 1962.

CASTAÑEDA, H. N., Actions, Imperatives and Obligations, Proceedings of the Aristotelian Society, 1967.

—, Acts, the Logic of Obligation and Deontic Calculi, Critica *1*, 1967, 77—99, and Philosophical Studies *19*, 1968, 13—26.

CHURCH, A., Introduction to Mathematical Logic, vol. I, Princeton, 1956.

CLIFFORD, J. E., Tense and the logic of change, Logique et Analyse *9*, 1966, 219—230.

FEIGL, H., and M. BRODBECK (editors), Readings in the Philosophy of Science, New York, 1953.

FEIGL, H., M. SCRIVEN and G. MAXWELL (editors), Minnesota Studies in the Philosophy of Science, 3 volumes, Minneapolis, 1956—1962.

GIBSON, Q., The Logic of Social Enquiry, London, 1960.

HANSON, W. H., Semantics for Deontic Logic, Logique et Analyse 8, 1965, 177—190.

—, A logic of commands, Logique et Analyse 9, 1966.

HEMPEL, C. G., Aspects of Scientific Explanation and Other Essays in the Philosophy of Science, New York, 1965.

HINTIKKA, J., Quantifiers in Deontic Logic, Helsinki, 1957.

LEMMON, E. J., Deontic Logic and the Logic of Imperatives, Logique et Analyse 8, 1965, 39—71.

NAGEL, E., The Structure of Science, London, 1961.

NAGEL, E., P. SUPPES and A. TARSKI (editors), Logic, Methodology, and Philosophy of Science, Amsterdam, 1962.

POPPER, K. R., The Logic of Scientific Discovery, New York—London, 1959.

PRIOR, A. N., Formal Logic, Oxford, 1955.

—, Time and Modality, Oxford, 1957.

—, Past, Present and Future, Oxford, 1967.

—, Papers on Time and Tense, Oxford, 1968.

PRZELECKI, M., The Logic of Empirical Theories, London, 1969.

QUINE, W. V. O., Methods of Logic (2nd ed.), London, 1962.

—, From a Logical Point of View, Cambridge, Mass., 1953.

—, The Ways of Paradox, New York, 1966.

—, Set Theory and its Logic (2nd ed.), Cambridge, Mass., 1969.

REICHENBACH, H., The Philosophy of Space and Time, New York, 1957 (orig. Berlin, 1928).

—, The Rise of Scientific Philosophy, Univ. of California Press, 1951.

RESCHER, N., The Logic of Commands, London, 1966.

—, Topics in Philosophical Logic, Dordrecht, 1968.

ROSSER, J. B., Logic for Mathematicians, New York, 1953.

SCHILPP, P. A. (editor), The Philosophy of Rudolf Carnap, La Salle, Illinois, 1963.

STENIUS, E., The Principles of a Logic of Normative Systems, Acta Philosophica Fennica 16, 1963, 247—260.

SUPPES, P., Axiomatic Set Theory, Princeton, 1960.

TARSKI, A., Introduction to Logic and to the Methodology of Deductive Sciences, Oxford, 1946.

—, Logic, Semantics, Metamathematics, Oxford, 1956.

WRIGHT, G. H. VON, An Essay in Modal Logic, Amsterdam, 1951.

—, A Treatise on Induction and Probability, London, 1951.

—, Logical Studies, London, 1957.

—, Norm and Action, London, 1963.

—, A New System of Deontic Logic, Danish Yearbook of Philosophy 1, 1964, 173—182.

—, A Correction to a New System of Deontic Logic, Danish Yearbook of Philosophy 2, 1965, 103—107.

—, Deontic Logics, American Philosophical Quarterly 4, 1967, 136—143.

WRIGHT, G. H. VON, An Essay in Deontic Logic and the General Theory of Action, Amsterdam, 1968.

—, Deontic Logic and the Theory of Conditions, Crítica 6, 1968, 3—25.

—, On the Logic and Ontology of Norms, in: J. W. DAVIS et al. (editors), Philosophical Logic, 1969.

ÅQVIST, L., Interpretations of Deontic Logic, Mind 73, 1964, 246—253.

—, "Next" and "Ought". Alternative foundations for von Wright's tense-logic, with an application to deontic logic, Logique et Analyse 9, 1966, 231—251.

B. Legal Philosophy

ALCHOURRÓN, C. E., Juristische Schlüsse a fortiori und a pari, Archiv für Rechts- und Sozialphilosophie, Beiheft 41 (Neue Folge 4), 1965, 5—25.

AUSTIN, J., The Province of Jurisprudence Determined, London, 1954 (first published in 1832).

BACQUÉ, J. A., Une pyramide aplatie, Archiv für Rechts- und Sozialphilosophie 50, 1964, 105—110.

BENTHAM, J., Of Laws in General, London, 1970.

BOBBIO, N., Lacune del Diritto, Novissimo Digesto Italiano, vol. IX, 419—424.

—, Teoria dell'ordinamento giuridico, Torino, 1960.

—, El problema del positivismo jurídico, Buenos Aires, 1965.

—, Studi per una teoria generale del diritto, Torino, 1970.

BULYGIN, E., Sobre la estructura lógica de las proposiciones de la ciencia del derecho, Revista Juridica de Buenos Aires 4, 1961, 215—223.

—, Der Begriff der Wirksamkeit, Archiv für Rechts- und Sozialphilosophie, Beiheft 41 (Neue Folge 4), 1965, 39—58.

—, Zwei Systembegriffe in der rechtsphilosophischen Problematik, Archiv für Rechts- und Sozialphilosophie 53, 1967, 329—338.

—, Sentenza giudiziaria e creazione di diritto, Rivista Internazionale di Filosofia del Diritto 44, 1967, 164—180.

CAPELLA, J. R., El derecho como lenguaje, Barcelona, 1968.

CARNELUTTI, F., Teoria generale del diritto, Milano, 1940.

CARRIÓ, G. R., Notas sobre Derecho y Lenguaje, Buenos Aires, 1965.

—, Sul concetto di obbligo giuridico, Rivista di Filosofia 57, 1966.

—, Principi di diritto e positivismo giuridico, Rivista di Filosofia 61, 1970.

—, Algunas palabras sobre las palabras de la ley, Buenos Aires, 1971.

CONTE, A. G., Saggio sulla completezza degli ordinamenti giuridici, Torino, 1962.

—, Décision, complétude, clôture. A propos des lacunes en droit, Logique et Analyse 9, 1966, 1—18.

—, Completezza e chiusura, Studi in memoria di Widar Cesarini Sforza, Milano, 1968.

COSSIO, C., La plenitud del ordenamiento juridico (2nd ed.), Buenos Aires, 1947.

—, Teoria de la verdad jurídica, Buenos Aires, 1954.

—, La teoría egológica del derecho y el concepto jurídico de libertad (2nd ed.), Buenos Aires, 1964.

DWORKIN, R., Is a law a system of rules? In: F. SUMMERS (editor), Essays in Legal Philosophy, Oxford, 1968.

ENGISCH, K.: Der Begriff der Rechtslücke, Sauer-Festschrift, 1949.

—, Einführung in das juristische Denken, Stuttgart, 1956.

ESSER, J., Grundsatz und Norm in der richterlichen Fortbildung des Privatrechts, Tübingen, 1956.

FIEDLER, H., Juristische Logik in mathematischer Sicht, Archiv für Rechts- und Sozialphilosophie 52, 1966, 93—116.

—, Derecho, Lógica, Matemática, Buenos Aires, 1968.

GARCÍA MÁYNEZ, E., Introducción al estudio del derecho, México, 1955.

GARZÓN VALDÉS, E. F., Derecho y «naturaleza de las cosas» (2 volumes), Córdoba, 1971.

GAVAZZI, G., Delle antinomie, Torino, 1959.

GIOJA, A. L., El postulado jurídico de la prohibición, Buenos Aires, 1954.

HART, H. L. A., Definition and Theory in Jurisprudence, Oxford, 1953.

—, Positivism and the Separation of Law and Morals, Harvard Law Review 71, 1958, 593—629.

—, The Concept of Law, Oxford, 1961.

HECK, P., Begriffsbildung und Interessenjurisprudenz, Tübingen, 1932.

HOHFELD, W. N., Fundamental Legal Conceptions, Yale University Press, 1964 (orig. New Haven, 1923).

KALINOWSKI, G., Introduction à la logique juridique, Paris, 1965.

—, La logique des lacunes en droit, Archives de Philosophie du Droit 13, 1969, 353—362.

KANTOROWICZ, H., Der Kampf um die Rechtswissenschaft, Heidelberg, 1906.

KELSEN, H., General Theory of Law and State, Harvard University Press, 1943.

—, Théorie Pure du Droit, Neuchâtel, 1953.

—, Reine Rechtslehre (2nd ed.), Wien, 1960.

—, Contribuciones a la Teoria Pura del Derecho, Buenos Aires, 1969.

KLUG, U., Juristische Logik (3rd ed.), Berlin, 1966.

—, Rechtslücke und Rechtsgeltung, Festschrift für Hans Carl Nipperdey, München—Berlin, 1965.

—, Observations sur le problème des lacunes en droit, Logique et Analyse 10, 1967, 98—115.

LARENZ, K., Methodenlehre der Rechtswissenschaft, Berlin, 1960.

MIRÓ QUESADA, F., Lógica jurídica, Lima, 1956.

NINO, C. S., Notas sobre la dogmática juridica, México (forthcoming).

NOWAK, L., De la rationalité du législateur comme élément de l'interprétation juridique, Logique et Analyse 12, 1969, 65—86.

OPALEK, K., On the logical-semantic structure of directives, Logique et Analyse *13*, 1970, 169—196.

PECZENIK, A., Empirical foundations of legal dogmatics, Logique et Analyse *12*, 1969, 32—64.

PERELMAN, CH. (editor), Antinomies en droit, Bruxelles, 1965.

PERELMAN, CH. (editor), Problème des lacunes en droit, Bruxelles, 1966.

RAZ, J., The Concept of a Legal System, Oxford, 1970.

RENAULD, J. G., La systematisation dans le raisonnement juridique, Logique et Analyse *1*, 1958, 168—183.

ROSS, A., On Law and Justice, London, 1958.

—, Directives and Norms, London, 1968.

—, El concepto de validez y otros ensayos, Buenos Aires, 1969.

SCARPELLI, U., La définition en droit, Logique et Analyse *1*, 1958, 127—138.

—, Contributo alla semantica del linguaggio normativo, Torino, 1959.

SCHREIBER, R., Logik des Rechts, Berlin, 1962.

—, Die Geltung von Rechtsnormen, Berlin, 1966.

SOLER, S., La interpretación de la ley, Barcelona, 1962.

—, Las palabras de la ley, México, 1969.

TAMMELO, I., On the logical openness of legal orders, The American Journal of Comparative Law *8*, 1959, 187—203.

—, Outline of Modern Legal Logic, Wiesbaden, 1969.

VERNENGO, R. J., La función sistemática de la norma fundamental, Revista Jurídica de Buenos Aires *3*, 1960, 207—225.

—, About some formation rules for legal languages, Law, State, and International Legal Order, Essays in Honor of Hans Kelsen, Knoxville, 1964.

VIEHWEG, T., Topik und Jurisprudenz (3rd ed.), München, 1965.

WEDBERG, A., Some problems in the logical analysis of legal science, Theoria *17*, *1951*, 246 ff.

WEINBERGER, O., Einige Betrachtungen über die Rechtsnorm vom Standpunkt der Logik und der Semantik, Logique et Analyse *7*, 1964, 212—232.

—, Rechtslogik. Versuch der Anwendung moderner Logik im Recht, Wien—New York, 1970.

—, Normenlogik anwendbar im Recht, Logique et Analyse *13*, 1970, 93—106.

WRÓBLEWSKI, J., Legal reasonings in legal interpretation, Logique et Analyse *12*, 1969, 3—31.

ZIEMBIŃSKI, Z., Les lacunes de la loi dans le système juridique polonais contemporain et les méthodes utilisées pour les combler, Logique et Analyse *9*, 1966, 38—51.

ZITTELMANN, E., Lücken im Recht, Leipzig, 1903.

Index